PU

SONIC™
THE HEDGEHOG

Adventure Gamebook 2

Zone Rangers

Adventure Gamebook 2

Zone Rangers

JAMES WALLIS

PUFFIN BOOKS

PUFFIN BOOKS

Published by the Penguin Group
Penguin Books Ltd, 27 Wrights Lane, London W8 5TZ, England
Penguin Books USA Inc., 375 Hudson Street, New York, New York 10014, USA
Penguin Books Australia Ltd, Ringwood, Victoria, Australia
Penguin Books Canada Ltd, 10 Alcorn Avenue, Toronto, Ontario, Canada M4V 3B2
Penguin Books (NZ) Ltd, 182–190 Wairau Road, Auckland 10, New Zealand

Penguin Books Ltd, Registered Offices: Harmondsworth, Middlesex, England

First published in Fantail Books 1993
Reissued in Puffin Books 1995
3 5 7 9 10 8 6 4 2

Text copyright © James Wallis, 1993
Illustrations © Arkadia, 1993
Sonic the Hedgehog © Sega Enterprises Limited, 1993
Licensed by Copyright Promotions Limited
All rights reserved

Typeset by Datix International Limited, Bungay, Suffolk
Filmset in 12/13 Palatino
Printed in England by Clays Ltd, St Ives plc

Except in the United States of America, this book is sold subject
to the condition that it shall not, by way of trade or otherwise, be lent,
re-sold, hired out, or otherwise circulated without the publisher's
prior consent in any form of binding or cover other than that in which
it is published and without a similar condition including this
condition being imposed on the subsequent purchaser

Dedicated to Raoul Vaneigem
(Sorry, dude)

INTRODUCTION

This is not a normal book, it's a gamebook. You don't read through it like a normal book, starting at the first page and ending with the last. Instead, *Zone Rangers* lets you decide how Sonic and Tails will solve puzzles, collect rings, defeat their enemies, release their friends, and put an end to the sinister schemes of Dr Robotnik. If you make the right choices, they'll win. If you make the wrong choices – well, that's too horrible to think about.

Before you start playing the game, read through the simple rules on the next few pages. The rules are almost exactly the same as the ones in the other Sonic gamebook, *Metal City Mayhem*, but read through them because there are a few differences. You will also need one ordinary die, and a pen or pencil.

Playing The Game

In *Zone Rangers*, you help to guide Sonic and Tails through the action. Every so often they will need advice and you must help them out. Their adventure will succeed or fail depending on your choices.

The book is divided into three hundred sections, each one with a number. The first one is **1**, the last one is **300** but you don't read through them in order. Instead, each section ends with several different things that Sonic and Tails could do next, and a number for each option. Once you have decided what you want Sonic and Tails to do, turn to the section with that number and read it. Continue doing this until you have either finished the adventure, or come to a 'GAME OVER' along the way.

Before you start, you have to decide how good Sonic and Tails are at doing certain things. Everybody knows that Sonic's very fast and very cool, but do you know exactly how cool, or how fast? This is your chance to decide.

What Is He Like?

If you turn to pages 12-13 and 14-15, you will find the *Vital Statistics* sheets for Sonic and Tails – a list of what they can do, what they are carrying, how many lives they have left, how many rings they have collected, and a few other things.

In the centre of each page are Sonic's (or Tails's) abilities. There are six of these: Speed, Strength, Agility, Coolness, Quick Wits and Good Looks. Beside them is a description of the ability and a box, which is empty at the moment.

Fill in Sonic's *Vital Statistics* sheet first. Read the descriptions of his abilities. Choose the one that you think he should be best at, and write a '5' in that box. Put a '4' in the next best, a '3' in the third best and '2' in all the rest. The different numbers show what Sonic's strengths and weaknesses are. Then do the same on Tails's sheet.

Doing Things

Some sections of the book will ask you to roll on one

of Sonic or Tails's abilities to beat a particular difficulty number. This means that you should roll one die, add the number you've written by that ability, and compare the total to the difficulty number. If the total is equal to or higher than the difficulty, Sonic or Tails has succeeded (yes!). If the number is lower, they have failed (oh no!). Follow the instructions in that section to find out what happens next. Sometimes the section will give you other numbers to add to your roll, so read each one carefully.

Fighting

Sonic and Tails can also use their abilities to fight enemies. Sometimes defeating them is so easy that you won't have to roll a die at all, but at other times you'll be asked to roll on a particular ability. Usually it's Strength or Speed, but it can be any of the others depending on the enemy and the type of attack.

All of Sonic and Tails's enemies have a rating, a number usually between four and ten. To fight an enemy, roll one die and add it to whichever ability either Sonic or Tails is using in that fight: the section will tell you. If the number you roll is higher or equal to the enemy's rating, the enemy is beaten (pow!). If not, the enemy has a chance to strike back against Sonic or Tails. Roll a die and add it to the enemy's rating. If the total is more than 10, they have hit the relevant hero (ouch!). If the total is less than 10, the enemy has missed and Sonic and Tails can attack again.

Sometimes Sonic and Tails will fight the same enemy at the same time. When this happens, add their two abilities together, and add the total to your die roll. If it's higher than the enemy's rating, the enemy has been hit (wham!). If not, then the enemy strikes back by adding one die to its rating, trying to get higher than 15. If the roll is higher, roll a die to see who has been hit. If you roll a 1, 2 or 3 it's Tails; 4, 5 or 6 and it's Sonic. If the enemy misses, it's our heroes' turn to attack again.

When Sonic or Tails is hit by an enemy or a trap, two things can happen. If they are carrying any rings, they lose them all and must try to get past the enemy or trap again. If they are not carrying any rings (because they haven't found any yet, or because they haven't picked any up since the last time they were hit) they lose a life, and must go back to earlier in the adventure to try again. The section will tell you where to turn.

Lives

Sonic and Tails start the book with three lives each. If either of them loses all his lives, you have failed and must start the adventure again from the beginning. There are two ways to get extra lives: the two characters can find them concealed along the way, or, if either Sonic or Tails ever has more than 100 rings at one time, then they automatically get an extra life.

Carrying Stuff

Both the characters start the game carrying a few items. The book will tell you if and when they can use these. They may also pick up new items along the way, or lose some in the course of the adventure. Always write rings, lives and new items down on Sonic or Tails's *Vital Statistics*, and cross off the ones they don't have any more.

That's everything you need to help Sonic and Tails through the perils that await them as they range across the Zones of the planet Mobius – and beyond. Now turn to Section **1** and read on.

SONIC'S VITAL STATISTICS

SPEED

Sonic's really fast. His training and his special shoes make him the fastest there is, and he loves the feeling of speed. But that can lead to trouble. Sometimes he's going so fast he doesn't notice things, or can't see when he should stop — or even can't stop and collides with things.

STRENGTH

Sonic's pretty tough and he knows it. He can run all day and smash Robotnik's traps just by bouncing on them. But he relies on his strength too much and doesn't always think about problems — it's much easier to bounce on them. That attitude can put him in dangerous situations.

AGILITY

Sonic's a natural gymnast. Climbing, jumping, swinging, swimming, diving, exploring — he can do it all, and he loves to show off his abilities by exploring and going where his friends can't. But he must be careful; just because he can get into some places doesn't always mean he can get out again.

COOLNESS

With those spikes and that attitude, how can Sonic be anything but cool? But he's cocky as well, and thinks he can do things he can't. And sometimes he'd rather have fun than do something important that has to be done.

← QUICK WITS ←

When something happens, Sonic's always the first to react to it. But he doesn't like hanging around and hates waiting for things – or people. Sometimes that means he's not prepared for what might happen next.

← GOOD LOOKS ←

Sonic looks good, and he knows that when he meets people, if he's charming and polite, he can wow them. But he is a bit vain; he takes care of his appearance and doesn't like doing things that'll mess up his spikes or his trainers.

LIVES LEFT:

RINGS: COLLECTED:
(If Sonic has more than 100 rings, he gets an extra life)

SONIC'S STUFF:
(Keep a list of equipment, gadgets and food that Sonic will collect in his adventures here)

Red trainers   White gloves

TAILS'S VITAL STATISTICS

SPEED

Tails is almost as fast as Sonic — in fact, if it wasn't for Sonic, he'd probably be the fastest creature on Mobius. But because he tries so hard to be better than his hero Sonic, he often doesn't notice things, and trips over them, or can't steer around them in time.

STRENGTH

Tails tries to be like Sonic and therefore likes to show how strong he is. He's good. at smashing traps and bouncing on enemies, but he has a habit of getting things wrong and making mistakes.

AGILITY

Tails has one thing that makes him a great gymnast — his twin tails. He can use them to hover like a helicopter, or with a quick flick he can change direction or spin through the air. He's so proud of this that he shows it off too much, and sometimes he uses it when there are better things he could have done instead.

COOLNESS

Nobody's as cool as Sonic, but Tails tries hard, and he's been hanging around his hero for so long that some of it is beginning to rub off. There's no way that two bushy tails will ever be as slick and streetwise as cool blue spikes, but Tails is no slouch in this department.

QUICK WITS

Tails isn't the quickest-thinking guy on the planet Mobius, but he has his natural foxy reactions, and when danger threatens he can sometimes move faster than Sonic. 'Act first – think later' is his motto.

GOOD LOOKS

Which would you rather cuddle up to – a spiky hedgehog or a smooth orange fox, with a sleek fur coat, two gorgeous bushy tails, that cute flick of hair and his white whiskers? In fact, Sonic is everyone's favourite, but Tails tries hard.

LIVES LEFT:

RINGS COLLECTED:
(If Tails has more than 100 rings, he gets an extra life)

TAIL'S THINGS:
(Keep a list of equipment, gadgets and food that Tails will collect in his adventures here)

Red trainers   White gloves

It's a cool spring morning in the Green Hill Zone, and Sonic and Tails are lying under a palm tree, sleeping as hard as they can. Sonic is dreaming of receiving the Mobius Prize For Being Best At Everything, while Tails is dreaming of hunting wild chocolate eclairs, armed only with a toothbrush. The two friends were up late the night before, watching television. The film *Zone Alone* was being shown on TVPM (Television Planet Mobius) for the first time and Sally Acorn had invited everyone to a party to watch it. Sonic and Tails had seen the film before and didn't like it, so they left the party before the film started and spent the rest of the evening eating microwaved snacks and watching monster movies on video. They didn't get to sleep until they'd watched their favourite, *Mobzilla Fights Outer-Space Monsters From Planet Z* twice. Still, they can doze as much as they want — heroes like them don't have to get up to go to school or work, and they don't have anything special to do today. Everything's quiet, which usually means that Sonic's enemy Dr Robotnik is plotting something, but Sonic and Tails beat him thoroughly last time and they are pretty sure that he won't be back for a while.

Tails grunts and turns over. He's dreaming that a herd of cream eclairs are hiding behind the Cosmic Washing Machine and he's wading through strawberry jam to get to them, carrying his trusty toothbrush like a quarterstaff. Sonic isn't dreaming, he's floating half-way between being asleep and waking up. He's warm and comfortable but there's an annoying noise at the edge of his hearing. It's a sort of buzzing, roaring, grinding sound and it won't go away.

Imagine that you are Sonic – what would you do? Do you think he should ignore the rumbling, roll over and go back to sleep? If you do, turn to section **233**. If you think he should get up and wake Tails as well, turn to section **78**. If you think Sonic should go and investigate the sound on his own, turn to section **114**.

2

The leader of the wart-hogs looks at Tails and Sonic for a long time. Finally he speaks. 'We have wasted too much time with these two,' he grunts. 'If they will not help us, we will not help them. Chase them into the jungle, and let them hope the crocodiles do not find them.' Sonic and Tails find themselves surrounded by more spear-points than they want to count. The wart-hog warriors advance, pushing the two heroes out into the dark jungle; then they turn and rush away, their leafy clothing blending with the foliage to camouflage them perfectly. In a few seconds there is no sign of them. Turn to **136**.

3

The signs lead to the escape pods' entry hatches, and a crowd of androids gathered outside them. There is a hubbub of confused conversation and nobody seems to know what's going on. Several of the androids have holes in their chest areas with wires trailing out, and are being supported by their comrades. Sonic and Tails dart between the androids, heading for the escape pods. When they reach the outside wall, Sonic looks up, noticing an alarm button on the wall. The glass over it has been broken, and a light flashes on and off just above it. However, it could be a circuit failure, leading to a false alarm. If Sonic and Tails still want to head for the escape pods, turn to **127**. If they hope it's a false alarm and rush back after the red robot, turn to **191**.

4

'We don't want to hurt you,' says Sonic, crossing his fingers, 'but you and your tribe have been acting real mean. It's got to stop.'

'Yes,' says Tails. 'We can't let you rush around attacking the other inhabitants of the jungle. It's not neighbourly, and it's not nice.'

'So,' says Sonic, 'the coolest thing would be for you to stop. If you agree and give us that Chaos Emerald, we'll go away and won't bother you any more.'

'But,' says the chieftain in a voice like gravel, 'but the rock says that I can rule the jungle. It says I'm supposed to. Who should I believe?' He's very confused by all this. Should Sonic and Tails attack him while he's confused (turn to **255**) or stop being friendly and start being nasty to him (turn to **56**)?

5

Sonic is standing on the ledge by the cell window. Outside is the city, bathed in early evening sunlight, but unfortunately there are strong iron bars in the way. To bend the bars far enough for him to squeeze his hedgehog body through, Sonic must roll on his Strength to beat an 8. If he makes the roll, turn to **242**. If he fails, the bars are too strong and he falls back into the cell, exhausted; he lands on the see-saw plank, snapping it in two. Now he can't try that trick again. Should he climb the walls of the cell (turn to **222**), overpower the guard outside the cell (turn to **133**) or, if he has some rope, lasso the hook in the ceiling with it (turn to **76**)?

6

The two animals dive into the swirling ocean. Behind them the ship fills with water and sinks with a gurgle. None of the robots are paying any attention to them; they're too busy carrying the Chaos Emeralds down into the submarine. The swim is further than it looks, and by the time Sonic and Tails haul themselves up onto the submarine, the robots have disappeared inside it with the Emeralds, and the hatches are closed. One gold ring lies there (write it down). There is a hiss as air bubbles up from around the submarine and it begins to sink.

'It's sinking!' says Tails, stating the obvious.

'No — it's submerging,' says Sonic. 'We have to get inside before it disappears.'

If Sonic has picked up a crowbar in his travels, he can use it to prise open the hatch (turn to **84**). Otherwise, he and Tails can use their brute strength to force the hatch open (turn to **256**), or they can be polite and knock (turn to **155**).

7

'I'm innocent! I've only just arrived! And I've never heard of the Outcasts,' replies Sonic.

'A likely story,' Galen says. 'I submit before the court two crucial pieces of evidence. One —' he holds out the Chaos Emerald, '— this Chaos Emerald, remarkably similar to the one which powers our own city. This one may be a fake, or it may be genuine, but one thing is certain: it should not be in the possession of this spy!' All the cats applaud. 'Now, the second piece of evidence,' continues Galen. 'I ask you to cast your eyes over this invading reprobate. What do you see, fellow citizens? There is a certain cat-like appearance to him, but he is BLUE! As we all know, only mutants are blue, and all mutants are Outcasts here. Guilty as charged! Guards, take him away.'

Oh dear. Turn to **259**.

8

-ZZZZZZZZZAAMM! The white light flicks off and Sonic and Tails fall into a bush. They're outside, somewhere. Around them are tall trees blocking out the sun, flowering plants of vivid colours, and shrubs bearing multicoloured fruit. From high in the tree branches comes the constant warbling of birds, and small creatures rustle in the undergrowth.

'Wow!' breathes Tails, getting out of the bush he landed in and looking around. 'Where are we, Sonic?'

The hedgehog carefully climbs out of his bush as it's a thorn bush, and sniffs the air. 'It's the Jungle Zone,' he says.

'I haven't been here before,' Tails observes.

'I have, Tails,' Sonic nods. 'You've got to be careful here. It's a dog-eat-dog world in the Jungle Zone.'

'Not a cat-eat-dog world?' Tails asks.

'What are you talking about?' Sonic replies.

'Well,' says Tails, 'foxes are related to dogs, and there's a big cat over there that probably wants to eat me.'

'Bogus!' comments Sonic. Coming towards them is the huge face of a ravenous dagger-fanged Warcat. It opens its mouth wide, showing more teeth than most dentists see in their whole lives, and lets out a roar that shakes the trees. Do Sonic and Tails attack the Warcat (turn to 227) or run away from it (turn to 99)?

9

'Chaos Emeralds?' Ross asks. 'No problem. We'll put them into the Warps of Confusion.'

'Do what?' Tails asks, mystified.

'The Warps,' Sonic explains. 'They were the Special Zones around Mobius. You wouldn't remember — we hadn't yet started to hang around together.'

'That's right,' says Ross. 'Robotnik didn't build the Warps, but he used them to hide the Emeralds from Sonic. Once something is in a Warp, it's almost impossible to get it out.'

'So how do we put them there?' Sonic asks.

'Two ways,' Ross answers. 'Either we lend you a spacecraft and you can do it, which is risky because you don't know the way, or we'll do it for you. It's what we were designed for.'

Sonic and Tails can offer to do it themselves (turn to 288), let Ross do the job (turn to 262) or ask him if there's another way out of the space station (turn to 74).

10

Tails dashes in to attack and the figures turn in surprise. 'Look! It's Tails!' shouts one of them.

'Wow! Sonic's pal Tails? Wow!' replies another. Tails sees they're monkeys, half-frozen with the cold. He screeches to a halt, slipping a little on the ice. 'It IS

Tails!' the monkey continues. 'Fantastic! He'll save us – although Sonic would be even better. Is he here, Tails?'

'No, he's not,' the fox responds crossly, 'but I can do anything he can. What's your problem?'

'That's the problem,' says the monkey, pointing. With a splash, a huge metal machine shaped like a shark surfaces in the open water. Does Tails help the monkeys by attacking the shark (turn to 268) or look around for a teleporter device (turn to 145)?

11

'DON'T JUST STAND THERE!' yells Robotnik. 'React! Show how angry you are! I want to watch you realize how eggs-cruciatingly powerless you are!' Sonic and Tails don't even blink. 'Aw,' Robotnik says, 'you're no fun.' He flicks a switch and the energy coils around the barrels of the Zap Cannon begin to glow. 'I'm not bluffing,' he says. 'Do something or I'll fry you.' Still the two animals refuse to respond. 'Ah well,' sighs Robotnik. Energy flashes from the Zap Cannon, and the two heroes vanish. 'Let's eggs-ecute the plan,' mutters Robotnik, disgruntled. With nobody to stop him, the demented doctor has won.

GAME OVER

12

The vines snap with a twang and the drawbridge plummets into the moat. Sonic jumps down onto it and grabs four gold rings lying there (write these down). Wart-hog warriors run towards him through the opened outer gate. 'Come on! We're in!' Sonic shouts, and charges into the stronghold, dodging the rotten fruit that the guards are firing at him. Turn to **44**.

It's a race against the bulldozer, and it has a head start! Sonic hits top speed so fast that he leaves scorch-marks on the grass as he hurtles ahead of the huge yellow machine, dashing in front of it to grab the sleeping fox by his twin tails and drag him out of the way. The bulldozer thunders past, its treads thrashing the ground mere centimetres from Tails's head.

Tails opens one eye. 'You've saved my life again,' he says. 'Thanks, Sonic. You're a true friend.'

'I know,' says Sonic, not embarrassed by his friend's praise. Well, Tails is not the most careful of foxes and Sonic saves him about twice a day, so he's used to being thanked for it. Now the two friends have to work out what to do next. Select one of the choices from the list and turn to that section:

Chase the bulldozer and attack it?	Turn to **212**
Chase the bulldozer and jump on board?	Turn to **26**
Follow the black road to see where it goes?	Turn to **107**
Explore the rest of the Zone?	Turn to **170**

14

The three Outcast agents look at him again. 'You're right,' says the bird, Number Two. 'He has to be an Outcast like us. The cats would never let anybody blue and spiky into their city. Welcome to our organization, Number Four.'

'I still think he looks like Sonic the Hedgehog,' growls the dog.

Sonic knows that one of the agents in the room is an agent for Galen and the cats who run the city, but he knows that if he tries to warn them, he might end up talking to the spy. What does he do?

Talk to Number One, the badger?	Turn to 38
Talk to Number Two, the tall bird?	Turn to 126
Talk to Number Three, the dog?	Turn to 253
Ask them all what their plan is?	Turn to 101

15

The Emeralds are giving off so much heat and light that it's hard even to look at them. Sonic half-closes his eyes and speeds across the floor towards the spinning, flashing shapes. Suddenly two bolts of light streak out from them, one blue and one green, and shoot across the room. If Sonic has more than two friends with him, turn to 295; if not, turn to 163.

16

With his speed slowed, Sonic can change the direction he's falling. Below him he can see what looks like a pool of water on top of a building – just the thing for a safe landing. He twists in the air and falls towards it. 'Aaaaaaaaaaaaah!' he screams as he realizes that it's not a pool of water, but a huge sheet of glass. Desperately he tries to steer away from it, but he's too close. There is a colossal CCRRAASSHH as he hits the glass and it shatters into billions of pieces which fall with him into the room below.

There is a party going on in the room – or there was until Sonic dropped in. Nobody was hurt, but all the guests are covered in broken glass and the food is filled with shards and splinters. Sonic pulls himself out of a huge sponge cake and looks up. There is no noise apart from the tinkling of a few final fragments of glass. Everybody in the room is looking at him and they all seem to be large cats. What should he do?

Be cool about it? Turn to 110
Offer them the Chaos Emerald as a
   gift? Turn to 245
Attack the most important-looking
   person there? Turn to 291

17

Tails dashes towards the fridge-machine. The mammoth turns, points its long trunk at him and blows. A cloud of frozen icicles shoot out, whizzing through the air like darts.

'That's not fair!' Tails complains. 'Nobody told me he could do that!' He must roll against his Agility to beat a 6 to dodge all the icicles. If he fails the roll, one of them hits him and he loses all his rings or, if he has no rings, a life (turn back to **125**). If he dodges successfully, does he smash the fridge (turn to **175**), attack the mammoth (turn to **102**) or keep going for the Chaos Emerald (turn to **297**)?

18

The two heroes wait at the edge of the clearing. After a few minutes two crocodiles appear from the jungle, walking upright on their hind feet and carrying wooden crossbows.

'When are we going to stomp out that wart-hog village?' one of the crocs says.

'Soon,' replies the other. 'Tomorrow, maybe.' They walk towards the gate, and one looks around warily while the other unlocks it. Sonic and Tails must roll on their Good Looks, to beat a 9. This time it's different from usual, though, because they're trying to get 9 or *less*. If they roll 9 or less, the crocodiles don't spot them; turn to **52**. If they roll 10 or more, they've been spotted and the crocs rush towards them; turn to **181**.

19

The android looks up. 'Tonic! Sails! I'm a big fan of yours,' it says weakly. 'I was bringing you a cup of tea when a red thing dashed past me carrying some Chaos Emeralds, and then another one jumped out of — oh dear.' It looks sadly at the hole in its chest.

'Which way did the one with the Emeralds go?' Sonic demands.

'To the right,' the android points. 'The other one ran off to the left.'

Sonic and Tails aren't stupid enough to split up, so which way do they go: left (turn to **169**) or right (turn to **232**)?

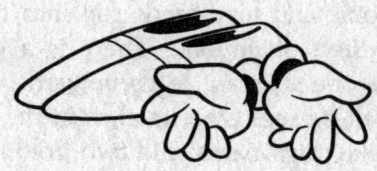

20

'You must be lying!' Robotnik exclaims. 'How else could you have known that I would be broadcasting secret mind-control signals in the middle of *Zone Alone* last night, then deliberately not watch it so you slept through the hypnotic programming early this morning. Ha ha ha! Brilliant! What you don't know is that I have used my teleporter devices to place Chaos Emeralds all over Planet Mobius, where they will cause confusion and disruption! Ha ha ha! I'm a genius! By tomorrow I will rule Mobius!' He glowers at Sonic and Tails. 'But now you know too much. I must get rid of you immediately! Guards! Remove their gloves and shoes!'

'No way!' gasp Sonic and Tails together. Sally Acorn and Porker Harris move towards them. Should Sonic and Tails resist (turn to **129**) or let themselves be stripped of their shoes and gloves (turn to **71**)?

21

Nobody stops Sonic and his companions on the way to the High Tower. The streets are deserted and the blue-green light from overhead casts an eerie pall over the city. There is only one entrance to the tower: a heavy wooden door reinforced with iron bars. It stands open, and Sonic and his friends slip into the hallway. There is no sign of anyone. There is a closed door here, and a stone staircase leads upwards. Sonic looks around, but all he sees are scratches in the stone walls which look like claw-marks, and two gold rings on the floor (he can take these). Should he and his companions open the closed door (turn to **228**) or climb the stairs (turn to **150**)?

22

There isn't much space for a run-up, but Tails sprints to the edge and jumps off into the air. A grey shape leaps out of the water and the metal shark's jaws clash shut millimetres below his feet. Tails yelps, but manages to land safely on the main ice-field as the shark splashes back into the sea. The figures wave to him and cheer. Should Tails look for a teleporter device (turn to **145**) or attack the shark (turn to **268**)?

23

'A robot!' shouts Sonic. He swings and knocks the robot's head off. It bounces to the floor, and the silver being picks it up and refits it on its neck.

'That wasn't very polite,' it says. 'I was about to welcome you to our space station and tell you that I am RO-55, or Ross to my friends, but I shan't now. So there.'

Sonic and Tails are taken aback by this self-reconstructing, petulant android, but Sonic retains enough presence of mind to think of a question or two. What does he ask?

'Who built you?' Turn to **159**

'How do we teleport out of here?' Turn to **74**

'Do you know how to dispose of
unwanted Chaos Emeralds?' Turn to **9**

24

'Attack when I shout three,' Sonic says. 'THREE!' Spinning blue and orange balls hurtle towards the door of the fort, and it explodes into sawdust. Sonic and Tails unwrap themselves and stand in the hallway of the building. There's a staircase leading up and down, and under it is a heap of strange objects, with two power-up monitors on top. Tails grabs them.

'Look!' he shouts. 'This one's got ten rings in it! And the other's got — oh wow! — a blue power-shield, the kind that protects the wearer from one injury. Cool! Which one do you want, Sonic?'

Choose who of the two gets the shield and who gets the rings, and write the items down on their *Vital Statistics*.

'I feel better already,' says Sonic. 'Where to now?' Choose whether they go up (turn to **142**) or down (turn to **296**).

25

'Okay,' says Sonic. 'I'm a spy. Just don't torture me.'

Ravis looks at him and sneers. 'You may be a spy, but you're certainly a craven coward. Such people are of no use to us.' He raises his voice. 'Guards! Take this pathetic creature out into the desert and tie him to a stake. He will make a tasty breakfast for the vultures.' The guards drag Sonic out into the night. Ravis turns away — and notices you. 'And as for you,' he says, 'just shove off, okay? Go back to the first section of the book. You'll have no more luck here.'

GAME OVER

26

Jumping onto speeding bulldozers is very dangerous, so don't try this at home. Sonic and Tails, on the other hand, are professionals and are sitting on the machine's bonnet, watching as it destroys more of the Green Hill Zone.

'I can see why they call it an earth-mover,' says Tails. 'Boy, that's some machine!'

'Let's get going,' says Sonic. 'We've got to stop it moving any more earth — or moving at all.' The two heroes can head for the driver's cabin at the top of the bulldozer (turn to section **204**) or for the engine (turn to section **251**).

27

The cell is like the one Sonic was in before, with a stone floor and one window set too high to see out of. There's a bed made of planks laid on piles of bricks, covered with a single blanket. In the middle of the ceiling is a large hook. Nothing is hanging from it, it's just there. Sonic and the others check every stone and brick but there are no secret ways out of this cell.

Sonic can ask what the other two are carrying (turn to **105**) or bang on the cell door (turn to **278**). Alternatively, if he has decided how he wants to escape, he can try the following:

Lasso the hook in the ceiling (if he has
   a rope).   Turn to 76
Make a see-saw catapult with the
   planks and bricks.   Turn to 182
Climb up to the window.   Turn to 222
Overpower the guard outside the cell.   Turn to 133

28

Tails and the small monkey are at the bottom of the
crevasse. Far above, the sky is a thin blue line between
the ice walls.

'Are we stuck?' asks the monkey.

'Not if I can help it,' Tails says. 'What would Sonic
do?'

'I don't know but I think we should ask the reader's
advice,' says the monkey.

Quite right too. Should Tails climb out of the crevasse
with the monkey on his back (turn to 183) or walk
along the bottom of the crevasse to see where it leads
(turn to 275)?

29

The door is solid metal, with a small sliding door set in the middle of it. Sonic bangs heavily on it and it slides open to reveal the ugly face of a cat guard. 'I don't care what you want,' he snarls, 'you're not getting it. Shut up and let me have some peace.' The small door slams shut. Does Sonic look out of the window (turn to **202**) or check out the bed (turn to **83**)?

30

Pulling the spacecraft out of a dive, Sonic spots a red speck against the starry sky. It's the small robot's ship, quite some distance ahead. Sonic kicks in the ship's afterburners and speeds after it. The smaller ship jinks, zigzags and dives towards a field of asteroids ahead of it. From the way it's flying, the two animals can tell that it's agile enough to zip between the floating, spinning rocks. They don't know if theirs is, and there's only one way to find out. Do Sonic and Tails pursue the red ship through the asteroids (turn to **211**) or fly around the edge, hoping to find the target on the other side (turn to **189**)?

31

Sonic can charge at the gate (turn to **249**), climb the walls (turn to **120**), climb a tree beside the clearing (turn to **87**) or see if he can think of anything better (turn to **272**).

32

Sonic tells the Outcast leader how the Outcasts' spies were betrayed by Number One. Ravis listens carefully. 'Hear this,' he says. 'The Outcasts will attack the city tonight. I will lead our main assault on the gates of the city, but you shall go with two of my warriors to the city's rear wall. When you see a white flare in the sky, climb the wall. Your mission is to free our agents and then find the Chaos Emerald. Will you do it?' Sonic nods, and Ravis shakes his paw and gives him two gold rings (write these down). 'Wonderful! I will give you your weight in dates, and many goats when we win,' he proclaims. Sonic politely refuses the last offer, and goes to meet his warriors. Mark down '2 warriors' on Sonic's *Vital Statistics*, and turn to **119**.

33

Bruised and surprised, the Warcat gives a long howl and disappears into the depths of the jungle. Suddenly six figures appear from behind trees. They're dressed in clothes made of leaves, wear large, carved wooden masks and carry spears. They seem impressed by Sonic and Tails and keep their distance. One or two of them keep their spears lowered. It's hard to tell if they're going to attack Sonic and Tails, or if they're afraid the two heroes might attack them. Should Sonic and Tails attack (turn to **81**) or show that they're friendly (turn to **298**)?

34

The streets are quiet at this time of the evening, and Sonic sneaks easily towards the High Tower without being noticed. The strange light continues to pour out of its windows, lighting up the whole city, and the longer Sonic watches it, the more uneasy he feels. Suddenly there is a scream from up ahead, and then another. A crowd of people are charging down the street towards Sonic, but they haven't noticed him because something large and ferocious is chasing them! Sonic can't see what it is but he can hear it howl. The crowd is getting closer and there is nowhere to hide. He must get out of the way or be trampled. If Sonic sprints in front of the crowd, heading towards the gates, turn to **289**. If he sneaks through the shadows towards the gate, turn to **154**.

35

Sonic fires the ship's engines and pushes the throttle forward. The spacecraft shoots across the water and rams the massive submarine amidships. A gaping hole appears in it and it begins to tilt to one side as water pours in. Sonic and Tails cheer loudly — then stop as water begins to fill their own ship, gushing in from a crack in the cockpit canopy.

'Computer!' shouts Sonic. 'COMPUTER! Open the cockpit!' There is no answer except an electrical fizzing. The water closes over the ship and it sinks slowly to the bottom of the ocean, far below.

GAME OVER

36

'Hi,' Sonic says, standing up in the remains of the cake. 'I'm Sonic and I've just dropped in — awk!' His arms are grabbed by two large cat-guards, who haul him out of the cake. The Chaos Emerald falls to the floor, and one of them picks it up and passes it to the most impressively dressed cat-person in the room.

The impressive cat looks at the Chaos Emerald, and then at Sonic. 'Sonic,' he says. 'Sonic the Turtle —'

'HEDGEHOG!'

'Shut up. We have heard of you, Sonic the Turtle. We don't know why you are here, but we will find out.' He raises his voice. 'Start the trial!' Turn to **69**.

37

Whether they took the wrong course, whether they were just too slow, or whether it disappeared in the middle, there is no sign of the red ship, its pilot or its contents when Tails and Sonic arrive on the far side. It's gone, and the Chaos Emeralds have gone with it. Sonic and Tails have failed to save Mobius.

GAME OVER

38

Sonic speaks to the badger, who is shuffling papers on the table. 'Someone here is a spy for Galen and the others who run the city,' he says.

The badger looks at him. 'A spy? Don't be ridiculous. I've known Number Two and Number Three for ages, and I trust them as far as I can spit.' He looks at Sonic through narrowed eyes. 'The more I learn about you,' he says, 'the less I like you.' Does Sonic talk to Number Two (turn to **126**) or Number Three (turn to **253**), or ask the group about their plans (turn to **101**)?

39

Sonic grabs the pole that Galen was using as a club. Above him, the Chaos Emeralds are twisting and spinning faster and faster, and the light from them is so bright it hurts his eyes. Sonic can tell something really bad will happen if he can't stop it, but the Emeralds are so hot he can't even jump close to them, let alone grab them. Does he use the pole to knock the Chaos Emeralds together (turn to **282**) or apart (turn to **213**)?

40

The side of the building isn't finished, and Sonic and Tails have no problem getting to the top. None of their friends or any of the robots working on the building pay any attention to them. It's as if they weren't there. Soon they stand on the tallest girder, looking out over the Zone. It's not a nice view. Ugly buildings have appeared, many with tall chimneys pouring out grey smoke. Roads zig-zag across the landscape and vehicles move along them. This isn't the Green Hill Zone that Sonic and Tails call home; it's been changed! It makes the two heroes very unhappy to see their favourite place like this. In the distance, at the end of a new road, is a very large, ornate building made entirely of metal. On its roof between towers and fortifications is a huge satellite dish. There is a lot of movement around the building. Sonic and Tails watch for a while, and then climb down. Once the friends have reached the bottom, should they walk along the road towards the building (turn to **107**) or talk to one of their friends (turn to **293**)?

41

Tails and the rescued monkey stare across the crevasse at the others, stranded on the other side. 'Can you jump that gap?' he asks them.

'Not a chance,' the monkeys reply. 'We're exhausted.'

'We could jump back,' says Tails, 'but we have to get to the top of the mountain, and only we two are on the right side for that. We'll keep going; you see if you can find some shelter or some food.' He and the monkey set off up the glacier. 'Don't worry, we'll be okay,' he says. 'What's your name, young lad?'

'Mildred,' says the monkey, 'and I'm not a lad. If you paid more attention you'd notice that, like you might have noticed that weird plant ahead of us.'

It *is* a weird plant. Its twisted stem sticks out of the snow and divides into six branches. Three of them have orange flowers with big fleshy petals, and the other three dive back into the snow. The plant shudders, as if it was shivering. Should Tails and Mildred investigate it (turn to **286**) or avoid it (turn to **111**)?

42

The monkeys crowd around Tails and thank him. 'You were excellent!' they say. 'You're as good as people say. We wish we could see Sonic in action too.'

'Well, this is sort of a solo mission,' says Tails. 'You haven't seen Sonic, then?'

'No,' says one of the monkeys, 'we haven't seen much since we woke up this morning, only this snow and ice everywhere. It's very confusing.'

What else does Tails ask the monkey?

'Where are we?'	Turn to **158**
'Who are you?'	Turn to **274**
'Have you seen a Chaos Emerald?'	Turn to **216**

43

An accented voice filters out of a small speaker on the instrument panel. 'Lasers n-n-n-not fitted to prototype *T-t-t-toho*. So sorry. T-t-t-turn to section 3-3-3-30,' it says.

'Bother!' says Tails. 'What was that about section numbers?'

'You'll learn,' says Sonic. 'That's one smart computer. Did it say 30 or 330? I hope it was 30, because there are only three hundred sections in this book.' He flips the *Toho* through a loop and dives towards section **30**.

44

The scene inside the stronghold is chaotic. Wart-hogs rush across the drawbridge to attack the crocodiles, but they have only spears while the defending reptiles have crossbows that fire overripe fruits at the confused wart-hogs. Things are getting messy and the ground is covered with peel and pulp, making it slippery. Crocodiles are moving to defend the two buildings inside the stronghold: the large and important-looking fort, and the stockade where the crocodiles keep their prisoners. If Sonic knows that the crocodiles have a prisoner he wants to free, turn to **106**. Otherwise turn to **214** to attack the fort.

45

Sonic and his soldiers must fight the beast. Sonic will have to use his Strength, but he can add 1 point for each soldier with him. The beast has a rating of 10. If it scores a hit on Sonic's side, roll a die. On a 1, 2 or 3, Sonic has been hit and loses all his rings. If he has no rings, he loses a life; turn back to **277**. If you roll a 4, 5 or 6, one of Sonic's soldiers is hit and knocked out. Cross him off Sonic's *Vital Statistics* and continue with the combat. If Sonic and his warriors win, turn to **157**.

46

Sonic and Tails sprint away, heading deep into the jungle.

'Where are we going?' Tails pants.

'Away!' replies Sonic, his words left behind as he hurtles through the forest. 'Can't you hear? That Warcat is right behind us!'

Tails can hear it. He can feel its hot breath on the back

of his neck. It must be so close it could almost bite him. Then he sees something ahead. Roll on Sonic's and Tails's combined Quick Wits, to beat a 10. If they succeed, turn to **118**. If they fail, turn to **174**.

47

The Emerald is incredibly hot! Tails can feel the heat through his gloves and he knows he has to get it away from the wires and cables around it as soon as possible. He dashes across and leaps towards the teleporter. There is a familiar flash of bright white light, and a FAZZZZZZZ! Turn to **277**.

48

The cabin is very cramped, and Sonic's spikes keep poking the other two. Chirps protests loudly and insists that he has to get on with making new roads all over the Green Hill Zone, but the other two ignore him. 'Look!' Tails announces. 'The television set was made by Nik Robot Industries. Nik Robot – Robotnik! He must be behind this.'

'That's nothing!' says Sonic. 'I've found these!' He shows off the five gold rings hidden under Chirps's seat. (Write them on Sonic's *Vital Statistics*, in the box marked 'Gold Rings'.)

'PUT YOUR PAWS IN THE AIR AND LEAVE THE VEHICLE,' declares a loud voice from outside. Sonic and Tails can see five animals — all friends of theirs, or so they thought — hovering over the bulldozer on airbikes. Each airbike has two machine-guns fixed to it.

'I guess we'd better do as they say,' says Sonic. 'There's too many — and they're our friends. We should be saving them, not beating them up. Maybe if we follow them we'll find out what's happening.'

The two heroes leave the cab, paws on their heads. The leading airbike swoops down and its pilot Sally Acorn sneers at them. 'Walk along the road, you renegades,' she says. 'Make any false moves and we'll shoot you.' The road is long and its surface is hot, and Sonic and Tails walk for ages. Eventually the road leads to a building made of metal. Its surface is studded with rivets, and there is a huge satellite dish on the roof. Over the door is a sign: 'Robotnik Broadcasting Company. We bring Mobius to you.' Turn to **124**.

49

You don't want to know what happens to people who enter the freezing vacuum of space without a space suit on. No, you don't. It's really, really gross. Put it this way, the phrase that astronauts use for it is 'Explosive Decompression'. See what I mean? Not nice at all. Just accept that it's **GAME OVER** for Sonic and Tails and close the book. Start again at the beginning.

50

Sonic must fight Number Two and Number Three, one at a time, using his Speed. Number Two has a rating of 7 and Number Three has a rating of 8. If Sonic loses a life during this fight, cross it off his *Vital Statistics* and turn back to **94**. If he wins, turn to **210**.

51

Add the number of rings that Sonic has to the number of rings Tails has. If the total is more than 50, turn to **185**. If they have fewer than 50 rings between them, turn to **70**.

52

'The rest of the warriors will join us soon,' says the wart-hog leader. Shortly Sonic hears creatures approaching through the twilight, and more wart-hogs appear. The leader turns to Sonic. 'You've seen things here,' he says. 'How should we attack?' What does Sonic suggest?

Climb the trees and swing across on the vines?	Turn to **87**
Climb the walls?	Turn to **120**
Batter down the gate?	Turn to **249**
Or does Sonic try to think of something better to do?	Turn to **272**

53

An accented voice fills the cabin. 'No l-l-l-lasers fitted to prototype *T-t-t-toho.* So sorry. Crash landing imm-imm-imm-imminent.'

'Whoops,' says Tails. Turn to **224**.

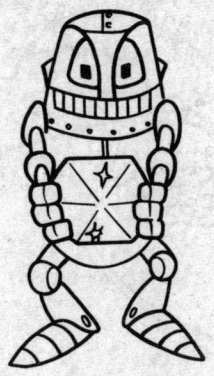

54

'Nobody, eh?' says the badger. 'And you just happened to drop in on our secret meeting, I'm sure. I think you've been eavesdropping for ages, listening to our plans. In fact, I think you're one of Galen's spies, sent to catch us.' The three back away. Will Sonic fight them (turn to **50**), say that he's Sonic the Hedgehog (turn to **195**) or claim he's a spy for the Outcasts (turn to **231**)?

55

Sonic leaps onto the gantry with Tails close behind. It's a long climb, but they reach the entrance to the rocket with seconds to spare. They dive in and the door slams shut behind them. From outside they can hear the last stages of the countdown: '5. 4. 3. 2. 1.'

'Did you know,' enquires Tails, 'that films invented rocket countdowns? The scientists really used count-ups, but countdowns were more exciting.'

There is a rumble below them and the rocket lifts off, gaining speed and height. The animals are pressed against the metal floor, their faces pulled out of shape by the g-forces. Slowly things return to normal, and they run to a porthole. The rocket's take-off has burnt up most of Robotnik's base. A small dot takes off from the blazing ruin and zooms away, trailing smoke: Robotnik in his Egg-o-matic.

'I hope you crash!' Sonic yells at him, and turns to Tails. 'Now we've got to work out how to stop the rocket delivering the Emeralds.' Our heroes can search the rocket (turn to **180**) or open the hatch (turn to **165**).

56

'Hey, scaly-face!' Sonic shouts. 'We thought wart-hogs were ugly but you take the biscuit in the "grossness" stakes!'

'Yeah!' Tails adds; 'you need need something to give you smoother skin – like sandpaper.'

'Or a mask,' Sonic taunts. 'The only way babes would want to be close to skin like yours is if you made it into a bag!'

'GRAWOWARRR!' replies the chieftain.

Roll on Sonic's and Tails's combined Coolness scores, to beat a difficulty of 8, to see how angry they have made the chieftain. If they succeed, turn to **112**. If they fail, they can attack him (turn to **153**) or be polite and friendly to him instead (turn to **4**).

57

The emeralds rattle out of the delivery device and Sonic and Tails rush to the porthole to watch them falling behind the rocket, towards the ground.

'Did we do the right thing?' asks Tails. 'Shouldn't we have found a place where Robotnik wouldn't be able to find them?'

Sonic is about to answer when he looks at the computer. A message is blinking on and off on its screen. 'EMERALDS DELIVERED – MISSION COMPLETED,' it reads. 'SELF-DESTRUCT SEQUENCE INITIATED.'

Sonic looks back at Tails. 'We've blown it,' he says, and the rocket explodes.

GAME OVER

58

Before long, Sonic sees a cluster of tents between two sand dunes. There are no lights or fires, no sign of an oasis or a well, and no movement. Does he scout around the outside of the camp (turn to **269**) or walk boldly into the middle (turn to **172**)?

59

Sonic lies still, ignoring the rumbling, thudding, grinding noise as it gets louder and closer. The horrible smell fills his nose and the ground begins to shake. Sonic puts his paws over his eyes and ears to blot it all out, and so he doesn't see the giant bulldozer before it squashes him flat as a pancake. Remember Sonic is never slow to act when there's a job to be done. Now turn back to section **1** and try again.

GAME OVER

60

Tails dashes to the edge and leaps into the air, trying to catch the monkey by the collar of its coat. Roll on his Speed to beat a **9**. If he makes it, turn to **139**. If he fails, turn to **226**.

61

As Sonic and Robotnik argue, Tails feels his fingers brush against something on the body of the robot holding him. He presses it and the robot's grip relaxes; it must be the 'Off' switch. He glances around and notices something lying beside the Egg-o-matic. It looks as if it's fallen out of the small machine. The fox ducks down behind a crate and sneaks forward. Robotnik is absorbed in his argument with Sonic, and doesn't notice as Tails creeps up to his seat, grabs the object –

it looks like a backpack, marked 'Emergency Parachute' – and sneaks back to the robot. He straps the parachute on and stands up, pretending the robot is holding him. Sonic has noticed all this happening, of course, but hasn't reacted in case Robotnik noticed too – what a hero. What should he say now to continue the argument?

'You're mad, Robotnik. Your plan
   will never work.'   Turn to **200**

'You're a genius, Robotnik. How is
   your rocket guided?'   Turn to **258**

62

'Hey!' Tails shouts. 'Who are you and what are you fighting?' The figures on the shore look up to see who was shouting. Tails ducks behind the snow-bank so they don't see him.

'Hey!' he hears in return. 'We're monkeys from the Hilltop Zone looking for our friends. Help us fight this monster!'

Tails knows that if he shouts again, he'll give away his position, so that's a bad idea. Instead, he can look for a teleporter device (turn to **145**), help the monkeys (turn to **168**) or attack them (turn to **10**).

63

'Whooooah!' Sonic shouts as he hurtles towards the ground.

'Whooooooooooooooooah!' Tails yells, not to be out-done.

'Whooooooooooooooooooooooooooooooo — hold on, this is stupid,' shouts Sonic. 'Which Zone are we falling towards?'

'It's the Green Hill Zone,' Tails shouts. 'Trees and waterfalls. I hope we don't land on anyone we know.'

They slam into the ground at several hundred metres per second, and lose all the rings they are carrying. If either of them has no rings then they lose a life. If it was their last life, it's **GAME OVER** — so near yet so far. If not, they're back in the Green Hill Zone, although badly hurt. Turn to 300.

64

Sonic swims to the bottom of the drawbridge. It's made from tree-tunks and is too sturdy to be smashed. Sonic can see the vines that hold it up, leading to a lever on the inside of the wall. Things would be easier if he could reach that, but if Sonic wanted an easy life he'd have been a plumber. Does Sonic cut the vines holding up the drawbridge (turn to 236) or use his strength to pull it down (turn to 188)?

65

With a flick of his tail, Tails dodges and the icicles smash into the side of the fridge-machine. Tails snatches one up and uses its sharp edge to hack away at the ropes holding the monkeys, freeing the three hostages.

'What now?' asks Mildred. Tails and his friends can

attack the mammoth (turn to **102**) or go for the Chaos Emerald on the fridge-machine (turn to **17**).

66

Sonic looks around and gives Tails a hefty shove. Tails staggers and falls over. Sally Acorn and Porker Harris turn and point their guns at him until he gets up, giving Sonic enough time to run to the pile of monitors. Sonic knows he has got only one chance as Sally and Porker will be alerted when the first monitor is smashed. It's too dark to see what the screens are showing, so he'll have to trust to luck.

Roll a die to see what Sonic gets:

1	Extra life
2–3	Shield: the next time Sonic is hit by an enemy, it has no effect (he doesn't lose any rings or a life)
4–6	Ten gold rings

Write down what Sonic found on his *Vital Statistics*, and turn to section **264**.

67

Sonic nods to Tails, and they break free from the robots holding them and dive towards the mad scientist. Robotnik sits back in the Egg-o-matic, watching them dash towards him.

'Ah well,' he sighs and flicks a switch. Energy blasts out from the Zap Cannon's twin barrels. Our two heroes are no more. Robotnik grins. 'Eggs-cellent! Now nothing stands in my way!' he shouts. 'HA! HA! HA!'

His laughter grows louder and louder, until it seems to ring out all over the planet – a planet without heroes.

GAME OVER

68

'What can we do?' says Sonic. 'If he open the doors, I might be able to dash past him . . .' He turns to Number Two. 'Pretend you're really ill,' he whispers.

Number Two looks at him quizzically, then starts moaning and groaning. 'Oooooooh. Aaaaaaaw. Owwww,' he goes. 'My stomach. Oo! It hurts.'

There is a rattling sound from the door. 'What's going on?' demands the ugly guard, appearing in the entrance. 'You must be fit for your execution, so if you're sick –' He steps forward and Sonic darts between his legs and into the corridor, running as fast as he can. He hurtles along corridors and down any stairways that don't lead to dead ends. Finally he dives through a door to find himself in an alley outside the prison. Turn to **91**.

69

The cats rearrange the tables and chairs to make a semicircle. In the middle sits the impressive cat, holding the Chaos Emerald, which sparkles and flashes with subdued energy, and Sonic, held by the two guards. The cat strides over to Sonic. 'I am Galen, High Judge and Commander of Scrap Brain City. You have broken into our banquet, probably on a mission of destruction, without an invitation, and improperly dressed. You,

Sonic the whatever-you-are, are accused of being an Outcast spy. We know they have spies in our city, because our agents have infiltrated them and tell me their every move. Do you plead innocent or guilty?' He stares at Sonic. Well?

Innocent?	Turn to 7
Guilty?	Turn to 140

70

The two heroes spin through the maze of lights and sounds, bouncing off walls and twisting past turnings and corners. Eventually they stop, dazed and confused.

'I'm exhausted. This is really tiring. Can't you think of a single way to get out of here?' Tails asks, with a note of desperation in his voice.

Sonic scratches his head. 'Well, yes, but it's a desperate one. Only for the direst of emergencies.'

'Is it dangerous?' Tails asks nervously.

'It's not dangerous for us,' says Sonic. 'The reader might get angry, because we have to break the First Rule of Gamebooks.' He pauses as Tails looks at him. 'The rule is: "Don't go backwards".'

'Backwards in space, time or through the sections?' Tails asks, his eyes full of wonder.

'All of them. Lie down, close your eyes and imagine you're lying under a tree in the Green Hill Zone.' They lie down on the weird undulating surface of the Warp. 'Relax,' says Sonic. 'Now recite after me: "It's a cool spring morning in the Green Hill Zone, and Sonic and Tails are lying under a palm tree, sleeping as hard as they can . . ."'

Turn to section 1.

71

'How easily you hard-boiled heroes submit in the face of true power!' says Robotnik, 'Just step onto the white cross on the floor, under the sinister device hanging from the ceiling — my new fast automatic shoe-removing ray, trademarked and patent pending. Honestly. Would I lie to you?'

Sonic and Tails are pushed at gunpoint towards the device by their former friends. Tails looks worried. 'It doesn't look much like a shoe-remover to me,' he mutters to Sonic as they are forced to stand under it.

'It's not! I *did* lie to you! Ha ha!' laughs Robotnik hysterically, and throws a huge switch. The device on the ceiling pulses and shoots a beam of whiteness straight down at them. Everything goes blank, except for a strange sound that goes FAZZZZZ-. Turn to section 8.

72

To escape from the robots, Sonic and Tails must each roll on their Speed, to beat an 8. If they fail, turn to 230. If they make it, they realize that they cannot hide on the crowded docks and they must run down one of the two tunnels. Do they choose the large one (turn to 217) or the small one (turn to 137)?

73

Sonic and Tails are given leafy clothes for camouflage and five gold rings each, then set off with the scouting party. They travel through thick jungle until the leader motions the group to stop. 'We are near the stronghold,' he says. 'Sonic and Tails, you look first. Don't get too close; there are guards around.'

The two creep to the edge of the clearing, and peer out. In front of them is a stronghold with walls made of sharpened tree-trunks stood on end. There is a large gate, firmly closed. Sonic and Tails can climb a tree for a better look (turn to **290**), they can watch for a while (turn to **18**), they can get close to the gate (turn to **108**) or they can rush to the wall and tunnel under it (turn to **218**).

74

'Sorry,' says Ross, 'there's no teleport out of here.'

'But we teleported in!' exclaims Tails. 'There must be a way out.'

'There's a way out but not by teleport,' says Ross. 'We can give you a spaceship. There's a planetary landing craft in our shuttle bay right now, and you can fly back to Mobius in it.'

'Isn't it difficult to pilot a spacecraft?' asks Tails.

'It's just like playing a video game,' replies the android. Sonic grins as he realizes he's going to be very, very good at it. The two heroes can ask to go to the spacecraft (turn to **288**), or they can ask Ross who built him (turn to **159**) or if he knows how they can get rid of their Chaos Emeralds safely (turn to **9**).

75

'You go left, I'll go right,' says Sonic, 'and I'll see you back here.' They dash around the building in different directions. Halfway round they pass each other and meet up again by the door.

'Did you spot anything?' asks Sonic.

'Only you,' says Tails. 'There's no other doorway.'

Should the heroes attack the door with a spin attack (turn to **24**) or throw things at the guards on the roof (turn to **176**)?

76

Sonic takes the rope, makes a loop in one end and throws it towards the ceiling. After three tries it lands on the hook and Sonic climbs up until he's level with the window. It has bars on it, but he can see out.

'Can you get out of the window?' shouts Number Three. Sonic tries to reach the window-sill, but it's too far. He can't swing the rope enough to get to it, and he knows he couldn't jump far enough. Disheartened, he climbs down.

'I've got an idea,' says Number Two. Sonic can take his advice (turn to **201**), or he can try one of his own plans:

Build a see-saw catapult from planks
   and bricks. Turn to **182**
Overpower the guard outside the cell. Turn to **133**
Climb the walls. Turn to **222**

77

Sonic steers to one side of the Warps. Is his ship fast enough to beat the red robot to the other side? Roll on Sonic's Speed, to beat a 9. If Sonic is piloting the *Kubrick* subtract 1 from his score; if he is piloting the *Yuzna* subtract 2. If he saw a star-chart on Space Station Eyrie, add 1 to his score. If he makes the roll, turn to **299**. If he fails, turn to **37**.

78

Sonic puts one gloved paw on Tails's shoulder and shakes his friend. Tails makes a snoring sound and turns over. The rumbling sound is getting closer. Sonic grabs hold of Tails's twin tails and pulls. Tails gives a yelp and jumps into the air.

'Why did you do that?' he asks. 'I was just getting to the good bit of my dream.'

'Look!' exclaims Sonic.

Rushing across the Green Hill Zone towards them is a monstrous yellow bulldozer. It's tearing down trees, pounding the ground flat and belching out thick, bad-smelling smoke. As it moves, it leaves a shiny trail behind it like a slug. Sonic and Tails can get closer to the bulldozer (turn to section **156** if you think that's a good idea) or they can get out of its way (turn to section **170**).

'Get outta here,' says Sonic. 'That is the most hare-brained scheme ever. It's so hare-brained that no hare with half a brain would have anything to do with it. I'll get my Chaos Emerald back on my own.'

'Wait!' says Number Two. 'You don't understand! If the cats are getting power from both Chaos Emeralds, they'll exceed the proximity effect and overload the —' he is too late. Sonic leaves the room, into the darkness outside. He bumps into something solid and furry.

'What on mmmph?' he says. Someone has covered his face with a cloth smelling of chemicals. Sonic tries to breathe, and passes out.

When he comes round, he's in a cell. Number Two and Number Three are staring glumly at him. 'What happened?' asks Sonic.

'The secret cat police grabbed us,' answers Number Three. 'They threw us in here, and took Number One away. They may be torturing him.'

'Or he might be the one who told them where we were,' adds Number Two.

'We can't sit here!' says Sonic. 'Someone has to tell the Outcasts in the desert what's going on, and I volunteer. Help get me out of here.' What should Sonic do?

Search the cell?   Turn to **27**
Ask what Number Two and Number
   Three are carrying?   Turn to **105**
Bang on the cell door?   Turn to **278**

80

Ross crumples to the floor. 'What was that?' he asks faintly. 'I've never seen it before. Chase after it, please.'

'We were about to,' replies Sonic. The two animals grab their helmets and dash out. Turn to **135**.

81

Sonic and Tails must fight two of the natives each, one at a time. Play through Sonic's first fight, then Tails's first fight, then Sonic's second and lastly Tails's second. The first two fights will take the natives by surprise and Sonic and Tails will use their Speed ability to fight them; for the second two fights the defenders are ready for them, and our two heroes must use their Strength instead. Each of the natives has a rating of 7. If either Sonic or Tails loses their rings or a life, cross it off their *Vital Statistics* and turn to **281**. If they defeat the four warriors, turn to **190**.

82

YOWCH! The Emeralds are so hot that Sonic can't hang onto them for a second longer. He lets go and they spiral up towards the roof, spinning around each other. Sonic watches as they twist in weird hypnotic patterns, and he's completely surprised when Galen and Number One jump on him from behind. He must fight them to survive. Turn to **239**.

83

The bed is as uncomfortable as it looks, with only one blanket on it. Suddenly Sonic realizes the only place to hide anything in this cell would be under the bed. He kneels on the floor and feels around and yes, there's something under there. He pulls out three gold rings (write them down), then realizes that part of the floor is wobbly, so perhaps something could be hidden under it. Sonic slides under the bed, lifts the loose flagstone and moves forward to see what is there — WHOOOOAH! He's rolling out of control down a stone chute that twists, turns and bumps him until he's dizzy and bruised. Suddenly he rockets out of the end of the chute into a small room, and into a group of animals, who spring back and draw wicked-looking swords, ready to attack! Turn to **123**.

84

The hatch pops open. Sonic and Tails jump in and slam it closed behind them. The submarine is filled with robots, all tending to different complex instruments. The hedgehog and fox sneak past them, until they come to a cupboard.

'In here,' says Tails. 'We've got to find out where the sub is going, so we'll hide in here until it gets there.'

The cupboard is cramped but they do find six gold rings (three each). The journey seems to last an age, but finally the submarine stops. 'I don't know where we are,' says Sonic, 'but I think we're there.' The heroes scramble over to the nearest porthole.

The submarine has surfaced inside a huge dome, and is moving towards a dockside which covers half of the base of the dome. There are two tunnels leading off it. The place is filled with robots, all attending to different tasks. A voice recites numbers backwards through a loudspeaker: '106. 105. 104.' Do Sonic and Tails leave the sub and swim to the dock (turn to **252**) or stay on the submarine to see what happens (turn to **104**)?

85

'Chirps!' Sonic says. 'Don't you recognize us?'

'No,' Chirps says. 'What are you doing in my cab?'

'But we're your friends,' Tails says. 'I'm Tails and he's Sonic. Remember?'

'Sonic and Tails?' Chirps exclaims. 'The enemies of President Robotnik?' Before Sonic or Tails can react, he presses a red button and a high-pitched shriek fills the cab. The television screen clears and Porker Harris, Sonic's piggy pal, appears.

'What's the problem, Bulldozer Three?' he asks.

'Sonic and Tails. They're in my cab. Help!' shouts Chirps.

'An emergency squad is on its way.' Porker disappears and the screen fills with static. Should Sonic and Tails leave the bulldozer (turn to **170**) or search the cab (turn to **48**)?

86

Sonic tells Ravis that the city is now powered by two Chaos Emeralds, and the Outcast leader frowns. 'That changes things,' he says. 'My army will attack the city tonight, but I must rethink our plans. I will lead an assault on the gates, but you must take four of my best warriors to the city's rear wall. Watch for a white flare in the sky, then climb over the wall and go to the High Tower. Get the Chaos Emeralds — we will not win unless you do it. Will you help us?' Sonic nods, and Ravis slaps him on the back. 'Excellent! Have these ten gold rings as a token of my trust. I will give you your weight in silver and many rugs once we have won,' he proclaims. They go outside to join the rest of the Outcast army. Mark down '10 rings' and '4 warriors' on Sonic's *Vital Statistics*, and turn to **119**.

87

Sonic jumps to a nearby tree and climbs up into the branches. From here he can see the inner wall of the stronghold, and the moat between the two. Several vines hang here and he grabs one, before looking down at everyone on the ground below.

'If this works,' he shouts, 'follow me. If it doesn't work, attack the gate.' Giving a huge yell, he jumps off the tree, and the vine swings him over the outer wall, the moat and the inner wall. With hedgehog-like grace, he leaps from the creeper and lands in the middle of the stronghold. Behind him, wart-hog warriors start swinging across after him. There are two wooden buildings in the stronghold. One is large and well-guarded, with a strange glow coming from its lower windows. The other looks like a stockade where prisoners are kept. Crocodile guards are rushing between the two and climbing the walls to fend off attackers. If Sonic saw the crocodiles taking any prisoners and he wants to free them, turn to **106**. Otherwise he can attack the large building (turn to **214**) or rush to the gate and let down the drawbridge (turn to **263**).

88

A digital voice fills the cockpit. 'Are you mad?' it says. 'What do you want to deploy the parachutes for? We're still in space.'

'So much for that,' Sonic mutters. Turn to **30**.

89

'Who said that?' Tails asks, looking around nervously. He pulls himself out of the snowdrift, brushes the snow off his fur and rushes towards the fighting. He can see a group of figures, possibly monkeys but he's not sure, standing on the edge of the ice and jabbing with spears at something large and grey in the water beyond. They look very aggressive. Should he attack the figures (turn to **10**), attack the thing in the water (turn to **168**) or go and look around for a teleporter device (turn to **145**)?

90

'Cool,' says Sonic. 'That sounds neat.'

'Clever? You wouldn't know clever if it stole your pyjamas! I didn't send you and your orange friend to the egg-citing places where I'd placed my beloved Chaos Emeralds by accident. No! I knew that a so-called hero like you would recover them all, and then I could steal them from you with the robots I'd planted on the space station built by my twin brother, Ovi Kintobor.'

'But you are Ovi Kintobor — or at least you were until the Chaos Emeralds changed you into Robotnik!' says an astonished Sonic.

'I said "My *twin brother*, Ovi Kintobor". You want to argue about it?' Robotnik asks, flicking the switch of the Zap Cannon meaningfully. Sonic shuts up. 'As I was saying,' continues the mad genius, 'I needed two agents whose brains wouldn't be scrambled by the mutating effects of the Chaos Emeralds. You two are perfect! A blue hedgehog and a fox with two tails — the Chaos Emeralds couldn't mutate you because you're already mutants!'

Tails looks at Sonic. 'Do you feel like a mutant?' he asks.

'No, I feel like a snack,' Sonic says. 'Remember that he's a complete lunatic. We can still escape if we humour him.'

'Ha ha ha ha ha!' continues the complete lunatic. 'In two minutes my beautiful rocket will blast off, programmed to drop the Emeralds you so kindly recovered into every Zone on the planet. By morning I shall control Mobius!'

What do Sonic and Tails do?

Look around the room?   Turn to **61**
Ask Robotnik who will pilot the
   rocket?   Turn to **258**
Tell Robotnik he's mad?   Turn to **200**

91

The city is darkening as evening falls. There aren't many people around on the streets, but Sonic knows that if he's seen, he'll be captured and thrown into an even more secure cell, so he must be careful. Should Sonic sneak through the shadows, towards the city gates (turn to **154**), should he dash through the streets to the gate as fast as possible (turn to **289**) or should he search for the Chaos Emeralds in the city (turn to **178**)?

92

Sonic and Tails duck behind a pile of scaffolding poles and watch. The animals coming in and out of the building are behaving very oddly: they stare straight ahead without talking. Even when two of them bump into each other, they don't react or say anything at all. It's really eerie. Sonic and Tails must roll on their combined Quick Wits, to beat a 10: add their Quick Wits scores together, then roll a die and add that as well. If the total is 10 or more then they've done it; turn to section **257**. If the total is less than 10 then they've failed; turn to section **134**.

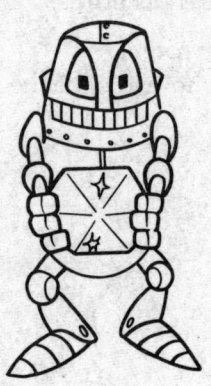

93

The door of the prison is locked, but there's a barred window next to it. 'You,' Sonic says to the toughest warrior, 'bend the bars so we can get in.' The soldier grips the bars, heaves and twists them as if they were made of warm wax. Sonic turns to look at you. 'Don't you *love* being in control?' he asks.

The gap is too narrow for the warriors, but Sonic climbs through, retraces his steps to the cell where he was imprisoned, and undoes the bolt on the door. Inside are Number Two and Number Three. 'Number Four!' shouts Number Two.

'Sonic!' shouts Number Three. 'What's going on?'

'Your dad's invading the city,' says Sonic. 'And he needs our help!' Suddenly the doorway is blocked by a furry blue-green shape. It looks vaguely feline, only much bigger, and as it turns to stare at Sonic, he recognizes it as the ugly guard, but double the size and twice as hideous now. It howls and kicks out at him. Sonic must fight it to leave the cell! He will use his Speed against the beast's rating of 10, and Sonic can add 2 points to his roll because Number Two and Number Three are fighting on his side. If Sonic loses a life, cross it off his *Vital Statistics* and turn back to **119**. If Sonic and the Outcasts win, turn to **144**.

94

'Of course I'll help,' agrees Tails. 'Any hero would.' He sets off towards a mountain peak that looms in the distance, with a mighty glacier making a frozen path to its summit. Tails points to it. 'That's the easiest way up,' he says. 'From the mountaintop we'll get the best view to look for your friends.' They set off through the drifting snow and the wind.

Meanwhile, back in the warmer climate of Scrap Brain City, Sonic is hot and bothered. He's surrounded by sharp sword-points, with three very angry animals holding them. One is a large badger, the second is a tall bird wearing glasses, and the third is a young dog, almost a puppy, with pointed ears. Sonic notices a pile of papers on the table, titled 'Secret Outcast Plans', and he realizes that he must have fallen into a meeting of Outcast spies. What's worse is that he knows one of them is an agent for the cats who run the city!

'Who are you?' asks the badger in a low, slow voice.

What does Sonic reply?

'I'm Sonic the Hedgehog; who are you?'	Turn to **195**
'I'm nobody in particular — just passing through.'	Turn to **54**
'I'm a spy for the Outcasts.'	Turn to **231**

95

Sonic carefully extends the net towards the twisting shapes of the Emeralds. With a sudden shake he flicks it over them, trapping them both inside its thick mesh and pulling them down to the floor. His friends go completely barmy with excitement and congratulations, and Galen and Number One begin to retreat and shrink. Suddenly there is a hissing sound from the net. A thin line of smoke rises from it, and a smell of burning fills the room. The net bursts into flames and the Emeralds break through it, spinning back into the air. Even at a distance, Sonic can feel their intense heat. The hedgehog hero can attack Galen and Number One (turn to **239**), grab the Emeralds in his paws (turn to **15**) or rush across the room to the teleporter (turn to **280**).

96

Sonic strains with all his might, but he can't force the two far enough apart to break the vines. He might do it if he had a few more seconds, but the crocodile guards have noticed what he's doing and are firing rotten fruit at him. Sonic drops back into the moat to dodge their missiles. He can cut the vines that are holding up the drawbridge (turn to **236**), he can climb the inner wall (turn to **223**) or he can swim back outside the stronghold and find another way of getting in (turn to **31**).

97

Running across sand dunes is very tiring, and as he gets closer to the lights, Sonic is glad to see tents surrounding an oasis, with grass and palm trees. It looks very inviting and refreshing. People in loose-fitting robes are moving between the tents and sitting around the fires, cooking in large iron pots, and suddenly he feels very hungry. He crests the final sand dune and approaches the circle of tents. A twig breaks under his foot and a figure beside the nearest fire sees him and stands up. Sonic walks closer.

'I'm looking for the Outcasts,' he says. 'Are you them?'

'Outcasts?' the figure replies. 'No, we're bandits.' He draws a curved sword from his belt and attacks. Sonic must beat three of the bandits in turn before the others back away. He is using his Speed to fight them, and their ratings are 6, 7 and 7. If he beats them all, turn to **294**. If he is hit once by the bandits, losing either his rings or a life, turn to **234**.

98

'No air? No problem!' shouts Sonic through his helmet radio. A few metres away Tails grins and gives him a thumbs-up. 'Let's head back to the station,' he radios back. Sonic thumbs his suit's controls, and feels a biting pain in his foot. It's not a malfunction, it's the red robot which has clamped its teeth onto him. If he doesn't get rid of it, it'll rupture his suit! Sonic must fight the robot, using his Quick Wits to do it. The suit slows him down and he must subtract 1 point from the roll of the dice. The robot's rating is 5. If Sonic loses a life, cross it off his sheet and turn back to **288**. If he beats the robot, turn to **248**.

99

Sonic and Tails turn and dash away through the undergrowth, running through the long jungle grass, leaping over fallen trees and sending small animals scurrying away. The Warcat crashes through the jungle behind them, splintering branches as it tears through trees that Sonic and Tails have jumped around. Suddenly the two heroes find themselves on a path that twists and turns around trees. They speed up, slowly moving away from the pursuing Warcat — until they abruptly turn a bend and come face to face with a group of six strange figures. They are dressed in leaves, carry spears and wear decorated masks that cover their faces. Two of them shake their spears at Sonic and Tails while the others talk in a strange language, probably wondering who these strangers are. Should Sonic and Tails approach these native warriors (turn to **151**), take their chances with the Warcat (turn to **227**) or run off into the jungle away from everyone (turn to **46**)?

100

The ship's controls resist as Sonic turns it towards the spinning lights and sounds of the Warps of Confusion. He's not sure he can steer his way safely through them, but he's going to find out. Roll against Sonic's Coolness, to beat a 7. Add 1 to his score if he's flying the *Toho*. If he fails the roll, turn to **241**. If he makes it, the ship hurtles out of the whirling madness of the Warps. Turn to **299**.

101

The three spies turn to look at him. 'Can we trust him?' asks Number One.

'Of course! He's Sonic the Hedgehog,' answers Number

Three. 'Besides, what are the chances of this plan working? Zero. Zilch. Nothing. Something always goes wrong. It can't hurt to tell him.'

'After all,' adds Number Two, 'Galen probably knows exactly what we're planning. Okay, Number Four, listen carefully. Scrap Brain City is powered by the Chaos Emerald, kept in the High Tower. It's closely guarded, but our technical expert — that's me — thinks that if we can isolate the Emerald, we can cut off the power to the city. Then we set off a flare, which is a signal to the Outcasts in the desert to attack. We don't want to take over the city or kill all the cats, we just don't think it's fair they should keep all the power and luxury for themselves, while we're stuck out in the desert with nothing.'

'How are you going to get into the High Tower?' asks Sonic.

'I haven't worked that out yet,' says Number Two. 'With Galen's spy around, as soon as I have the plan, he'll know it, so I was leaving that until the last moment. Will you help us?' Does Sonic agree to help (turn to **149**) or does he say it's the most hare-brained scheme he's ever heard (turn to **79**)?

102

Tails knows what he wants — he wants that Chaos Emerald and he wants to get out of here, and no hippy elephant is going to get in his way! With a yell that is 98 per cent aggression and adrenalin and 2 per cent coldness, tiredness and frustration, he charges. Tails

must use his Speed to defeat the lumbering mammoth.
It has a rating of 10, but Tails can add 1 point to his
roll for every monkey fighting beside him. If the
mammoth scores a hit on him, roll the die. On a 1, 2
or 3 it has hit Tails, who must lose all his rings (or, if
he has no rings, cross off a life and turn back to **125**).
On a 4, 5 or 6 it has hit one of the monkeys, who is
knocked out of the combat (remember to add a point
for any remaining monkeys). If Tails and the monkeys
win, they can either smash the fridge-machine (turn to
175) or go for the Chaos Emerald (turn to **297**).

103

The shark doesn't notice the ice-floe with its passenger,
but the figures on the shore do, and they wave at
Tails. 'Jump!' they shout, 'or it'll melt! Jump!' Tails
shakes his head; he's made up his mind, and he can't
see how such a large chunk of ice could melt so
quickly that he couldn't jump off it in time. When the
ice does melt a few seconds later, very suddenly, Tails

is most surprised to be dropped into the freezing water below. By the time he's stopped being surprised and started swimming up to the surface, the huge shape of the metal shark is already swooping down towards him. There is a single gulp and a robotic burp, and that's that.

GAME OVER

104

Through the porthole the two animals can see the robots unloading the submarine's holds. Two crates, marked 'Chaos Emeralds: Handle With Care', go ashore first, followed by five other unmarked boxes. 'I wonder what's in those?' whispers Tails.

'Computer parts,' declares a voice behind him. It is the small red robot, or at least a small red robot, and it has five other small red robots behind it, all carrying unpleasant-looking rayguns. 'Stoic and Nails,' says the robot. 'Come with us.' Sonic and Tails are led out onto the dockside, through the throng of robots unloading the submarine. The animals exchange a glance: it's just possible that they could get away from their captors in this confusion. Do they try it (turn to **72**) or follow meekly on (turn to **230**)?

'Turn out your pockets,' Sonic demands. The other two do as they are told, and Sonic watches as they produce the contents. 'What's this?' he asks.

'That's a copy of the key to the city gates,' answers Number Three. 'Next to it is a lucky talisman given to me by my — by the chief of the Outcasts. You can have both of them.'

If Sonic wants either or both of the items, write them down on his *Vital Statistics*. 'Is that it?' he asks.

'We were searched before they threw us in here,' says Number Three. 'All we have is the clothes we're wearing — no, wait!' From around his waist he unwinds a length of thin rope. 'I use it as a belt,' he explains. 'And I've got one gold ring in my pocket. Take it for good luck.' If Sonic should search the cell next, turn to **27**. If he should bang on the door, turn to **278**.

106

Sonic approaches the stockade, two wart-hogs beside him. There are two crocodile guards there; they aim crossbows at the advancing trio. Sonic and his companions must fight the guards. Sonic uses his Speed here, adding 1 point to his roll for each of the wart-hogs. The crocodiles each have a rating of 9, and Sonic must fight them one at a time. If a crocodile hits Sonic, roll a die. On a 1, 2 or 3, Sonic has been hit and loses his rings (if he has no rings he must lose a life and turn back to **31**). On a 4, 5 or 6 one of the wart-hogs has been hit and retires from the fight. Only add a point for each surviving wart-hog. If Sonic and the wart-hogs win, turn to **131**.

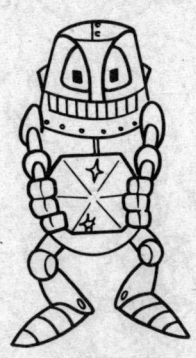

107

The road leads through the changed landscape of the Green Hill Zone, towards a building on the horizon. It's made of silvery metal, with large towers, fortifications and battlements. On top is a huge satellite dish pointing upwards into the sky. The building has two huge open doors, and Sonic and Tails can see animals from around the Zone going in and out of the building. They all carry tools or equipment. There's a sign above the doors, reading: 'Robotnik Broadcasting Company: We bring Mobius to you.' Do Sonic and Tails enter the building (turn to **193**), stand and watch the animals (turn to **92**) or explore the Zone (turn to **170**)?

108

Sonic and Tails creep to the main gate. It's made of heavy logs tied together with vines. There are cracks between the logs, and through them the heroes can see another wall on the inside and a water-filled moat between them. There's a drawbridge which is lowered at the moment – with two crocodiles coming across it, towards the gate that Sonic and Tails are outside! Do the heroes run (turn to **266**) or stand and fight (turn to **181**)?

109

The heroes yank their arms free of the robots holding them and dash for the exit. Blasts of energy sizzle around their ears but Robotnik is a rotten shot. They duck into the tunnel and emerge into a huge cavern containing an immense red-and-black rocket. A gantry stands beside it. The count gets lower: '19. 18. 17.' Do they destroy the rocket (turn to **235**) or get in it (turn to **55**)?

110

Sonic sits up in the sticky cake, and wonders how he can bluff his way out of this equally sticky situation. Roll on his Coolness, to beat a 7. If he succeeds, turn to **171**. If he fails, turn to **36**.

111

Tails and Mildred walk around the plant, watching it. It quivers and shakes harder if they get near. 'What is it?' asks Mildred.

'I've never seen anything like it before,' Tails replies. 'It could have come with the snow. Or, if there's a Chaos Emerald nearby, that could have changed it. Chaos is all about things becoming unpredictable and bizarre.'

'Let's get closer,' suggests Mildred. 'We can see if your theory is right.' Does Tails agree (turn to **286**) or do they carry on through the snow (turn to **161**)?

112

It's difficult for a crocodile to go red in the face, but this one manages it. He looks around for a weapon but there's nothing nearby, and Sonic and Tails are keeping out of range. Wild with rage, he hurls the Chaos Emerald at them. Sonic catches it. 'Thank you!' he shouts and dives for the teleporter. As he reaches it, he is surrounded by the familiar white light. Tails jumps into the beam a moment later. FAZZZZZZZZZ-. Turn to **229**.

113

A voice fills the cockpit. 'Parachutes have been deployed,' it says. 'Just in time.' The engines cut out and the *Yuzna* falls through the atmosphere of the planet. Far below, Sonic can see the ocean and the red robot's ship floating on the surface. There is no land in sight. As the *Yuzna* drops closer, he sees that the robot is standing on its ship, with the Chaos Emeralds beside it. The *Yuzna* falls into the ocean not far from the small red ship. The water around the ships begins to bubble as something rises up between them, and Sonic and Tails gasp as a huge golden submarine breaks the surface. Robots rush out from hatches on the submarine and jump across to the red ship. What should Sonic and Tails do?

Use the *Yuzna* to ram the submarine?	Turn to **35**
Abandon their spacecraft and swim to the sub?	Turn to **6**
Jump to the red ship?	Turn to **130**

114

Sonic leaps to his feet and dashes towards the source of the sound — there's nothing like a good run to wake you up in the morning, especially if you're a hedgehog. Ahead of him, a group of palm trees shake and sway, then fall to the ground, sliced into matchsticks, as a huge yellow machine ploughs through them. It looks like a bulldozer, except that Sonic has never seen a bulldozer this big before. Its motor coughs out thick clouds of oily smoke. On top of the massive machine is a driver's cab, and Sonic can see someone in there through the mirrored glass. The machine is spraying a black liquid behind it, making a hard, shiny surface that stretches into the distance. The bulldozer accelerates towards some nearby trees – the trees under which Tails is sleeping! Sonic has to save him, but how?

Run back and grab Tails before he's squashed flat?	Turn to **13**
Throw something to wake Tails up?	Turn to **243**
Let the machine run over Tails and explore alone?	Turn to **186**

115

Tails whizzes his tails and manoeuvres between the ice walls to the stranded monkey. 'Grab my paw!' he shouts. The monkey does, and Tails increases the speed of his spinning tails to lift them both out of this hole. Roll on Tails's Strength, to beat an 8. If he makes it, turn to **254**. If he fails, turn to **203**.

116

'We're not going to attack you,' says Sonic. 'We come in peace. Sort of. What is your name?' The strange beast growls and howls, and Sonic hears answering howls in the distance. In the moonlight he can just see its face, which looks oddly like a cat's, but its fur is a strange blue-green colour. 'Did the Chaos Emeralds change you into this?' asks Sonic. The beast roars with anguish, and staggers forward, smashing at them with muscled arms. Turn to **45**.

Number One slumps to the floor, beaten. As he falls, the Chaos Emeralds behind him spin faster and brighter. Bolts of brilliant blue-green light explode from them, shooting across the room. Roll the die twice and add the two numbers; that's how many bolts the Emeralds fire. Roll the die once for each bolt. Every time you roll a 1, a blue bolt hits the Galen-monster and increases his rating (which starts at 10) by 1 more point. For every 5 or 6 that you roll, a green bolt strikes one of Sonic's companions. A roll of 5 will be deflected by a contamination suit, if the victim is wearing one, but otherwise in a hideous few seconds he mutates into a monster with a rating of 7! The moment the lights stop flashing, Sonic's transformed companions attack. Sonic must use his Speed to fight them off. He adds 1 point to his roll for every unchanged companion he has. If he is hit during this fight, roll a die. On a 1, 2 or 3 Sonic is hit and loses all his rings (if he has none left, cross off a life and turn back to 21). On a 4, 5 or 6 one of his unchanged companions is hit and is knocked out of the fight (cross him off Sonic's *Vital Statistics*). Once the mutated companions are defeated, Galen roars and leaps towards Sonic, who must use his Strength to defend himself. Again, he can add 1 point to his roll for every companion who hasn't been knocked out of the fight. If Sonic wins, turn to 39.

118

'Jump!' shouts Tails, and Sonic does. There is a crash behind them as the Warcat, who doesn't speak English and didn't jump, falls through a thin layer of branches and leaves, into a deep pit. It roars in frustration, but it can't get out. A group of six creatures appear from behind some trees. They are all dressed in simple clothes made of leaves. Each one wears a carved wooden mask, and most of them carry spears. They're very pleased to see the Warcat trapped in the pit, but they keep away from Sonic and Tails, as if they are afraid of them. Two of the braver ones advance, jabbing with their spears. Do Sonic and Tails attack them (turn to 81) or show they mean these people no harm (turn to 298)?

119

The Outcast army is assembled outside. They are of all species and carry many different weapons, from swords to laser pistols, but Sonic can tell that behind their disordered appearance is a strength of spirit that makes them a fearsome fighting force. Ravis introduces Sonic to the soldiers who will be fighting alongside him. 'We are honoured,' they say. 'This will be the great-grandmother of all battles.' Ravis gives a command, and the army starts the long march across the desert. Sonic, walking with the others, can see a blue-green glow on the horizon in the direction of the city. The glow grows brighter as they get closer, but the high city walls hide its source. Ravis taps Sonic on the shoulder. 'Go to the far side of the city,' he says, 'and wait for our signal. We will attack in an hour.'

Sonic and his troops run off across the sand, leaving the army behind.

An hour is a long time if you're waiting for something, especially in the dark. Sonic is sure that the time has passed but he can't hear a battle — could Galen's forces have captured the entire army? It's possible, he thinks. The blue-green glow is making him jumpy. Does Sonic give the order to attack (turn to **237**) or does he wait (turn to **219**)?

120

'Follow me!' shouts Sonic and runs to the walls. They are carved from rough tree-trunks and climbing them is easy. He looks over the top and sees another wall on the inside, with a water-filled moat dividing the two. There are crocodile guards standing on the inner wall, and they are firing rotten fruit at the blue hedgehog, who is making an easy target. Sonic must roll on his Speed to beat an 8 to dodge the flying fruit. If he makes it, turn to **287**. If he fails, he is knocked off the wall; turn to **31**.

121

Roll on Sonic's Agility to beat a 7 to sneak past the guards. If he makes the roll, turn to **192**. If not, turn to **205**.

122

With a cooling Chaos Emerald in either paw, Sonic glances over his shoulder. The creatures mutated by the Emeralds are shrinking and sliding back into their normal forms and Sonic is sure that they'll be okay in an atmosphere untainted by chaos. He dashes to the teleporter and leaps under it, but there is no bright white light or FAZZZ- noise. Sonic looks desperately across to the other side of the room, where his friends are standing. 'How do I get this thing to work?' he shouts.

'Kick it!' comes the reply. Sonic gives the machine a good boot, and FAZZZZZZZZZZZZAM! He appears in mid-air and tumbles a few centimetres, landing on something soft. 'Oof! Gerroff!' it goes.

Sonic picks himself up. 'Tails!' he exclaims. 'What are you doing here?'

'I got here about five seconds ago,' complains the fox. 'I've had an adventure with ice and a robot shark and monkeys and a giant fridge. Am I a real hero yet?'

'Not yet,' says Sonic. 'Unless you can do better than these.' He shows him the two Chaos Emeralds, then looks around him. 'Where are we anyway?'

They are in a small room with bright white panels on the walls. In one corner lie two gold rings, which they can take. There is a single door which, as they watch, slides open. Someone steps into the room. It looks like a human being completely covered in silvery metal. Do Sonic and Tails attack it (turn to 23) or talk to it (turn to 273)?

123

Meanwhile, over on the other side of Mobius, Tails is buried up to his waist in a snowdrift. Unfortunately he's upside down, so his head is in the snow and his feet are waving in the air. A moment ago he material-ized a metre above the snowdrift, and you can work out the rest yourself.

'Sonic!' he shouts, his voice muffled by snow. 'SONIC! Where are you?' He listens for any reply. There's no trace of Sonic's voice — not surprising since he's in Scrap Brain City — but Tails can hear shouts and the sound of a fight. If you think Tails should burrow into the snow so that the fighters can't see him, turn to 240. If you think he should investigate what's happen-ing, turn to 283. If you think he should join in the fight, turn to 89.

124

The building is dark, cold and gloomy. As the group walks into the entrance hall, Sonic notices a large television set at the end of the room. It's not switched on, but there are smaller televisions and computer monitors piled around its base. Some of them look as if they might be power-ups, like the ones that Sonic and Tails find in the zones. Does Sonic try to grab one of the monitors without his captors noticing (turn to 66) or does he keep walking (turn to 264)?

125

From the heat of the desert to the cold of the Hill Top Zone. Tails and his friends have travelled far up the glacier towards the top of the mountain. The monkeys are getting tired in their heavy overcoats but Tails, with his furry coat, leads them onwards and upwards. Finally the monkeys cannot continue. 'Stop!' they shout. 'We have to rest. This flat place looks perfect.'

'Wait!' shouts Tails. 'That could be snow covering a —' but it's too late. The first monkey throws itself onto the snow. There is a cracking noise, the snow slips away and the monkey starts to slide down into a crack in the ice. ' — a crevasse,' finishes Tails. Should he dash and grab the monkey before it falls into the depths (turn to **60**), or should he wait before helping (turn to **208**)?

126

'Ah, Number Four,' says the bird.

'I am not a number, I'm a hedgehog!' shouts Sonic. 'I've got important information for you, so listen up. One of your group is an informant for Galen and the cats running the city.'

'I know!' says Number Two. 'Every time we try a new plan, the secret police are waiting for us. Last week we were planning to raid the High Tower with the Chaos Emerald in it —'

'Wait a second,' interrupts Sonic. 'There's one Chaos Emerald here already, before I arrived with the second one?'

'Yes,' replies Number Two, 'it's the city's power source. You brought another Emerald with you? Oh dear. Oh dear oh dear. Dearie, dearie me. I'll have to think about this. Dear oh dear oh dear . . .' Number Two sits down to think.

What should Sonic do next?

Talk to Number One?	Turn to **38**
Talk to Number Three?	Turn to **253**
Ask what their next plan is?	Turn to **101**

127

Sonic and Tails fight their way through the crush and into an escape pod full of androids. The door slams, there is a rumble and the pod leaves the station and flies off into space. Sonic looks through a porthole. He can see the station and it doesn't seem to be under attack. There's only one spaceship around: a small red one, flying straight for the escape pod. Sonic spots a familiar-looking robot in the cockpit, surrounded by Chaos Emeralds; then the ship's lasers flash and the pod explodes. Bang.

GAME OVER

128

The croc wraps a scaly arm around the dazed Tails, lifts him up and sprints through the gate. Sonic chases them but the wooden door slams shut in his face. 'Tails! Are you okay?' shouts Sonic. There is no reply. Sonic sniffs. 'My buddy's gone. If I wasn't a hero, I think I'd feel frightened. Tails is a hero too — he'll be safe. I hope.' He walks to where the leader of the wart-hogs is standing.

'Is there anything I can do?' asks the leader.

'Yeah,' says Sonic. 'You can start the attack *right now.*' Turn to **52.**

129

Roll on Sonic's and Tails's combined Speed, to beat a 13. That means you must add Sonic's Speed and Tails's Speed, then roll one die and add that as well. If the total is 13 or more, you should turn to **271.** If the total is 12 or less, turn to **71.**

130

Sonic and Tails leap towards the red ship, landing on its tail. The small red robot has been joined by four others, taking the Chaos Emeralds to the submarine.

Four of them form a wall in front of Sonic and Tails, while the fifth escapes with the gemstones. Sonic and Tails must each fight two robots, in turn, using their Speed. Each robot has a rating of 7. If either of the heroes loses either their rings or a life, turn to **198**. If they win the fight, turn to **6**.

131

Sonic and the wart-hogs smash down the stockade gates. Inside, tied up, are three more wart-hogs and Tails. Sonic pulls the ropes off him. 'Are you okay, Tails?' he says worriedly.

Tails smiles. 'Sonic,' he says. 'Boy, I'm glad to see you.' The two friends rush out of the stockade and over to the main fort. Turn to **214**.

132

Tails dashes towards the teleporter. Its wires are sparking, but that doesn't stop a determined fox. He leaps towards it. There is a crackling sound and the white light blasts down at him, stronger and hotter than ever before. Roll on Tails's Strength, to beat an 8. If he fails, the bright light fries him and he loses all his rings. If he has no rings, he loses a life and must turn to **125**. If he survives the beam, turn to **277**.

133

There's one problem with overpowering the guard: the solid door between him and Sonic. The hedgehog hammers on it. A little trapdoor in it slides open, and an ugly guard peers in. 'I don't want any trouble from you,' says the guard, 'or I'll show you real trouble. Now shut up. I'm trying to get some sleep.' The trapdoor slides shut. What now? Sonic can attract the guard's attention again (turn to **68**), climb the wall towards the window (turn to **222**), make a see-saw catapult out of the planks and bricks of the bed (turn to **182**) or, if he has a rope, try to lasso the hook in the ceiling (turn to **76**).

134

'Paws up! Turn around slowly.' As Sonic and Tails rotate they see their friend Sally Acorn, pointing a submachine-gun at them. Behind her is Porker Harris, also with a gun. They look mean.

'Good work, Five,' says Porker. 'Capturing the notorious Twin-Tails and Sonic the Wart-hog. President Robotnik will be pleased.'

'That's Sonic the HEDGEHOG,' explodes Sonic, 'and his – did you say *President* Robotnik?'

'We ask the questions,' says Sally. A confused Sonic and Tails are steered at gunpoint into the building. Turn to section **124**.

135

The corridor is lit by flashing alarm lights. Sonic and Tails almost trip over an android lying against the wall with a hole in its metal skin. There's no sign of the small red robot, or the Emeralds. Should Sonic and Tails go left (turn to **169**), right (turn to **232**) or talk to the android (turn to **19**)?

136

Sonic and Tails are alone in the darkening jungle. 'Night's coming. Let's find somewhere to sleep,' says Sonic.

'Won't all the good places have things living in them?' asks Tails. 'Creepy-crawlies and things with lots of teeth and legs?'

'Of course not,' says Sonic, striding ahead. 'Anyway, you're with me so you're perfectly safe. Just keep your wits about you and be carefu — aaaarrgghh!' The ground collapses beneath their feet, and they plunge into a pit. It's too deep for them to climb out and they're stuck there. Since they've annoyed the only people in the Zone who might help them, they may be trapped for a long time. By the time they get out, Robotnik will have conquered the whole world.

GAME OVER

137

Sonic and Tails creep down the tunnel. Ahead of them is a large chamber full of machines and equipment. At the far end is a big weapon, and the two heroes take a couple of steps into the room to get a better look at it. Mistake! They are grabbed by two silver robots and dragged to the centre of the room. The big weapon swivels towards them. It is Dr Robotnik in his Egg-o-matic machine, with a massive twin-barrelled gun fixed to the front.

'What's that?' asks Tails.

'Ha ha ha!' replies Robotnik. 'A Zap Cannon. Move and I shall fry you into Flambéd Fox.'

'You don't fry flambés, you burn them!' shouts the fox. 'Every cook knows that.'

'Well, your goose is certainly cooked!' replies the mad scientist. 'You never realized how I tricked you! Ha, ha, ha!' Over the laughter, Sonic and Tails can hear the voice counting backwards: '69. 68. 67.' What should Sonic and Tails do?

Stand there silently?	Turn to **11**
Demand that Robotnik tell them how he tricked them?	Turn to **152**
Pretend to be impressed by Robotnik's cleverness?	Turn to **90**
Attack Robotnik?	Turn to **67**

138

The bulldozer rumbles past the spot where Sonic and Tails were lying a moment before, flattening the earth with its blade and spraying it with a sticky liquid which sets hard, making a wide road that stretches into the distance. The bulldozer roars away. Sonic watches it go, and turns to look out of the pages of the book, up towards you. 'Hey!' he says, 'HEY, YOU, READER! This is supposed to be a thrilling adventure, but all we've done so far is wake up and roll out of the way of some machine that's wrecking our home. Me and Tails,' he gestures at Tails, who trips over the full stop at the end of the last sentence and almost falls off the page, 'we're brave adventurers, so give us something brave and adventurous to do. And make it fast, because that bulldozer is trashing the Green Hill Zone!' Choose one of the following things for the pair to do:

Try to destroy the bulldozer.	Turn to **212**
Run after the bulldozer and jump onto it.	Turn to **26**
Walk down the new road.	Turn to **107**
Explore the rest of the zone.	Turn to **170**

139

Tails grabs the monkey's collar and the two land safely on the other side of the ice canyon. Now the snow has fallen into it, they can see the crevasse stretches for kilometres, to the edges of the glacier. Turn to **41**.

140

'I'm guilty,' says Sonic. 'Can I have the Emerald back?'

'You admit your guilt,' says Galen. 'Take him away, guards. Show no mercy.' Turn to **259**.

141

'Hang onto my arm!' shouts Tails. He yanks the rip-cord and fabric pours out of the pack, billowing out to form a rainbow-coloured parachute. There is a jolt as it opens and Sonic loses his grip on his friend's arm. He slips, falls and grabs — and one gloved paw wraps around Tails's shoes. He hangs on with all his strength.

They are falling into a sparkling, shimmering cloud. 'It's full of rings!' exclaims Tails. 'It must be a Bonus Zone! Grab all the rings you can!'

Roll the dice. Whatever the number is, Sonic and Tails catch that many rings and can roll again if they want to, as many times as they like until they either decide to stop or they roll a 1. If they roll a 1, they lose all their bonus rings and fall through the cloud, down towards the Green Hill Zone below.

'It looks like home,' says Sonic.

'It'll be good to be back,' replies Tails. Turn to **300**.

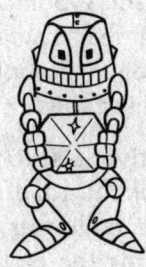

142

Sonic and Tails rush up the stairs to the roof and find themselves behind four crocodiles with crossbows, firing at the wart-hogs. One of the crocs turns around and takes aim at them. Sonic and Tails must fight the four crocodiles, two each and in turn. They get the advantage of surprise, so they will use their Speed, and the surprised crocodiles have a rating of only 7 each. If Sonic or Tails loses a life, cross it off their *Vital Statistics* and turn back to **31**. If they defeat all the crocs, they find six rings here, three each (write them down) and head down the stairs. Turn to **296**.

143

The two animals search the cab thoroughly. Tails finds ten gold rings hidden under the driver's seat and he gives five to Sonic (mark down five rings on each character's *Vital Statistics*). Sonic turns the television upside down, and sees that it was made by Nik Robot Industries. 'Nik Robot – Robotnik! he exclaims. 'I knew he had to be behind this.'

Tails stands on the driver's seat. 'There's a weird new building at the end of the road,' he says. 'Should we investigate?' Now the bulldozer is stopped, they can follow the road towards the building (turn to **107**) or explore the rest of the Zone, looking for their friends (turn to **170**).

144

'Let's get out of here,' says Number Two.

'Wait,' says Sonic. He opens a cabinet on the corridor wall, and inside are ten rings and a crowbar. If Sonic takes them, write them on his *Vital Statistics*.

The three go back to where Sonic's warriors are waiting. 'Where now?' they ask. Does Sonic head towards the High Tower (turn to **21**) or the gate (turn to **196**)?

145

There's no sign of a teleporter. Suddenly, there is a tremendous crash, and Tails whirls to see that a robot shark has smashed through the ice and has gripped a small monkey in its metal jaws. Does Tails attack the shark (turn to **268**) or the monkeys (turn to **10**)?

146

The hatch opens and the slipstream of air rushing past outside sucks the heroes out of the rocket. They tumble downwards, watching the rocket zoom away. It doesn't matter where they land; the Chaos Emeralds will be spread across Mobius and Robotnik will control the planet. Oh dear.

GAME OVER

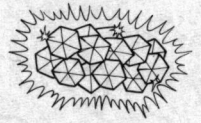

147

'Dr Robotnik?' asks the leader. He pronounces it 'Drrr'. 'I've never heard of him.'

'But you must have — haven't you seen his broadcasts?'

'No,' replies the leader. 'Unfortunately there's no electricity out here. I recognized you from a poster.'

'Oh,' says Tails, confused. He can ask why the tribe is so warlike (turn to **261**) or why the food is so awful (turn to **209**).

Tails slaps the button with his paw. The inner door closes, the outer one opens and the red robot squeals as it is sucked out of the airlock into space. Sonic and Tails watch it spin away from the space station.

'Why did you do that?' asks Sonic.

'It wasn't the robot with the Emeralds,' says Tails. 'The thief must still be here.'

Suddenly a voice fills the air. 'Attention. Your attention please,' it says. 'The space station is under attack. Evacuate immediately. Follow the flashing signs to the escape pods, please.' Do Sonic and Tails go to the escape pods (turn to **3**) or the way the robot with the emeralds must have gone (turn to **191**)?

'That makes sense,' says Sonic. 'What might happen if they've got two Chaos Emeralds in the High Tower?'

'If they're careful,' says Number Two, 'everything will be fine. If they're careless, the proximity effect might overload the — where's Number One?'

'What's that chemical smell and hissing sound?' asks Sonic.

'Wurgh!' replies Number Three, slumping to the floor.

'Augh!' remarks Number Two.

'Eeeugh!' adds Sonic as black dots dance before his eyes, and he passes out. When he comes round, he's in a cell with Number Two and Number Three. 'What happened?' asks Sonic.

'We were gassed,' answers Number Three. 'Number One betrayed us. Now there's a guard outside the door, and no way we can escape.'

'There's always an escape route,' says Sonic. 'Besides, we must warn the Outcasts about what's going on!' What should Sonic do?

Search the cell?   Turn to **27**
Ask what the others are carrying?   Turn to **105**
Bang on the door?   Turn to **278**

150

The stairs end in a steel door. Sonic grips the handle and can feel it vibrating as the door opens. Inside, the room is filled with bright blue-green light, coming from the middle of the room where the two Chaos Emeralds hang in mid-air, spinning round each other in a slow orbit. Gazing at them are two of the cat-beasts Sonic saw in the city. They look around at the hedgehog, and with a jolt Sonic recognizes them. One is Galen, hideously swollen and transformed, his fur now a lurid blue-green colour, and the other is not a cat, it's a badger: Number One. Around the walls of the room are strange machines and odd equipment — probes, read-outs, computer banks, stabilizers and trans-formers. On the far side of the room is what looks like a teleporter, although Sonic can't be sure. Galen bends to pick up a long metal pole from the floor. Grasping it like a club, he and Number One move towards Sonic's group. What should he do?

Run for the teleporter? Turn to **280**

If Sonic has the net, use it to grab the Emeralds? Turn to **95**

Grab the Emeralds in his paws? Turn to **15**

Attack Galen and Number One? Turn to **239**

151

The two spear-carriers advance on our heroes. The others are still discussing what to do. If Sonic and Tails should take no chances and attack, turn to **81**. If they should make friendly gestures, turn to **298**.

152

'You're an evil, twisted creep!' shouts Tails. 'I don't believe you tricked us.'

'Ah, but I did!' gloats Robotnik. 'I didn't send you to the same place as the Chaos Emeralds by mistake. I knew you would try to recover them all — something my robots couldn't do — and then I could steal them from you with the robots I'd planted on the space station. I chose you two because the Emeralds mutate ordinary people, but a blue hedgehog and a fox with two tails — the Chaos Emeralds couldn't mutate you because you eggs-ist as mutants!'

'*Are* we mutants, Sonic?' Tails asks.

'Mutants? No way!' says Sonic. 'Robotnik, you've cracked!'

'Pathetic!' Robotnik continues. 'By morning there will be a Chaos Emerald back in every Zone, and I shall control Mobius!' What do Sonic and Tails do?

Look around?   Turn to **61**
Ask Robotnik about the rocket?   Turn to **258**
Tell Robotnik he's mad?   Turn to **200**

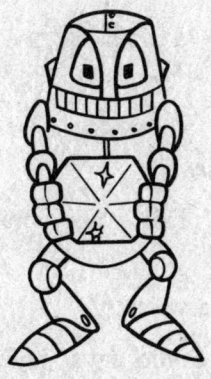

153

The two rush forward, but before they are close enough to hit the chieftain, bolts of fierce green light burst from the Emerald. Sonic and Tails must each roll on their Quick Wits to beat an 8 to dodge the beams of light. If either of them fail, the beams hit them and they lose their gold rings. (If they have no rings they do not lose a life.) The beams fade away, leaving spots flashing before their eyes. If they want to stay out of range and insult the chieftain, turn to **56**. If they want to be nice to him, turn to **4**.

154

Sonic reaches the gate; it's a metal barrier with a keyhole on one side. In front of it, two guards are talking about the new Chaos Emerald which, Sonic overhears, has been linked to the city's power system. If he has a key, he can sneak past the guards and unlock the gate (turn to **121**). If not, he must attack the guards (turn to **205**).

155

'After you,' Sonic says.

'No, no, after *you*,' Tails says. Sonic bends down and knocks hard.

'Who is it?' comes a voice.

'Two castaways,' Sonic says, trying to disguise his voice.

'Not now, Robinson. We're busy,' comes the reply, followed by hysterical robot laughter. The submarine sinks beneath the surface, and Sonic and Tails are left bobbing in the ocean with no hope of rescue.

GAME OVER

156

The massive bulldozer's tracks tear up the ground as it speeds across the Zone, leaving a shining path behind it. In front of its roaring engine is a driver's cab made of mirrored glass.

'Look!' exclaims Tails. 'That shiny liquid is drying! It's making a road.'

Sonic is looking around and sniffing. Something's very wrong in the Green Hill Zone and, since he's the resident hero, he'll be the one who has to sort it all out. There'll be danger and peril, robots to be beaten, Chaos Emeralds to be found, global threats to be overcome and, behind it all, most likely the mad Dr Robotnik! 'I love being a hero!' he shouts. Should Sonic and Tails follow the road (turn to section **107**), explore the Green Hill Zone (turn to section **170**), or should they jump on the bulldozer (turn to section **26**) or attack it (turn to section **212**)?

157

A bright flash explodes in the sky – the flare signal that they were supposed to wait for. Either Ravis and his forces were late, or Sonic was early. Sonic spots the tower that the others called the High Tower. Blue-green light floods from its windows, making it look like an eerie lighthouse. Do Sonic and his soldiers head for the tower (turn to **21**), the gates (turn to **196**) or the prison (turn to **93**)?

158

The monkeys look at him. 'This, believe it or not,' says one of them, gesturing at the surrounding snow and ice, 'is the Hilltop Zone. Snow started falling late last night. When we woke up today, it was like this.

We split up to find food, shelter and other survivors, but now we can't even find the others. Then that shark-thing attacked.'

'Will you help us, Mr Tails?' interrupts the smallest monkey. 'We're very cold and hungry and we're fans of you and Sonic — Sonic especially.' Will Tails agree to help them (turn to **94**), refuse (turn to **247**) or ask them if they have seen a Chaos Emerald (turn to **216**)?

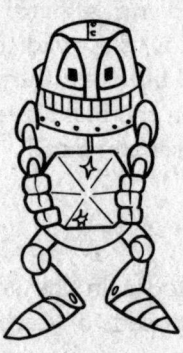

159

'Who built me?' echoes Ross. 'Your old friend, Dr Ovi Kintobor.'

'You mean Robotnik before he became Robotnik?' asks Tails.

'That's him,' replies Ross. 'Sonic knew him then. Ovi discovered the Chaos Emeralds too, although that was a mistake. He was trying to neutralize all the chaos in the world, but his machines overloaded and turned him into Robotnik. Now he's trying to undo all the good work he ever did. He built us to crew this space station,

Station Eyrie, to monitor Mobius's surface and to watch the Warps of Confusion. Later on Robotnik hid the Emeralds in the Warps so Sonic couldn't find them – but he did.'

'Of course,' says Sonic. 'I'm a hero.' What does he ask now?

'How can we teleport out of here?'   Turn to **74**

'Can you help us get rid of these Chaos Emeralds safely?'   Turn to **9**

160

'Wonderful!' the leader exclaims. 'There is no time to waste. We were planning to attack the crocodiles' stronghold tonight. Do you want to wait until then, or come on a scouting expedition to spy out the stronghold?' Do Sonic and Tails go scouting (turn to **73**) or wait (turn to **238**)?

161

Mildred shrieks as a snowball whizzes past her and she staggers into Tails, who falls over. The ground cracks and collapses, sending them plummeting downwards!

They land in an underground ice-chamber. At one side is a large, humming machine. It reminds Tails of a huge fridge. On top of it is a teleporter and, connected to it by wires and cables, is an orange Chaos Emerald. Tied around the fridge-machine are three monkeys. Mildred squeaks with joy and is about to run over when Tails stops her.

A dark shape comes lumbering in from a side-chamber. It's ten times as tall as Tails, with white tusks and a heavy coat. You might recognize it as a woolly mammoth, but Tails has never seen anything like it before. The mammoth stands in front of the fridge-machine, as if on guard.

Should Tails and Mildred attack the mammoth (turn to 102), free the monkeys (turn to 244) or make a dash for the Chaos Emerald and the teleporter (turn to 17)?

162

Sonic tries to twist the steering wheel away from Chirps. The chicken squawks and presses a red button, and a high-pitched shriek fills the air. The television screen blinks on, showing Sonic's friend Porker Harris, the pig.

'We heard your alarm, Bulldozer Three,' he says. 'An emergency squad is on its way.' Should Sonic and Tails search the cab (turn to 48) or get away from the bulldozer (turn to 170)?

163

Sonic ducks and the light shoots over his head. Galen and Number One step in front of the Chaos Emeralds, ready to defend them. Sonic can't stop and almost runs into their paws. He must fight them! Turn to **239**.

164

'You're right, Number Two,' says the badger. 'He has the shifty eyes of a secret agent.'

'Hey!' says Sonic. 'Watch who you're talking about.'

'And he's rude too,' adds the badger. 'You two subdue him.' The bird and the dog advance on Sonic. The badger slips through the door, closing it behind him. Does Sonic point this out (turn to **199**) or does he fight to get free (turn to **50**)?

165

The hatch is fastened tight. If Sonic and Tails are determined to open it, they must roll on their combined Strength to beat a 12. If they make it, turn to **146**. If not, the hatch stays closed; turn to **180**.

166

The drawbridge falls with a splash. The way into the stronghold is open. Sonic climbs onto it. 'This way!' he shouts and runs in. Turn to **44**.

167

'Torture me,' says Sonic. 'I'll never admit I'm a spy because I'm not. You can break my body but you can't break the truth.'

'Good,' says Ravis. He lifts Sonic off the floor. 'You have the spirit of a true hero. None of those who live in the city would ever be so brave. You said you knew what was happening in the city. Tell me all. Did you speak with my agents there? Quickly now,' he demands. If Sonic shows Number Three's talisman to Ravis, turn to **292**. Otherwise he can tell Ravis that his agents are in prison (turn to **32**) or that there are two Chaos Emeralds in the High Tower (turn to **86**).

168

A huge metal shark rears up, smashing through the ice. The monkeys back away, jabbing at it with their spears, but they're hardly even scratching it. Tails takes a run-up and leaps into the attack! He will use his Speed to fight the shark. It has a rating of 12, but Tails adds 1 point to his roll for each monkey and there are four of them. If the shark hits him, roll the die again; on a 1, 2 or 3 Tails loses all his rings or, if he has no rings left, a life (cross it off and turn back to

123). On a 4, 5 or 6 one of the monkeys is hit and knocked out of the fight (don't add a point for a beaten monkey). If the shark is beaten, turn to **42**.

169

The corridor leads to an airlock. The inner door is open, and inside is a small red robot. It has opened a panel in the wall and is twisting some wires together. By the inner door is a button marked 'Cycle Airlock'. Should Sonic and Tails attack the robot (turn to **270**) or press the button (turn to **148**)?

170

Sonic and Tails don't get far into the Zone before they find everything has changed. Hills have been levelled, roads have been built and new buildings have sprung up like toadstools. What is going on? The air is full of the roar of chainsaws, the crash of falling trees, the thumping of pile-drivers and the moaning of Tails. 'My head hurts,' he complains. In front of them stands a particularly ugly building. It's not finished and workers are swarming over it like ants. Some are robots but Sonic recognizes others – they're his friends! Flicky the Bluebird, Johnny Lightfoot, Joe Sushi, they're all here. Why would they build such a hideous thing in the Green Hill Zone? What should Sonic and Tails do now?

Ask one of their friends what's
  happening?   Turn to **293**
Climb the building for a better view? Turn to **40**
Follow the road?   Turn to **107**

171

'Hi there,' Sonic grins. 'This is a most excellent cake. Delicious. My compliments to the chef. It's traditional for people to jump out of cakes at big parties, so I thought I'd do something alternative, like jumping into a cake. It's different, it's hip and I enjoyed it.'

'Are you an Outcast?' asks an impressively dressed cat-person.

Sonic is sure that being an Outcast is bad. 'I'm new,' he says. 'I've just arrived. I like it here. Great cakes. I think I'll stay a while.'

'We'll just perform an immigration ritual we have here,' says the impressive cat, then raises his voice. 'Guards! Grab him!' Two huge cats grab Sonic by the arms and haul him out of the cake. The Chaos Emerald drops to the floor, and they pick it up and pass it to the impressive cat. Turn to **69**.

172

The camp seems deserted as Sonic strides between the tents. It's very eerie, as if the inhabitants of the camp have just disappeared. Sonic bends down to pick up a gold ring poking out of the sand (write it down) and the flaps of the tents fly open as warriors with swords leap out. In an instant he is surrounded. 'Don't move, cat spy!' says one.

Meanwhile, in the Hilltop Zone — 'Hey! that's not fair!' Sonic shouts. 'It starts getting exciting, and you leave me in the lurch. Come back!' Turn to **125**.

173

'Long-range radar on,' says a computerized voice and a display appears on the windscreen in front of Sonic, showing where everything is around him and whether they're friendly, hostile or neutral. If Sonic has to make any rolls to control the *Kubrick*, add 2 points to the dice roll for the advantage the radar gives him. Make a note of that, then turn to **30**.

174

Ahead of them is a clearing. The two animals sprint into it and shriek as the ground gives way and they plunge into a pit! Roll a die to see who hits the bottom first. If you roll 1, 2 or 3 it's Tails; if you roll 4, 5 or 6 it's Sonic. The first one to land loses their rings (cross them off their *Vital Statistics*). If they don't have any rings then cross off a life and turn back to **8**.

The Warcat leaps over the pit and snarls, but it's not going to risk being trapped as well and soon prowls off into the jungle. A minute later a vine drops into the pit, and the two heroes climb out. At the top are six creatures dressed in leaves, wearing wooden masks and carrying spears. They don't look very friendly. Most of them huddle on the far side of the pit, discussing what to do, while two approach with their spears raised. Do Sonic and Tails attack (turn to **81**) or make friendly gestures (turn to **298**)?

175

Tails dashes across the room and rams the machine with a spin attack. A pipe breaks inside it, spilling a cold fog out into the room. The machine stops humming and six gold rings fall out. Tails grabs them, then looks around, puzzled. 'What's happening?' he says. 'It's getting warm!' Water drips from the remains of the fridge, and the ice holding the captured monkeys melts, releasing them. A crack is forming in the chamber's ceiling, and it creaks ominously. 'Run!' shouts Tails. 'The whole place is going to collapse!' Mildred and the other monkeys rush away towards the outside. Should Tails run for the teleporter (**132**) or grab the Chaos Emerald (turn to **47**)?

176

Tails and Sonic start hurling fruit back up at the crocodiles on the roof. One mango scores a lucky hit, and the crocodiles start aiming at the heroic pair. Rotten bananas, papayas and grapefruit splatter down around them. Sonic and Tails must separately roll on their Agility to beat a 6. If either of them misses the roll, that one loses their rings. If they have no rings they must lose a life instead (turn back to **31**).

'This isn't working,' says Sonic. 'Think of something before they start firing coconuts and prickly pears.' The friends can try to smash the door down (turn to **24**) or look for another way in (turn to **75**).

177

Sonic stands over the keyboard. There is no password, just a menu showing choices. Sonic zips through them.

'Can it play *Cosmic Invaders II*?' asks Tails.

'No. Shut up and let me operate this thing!' snaps the hedgehog. Before long he has called up the menu he wants. There are four choices; which does he choose?

Self-destruct?	Turn to **206**
Open the hatch?	Turn to **146**
Change the rocket's course?	Turn to **246**
Jettison the Chaos Emeralds?	Turn to **57**

178

Sonic scratches his head. 'Search for two Chaos Emeralds in a city this size?' he says. 'You're an optimist.'

His attention is caught by an eerie glow coming from one of the towers. It is taller than the others and not as richly decorated. The strange blue-green light is flooding from the windows and spreading out across the city. There's something peculiar about it, and it gives Sonic an uncomfortable prickling sensation down his spine. He looks out of the page and catches your eye.

'I take it back,' he says. 'It took me three or four seconds to find them. But I'm not sure I want to get too close.' If you think Sonic should go towards the tower, turn to **34**. If he sneaks through the shadows towards the gates, turn to **154**, or if he sprints to the gates, turn to **289**.

179

Sonic stares at the television, feeling his mind whirling like the patterns on the screen, and he knows he must resist. He summons all his energy and leaps into the air, spinning like a dervish, and smashes into the TV. It explodes into pieces which shower across the room.

'Oo-er,' says Tails. 'I feel funny. There's a ringing in my ears.'

'That's not in your ears,' says Sonic, who can hear it too. 'We've set off an alarm.'

'Hands up!' says a voice behind them, and the two spin around to see their friends Sally Acorn and Porker Harris pointing machine-guns at them. 'Don't move,' continues Sally. 'Now follow us.'

'You told us not to move,' complains Tails.

'Shut up and walk,' says Porker, waving his gun. Sonic and Tails exchange a confused glance, and set off down the corridor. Turn to **264**.

180

The nose of the rocket doesn't have much in it: the hatch and two machines. One is a computer with a screen and a joystick. The other is a strange device attached to the rocket's hull, like a big grenade launcher or bomb rack. There's a panel on the side, which Tails pops open. Inside are the Chaos Emeralds. Sonic and Tails can operate the computer (turn to **177**), open the hatch (turn to **165**) or jettison the Chaos Emeralds (turn to **57**).

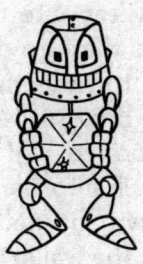

181

Sonic and Tails must fight the two crocodiles — one fight each. Play Sonic's battle first, then Tails's. Both crocodiles have a rating of 8 and Sonic and Tails use their Strength to fight them. If Sonic loses a life, cross it off his *Vital Statistics* and turn back to **160**. If Tails is hit by the crocodile he is fighting, turn to **128**. If both crocodiles are defeated, turn to **52**.

Sonic grabs the bed and pulls it apart. He makes a stack of bricks in the middle of the floor. Then he balances the longest plank across the bricks, and piles the rest of the planks against the wall.

'I've never really understood modern art,' says Number Three, 'but I'm sure it's very good. What do you call it?'

'I call it "Cool Way Out",' says Sonic. 'You two stand on the pile of planks. I stand on the low end of this plank and when I say "three", you jump onto the raised end of this plank. It'll flick me up and I'll grab the bars. Okay? THREE!'

The startled animals leap into the air and land on the end of the plank. As they go down, Sonic's end goes up and he is tossed towards the roof. Roll on Sonic's Agility, to beat a 7. If he succeeds, he lands neatly on the window-sill – turn to **5**. If he fails, he misses the window and falls back into the cell. He's not hurt but the plank splits down the middle, so he can't try it again. Does he climb the walls (turn to **222**), overpower the guard outside the cell (turn to **133**) or, if he has some rope, lasso the hook in the ceiling with it (turn to **76**)?

183

The monkey climbs onto Tails's back and the fox starts to climb the ice wall of the crevasse. It's hard going, and the weight of the monkey makes it harder. Roll on Tails's Agility, to beat a 6. If he makes the roll, he clambers out of the crevasse – turn to **41**. If he fails, then the ice wall is just too slippery for him and he slides back down to the bottom, where he can either use his tails as a helicopter to carry them both out (turn to **115**) or walk along the crevasse to see where it leads (turn to **275**).

184

Sonic hits the ground so fast that he loses all his rings (but he doesn't lose a life if he has none) and bounces back up into the air. 'Aaaah!' he screams as the city rushes up at him again. Turn to **16**.

185

'Sonic! What's that?' shouts Tails. He dives towards the glittering shape in the distance. It's a pink Chaos Emerald and the fast fox has it clasped firmly in his paws. A blot of colour appears and their spaceship re-grows and re-forms around them, as if someone had filmed a wax model melting and then shown the film backwards. 'Wow! Cool special effects! This is a big-budget gamebook!' breathes Tails. Sonic is already in the pilot's seat, accelerating to full speed. Turn to **299**.

186

The *real* Sonic the Hedgehog would never leave his friend Tails to be squashed by a rampaging machine. Sonic must have fallen under the mind-control rays of Dr Robotnik, and now there is nobody to save the world from the deranged dictator. The planet Mobius is doomed. Turn back to section **1** and try again.

GAME OVER

187

Sonic races towards the Emeralds. Galen and Number One step into his way, their arms outstretched to grab him. Sonic puts one foot on Galen's arm and one on Number One's shoulder and leaps straight towards the Emeralds. He hurtles between them and THWACK! THWACK! catches an Emerald in each paw. They're scorching! His gloves are smouldering and his paws feel like they're being roasted. Roll on his Coolness to beat a 9. If he succeeds, turn to **122**. If he fails, turn to **82**.

188

Sonic grabs the top edge of the drawbridge. He positions himself between bridge and wall, and uses all his strength to push the two apart. The vines creak and stretch, but does he have enough power to snap them? Roll on Sonic's Strength, to beat an 8. If he succeeds, turn to **12**. If he fails, turn to **96**.

189

The red ship disappears amongst the rocks. Sonic steers away from them, skirting the edge of the field and watching for meteors. Roll on Sonic's Quick Wits, to beat a 5. If he consulted a space chart on the space station, add 1 point to his score. If he is flying the *Toho*, add 1. If he is flying the *Yuzna*, subtract 1. If he succeeds, turn to **267**. If he fails, turn to **37**.

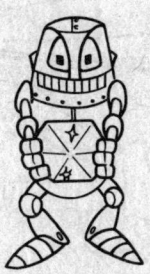

190

The other natives scatter into the forest, their leafy clothing blending in with the green background. They disappear almost immediately. 'Leave them to the crocodiles!' comes a faint shout, and then there is no more sign of the natives. Turn to **136**.

191

Down a short corridor is a vast room. Sonic and Tails step into it, to see a small red spacecraft hurtle through the opening at the other end, diving through a force-field and out into space. Three other spacecraft sit here: one huge and well-shielded, one squat and heavy, and one as thin and streamlined as a dart.

'What are they?' asks Tails.

'I don't know,' says Sonic. 'COMPUTER! Tell us about these three spaceships.'

'Certainly, Sonic,' says a voice. 'The first vessel is the *Kubrick*, a long-range spacecraft. The second is the *Yuzna*, an exploration ship designed for planetary landings. The third is the experimental prototype star-fighter *Toho*, ready for its first test-flight.'

Select a spacecraft for Sonic and Tails, write it down on Sonic's *Vital Statistics*, then turn to **250**.

192

The key turns in the lock. Sonic pushes hard against the gate and it opens just far enough for a slim hedgehog to slip out. The desert outside is dark and Sonic can see the constellations spread out across the sky. Above the horizon a single bright star winks. In another direction, Sonic can see the faint lights of campfires in the desert dunes. Should Sonic head towards the campfires (turn to **97**) or follow the star (turn to **58**)?

193

Inside is a large hallway, gloomy and dark. At the far end is a large, square shape that Sonic and Tails can just see. They venture further in. There is a click and the dark shape lights up: it's a television screen, with a pattern of whirling dots and twisting shapes on it. Tails and Sonic put up their paws to shield their eyes, but there is something about the way the shapes move, and the soft music in the background that makes them want to lower their paws, open their eyes and go out and make new buildings all over the Green Hill Zone. Roll on Sonic's and Tails's combined Coolness, to beat an 8. That means you should add Sonic's Coolness to Tails's Coolness; then roll a die and add that as well. If the total is 8 or more, they've succeeded; turn to **179**. If the number is lower than 8 they've failed; turn to **276**.

194

'What's this?' asks Tails, pointing at something vague and grey floating in front of him.

Sonic studies it carefully. 'It's nothing,' he says, 'nothing at all. It's a complete emptiness. Tails, you've cracked it — it's a space! And in the madness of the Warp, where there's a space, there must be a spaceship!' He jumps into the greyness and Tails follows him, landing beside Sonic, back in the cockpit, as the ship zooms out of the Warp! Turn to **299**.

195

'Sonic the Hedgehog?' says the bird. 'Not *the* Sonic the Hedgehog? Defender of the Green Hill Zone? Saviour of Planet Mobius?'

'The Sonic the Hedgehog who runs around with that cute, cuddly fox?' asks the dog, putting away his sword. 'I'm a big fan of his – I mean, yours.'

'I've never heard of you,' mutters the badger. 'You have disrupted our meeting. Same time tomorrow, everyone.' He starts tidying papers.

'Don't mind him,' says the bird. 'He's always grouchy. I'm Number Two, and my friend,' he points to the dog, 'is Number Three. You're Number Four.'

'I'd rather be Sonic,' says Sonic. 'Who is Number One?'

'You are Number Four,' says the bird sternly. 'Number One is the badger. We're Outcast agents. The rest of the Outcasts live in the desert – Galen and the cats won't let them enter the city. So we've sneaked in, to prepare for an invasion.' Sonic knows that one of the group is a spy for Galen, but he knows that if he chooses wrongly he'll be talking to the spy. Who does he talk to?

Number One?	Turn to **38**
Number Two?	Turn to **126**
Number Three?	Turn to **253**
Or does he ask them what their plans are?	Turn to **101**

196

As Sonic approaches, he can see the gates are swinging on their hinges, blown apart by an explosion, and Ravis and his army are inside the city. The Outcast leader spots Sonic and his soldiers. 'What are you doing here?' he splutters. 'Some secret sneak attack you are! You should be at the High Tower, cutting off the cats' power supply.'

'Hey, I thought you needed help, okay?' Sonic replies.

'I don't need any help,' Ravis growls, knocking out an attacking cat with the hilt of his sword. 'Just go and fulfil your mission.' Should Sonic head for the tower (turn to **21**) or free the Outcast agents from prison instead (turn to **93**)?

197

'We know your stupid plans,' lies Sonic. 'We can beat all of them.'

'As I thought,' sneers Robotnik, 'you're too dangeous to stay in the Green Hill Zone – you'd escape and smash all my beautiful new buildings. I have to get rid of you. Guards! Remove their shoes and gloves.'

'No, not those!' gasp Sonic and Tails in unison.

'Ha ha! Ha ha ha ha ha ha! Yes! Take them off !'

Sally Acorn and Porker Harris move menacingly towards our heroes. Should Sonic and Tails defend themselves (turn to **129**) or let themselves be stripped (turn to **71**)?

(turn to **129**) ... (turn to **71**)

198

The robots grab the stunned heroes and drag them on board the submarine. For machines so small, they're very strong. Sonic and Tails are pulled down corridors and thrust into a cell. Sonic has a familiar prickling feeling in his spikes, and he knows the Chaos Emeralds are close.

'When do we escape?' asks Tails.

'Not yet,' says Sonic. 'I'm certain we'll find Robotnik wherever this submarine is headed.'

Eventually the cell door opens and six robots stand outside. 'Come with us,' they say.

'Where are we going?' asks Tails.

'Come with us,' repeat the robots. Tails and Sonic shrug and follow the machines out onto the top of the submarine. It is moored to a dock inside a huge dome.

The whole place is filled with robots, all attending to different tasks. Two tunnels lead out of the dome. A loud voice is reciting figures backwards: '104. 103. 102. 101.' Do Sonic and Tails follow the robots (turn to 230) or run away from them (turn to 72)?

199

'Your buddy's left,' says Sonic, pointing to the door.

Number Two drops his sword and rushes over. 'It's locked!' he exclaims, and starts coughing and spluttering. Sonic can smell a chemical odour that makes him feel ill. The other two slump to the floor, which suddenly seems like an awfully sensible place to be lying. A dark fog floats over Sonic's eyes, and he passes out.

When he comes round, he's lying in a cell with Number Two and Number Three. 'I know what you're thinking,' says Number Two, 'and you're wrong. There's no way out. We've looked.'

'Never give up,' says Sonic. 'I'm an expert at this.' What should he do?

Search the cell?   Turn to 27
Ask what the other two are carrying?   Turn to 105
Bang on the cell door?   Turn to 278

200

'You're mad!' shout Sonic and Tails in harmony.

'You're toast!' replies Robotnik and fires the Zap Cannon. He walks over to where our heroes used to stand. 'Hmmm,' he muses. 'My life may be less eggs-citing from now on, but it'll be a lot easier!'

GAME OVER

201

Number Two shakes the rope loose. 'If you can loop the *middle* of the rope over the hook, you can hold onto the loop while Number Three and I pull you up to the window. You'll be able to swing across to it that way,' he suggests.

Sonic nods. 'It doesn't explain how I'll get through the bars on the window,' he says, 'but it's a start.' Looping the rope over the hook takes ages, but eventually it slips over. Number Two and Number Three haul on the rope, lifting Sonic up until he is level with the window. He starts to sway the rope, slowly at first and then more and more until finally he grabs the bars on the window. He's there! Turn to **5**.

202

The window has bars across it so narrow that not even Tails could squeeze through. Sonic can see most of the tall buildings in the city; power cables thread between them. One tower stands on its own in the middle, higher than the others, and most of the power cables lead towards it. Beyond the towers are the city walls. Sonic can see gates leading into the desert, and there are cat guards around them. It looks very hard to get into the city – or out of it. Sonic turns away from the window. Does he examine the door (turn to **29**) or the bed (turn to **83**)?

203

Tails whirls his tails as fast as he can. The fox and his passenger rise into the air, but almost immediately begin to sink back down. Tails lowers the young monkey to the ground, and sits down, panting. 'It's no good,' he says, 'I haven't got the muscles to lift us both – and I'm not going to fly out of here on my own. I'll get you out somehow.' Turn to **28**.

204

Sonic and Tails climb up to the cabin in seconds. Sonic stares at the mirrored glass that covers the door.

'Are you making a plan?' Tails asks.

'No, checking my spikes look smart,' says Sonic. He pushes the door open to reveal a plump figure who stares at Sonic and Tails. It's their friend, Chirps the chicken. There is also a large television set, turned to a dead channel.

'Who are you? What are you doing here?' he asks. What do Sonic and Tails do now?

Grab the bulldozer's controls?	Turn to 162
Turn off the television set?	Turn to 285
Talk to Chirps?	Turn to 85

205

The cat guards aren't paying attention to their duties and Sonic could sneak past them. Unfortunately he needs a key for the gate, and he can see one dangling from each of the guards' belts. 'Heads up!' he yells as he charges. Sonic must use his Strength to fight the two guards in turn; they both have a rating of 8. If he loses a life, cross it off and turn back to 91. If he wins, he grabs a key; turn to 192.

206

The rocket does.

GAME OVER

207

Sonic tries to dodge but his feet are stuck in mud. The drawbridge falls and lands on his head. Ouch! Sonic must lose all his rings. If he doesn't have any then he loses a life (cross it off his *Vital Statistics* and turn back to 31). Sonic hears wart-hog warriors rushing over the drawbridge and into the stronghold. He clambers up and follows them inside. Turn to 44.

208

The monkey slides away, slipping down the crevasse into its depths. Finally it reaches the bottom and stands up. It's not hurt, but it can't get out. The other monkeys gather on the other side of the crevasse, which stretches a long way in either direction. 'Well?' says one of them. 'You're the hero. How are you going to rescue our friend?' Tails can climb down (turn to **28**) or use his tails like a helicopter to fly down (turn to **115**).

209

'We apologize,' the leader says sadly. 'Since the crocodiles found their glowing rock, they have taken all the fruit, nuts and berries and keep them for themselves.'

'Crocodiles?' asks Sonic.

'Yes. A week ago they raided our village. They stand on two feet and spoke of a glowing rock they had found which had given them ideas of taking over the Zone. Will you help us fight back, and get rid of the glowing rock?' Sonic and Tails can agree to help (turn to **160**) or refuse (turn to **2**), or ask why the wart-hogs are so warlike (turn to **261**) or whether they have heard of Dr Robotnik (turn to **147**).

210

His defeated foes slump back, exhausted by Sonic's timing and brilliant tactics. He dashes to the door and rushes out — straight into the arms of a cat guard. A cloth smelling of chemicals is pushed over his face, dots swirl before his eyes and he passes out.

When he comes round, he's in a cell with Number Two and Number Three. 'Shhh,' Number Two hisses.

'There's a guard outside, so keep your voice down.'

'What happened?' Sonic asks.

'Number One betrayed us to the cats and now we're to be executed,' Number Three replies.

'Not if I can help it!' says Sonic. 'Let's get out of here.' What should he do?

Search the cell?	Turn to **27**
Ask what the other two are carrying?	Turn to **105**
Bang on the cell door?	Turn to **278**

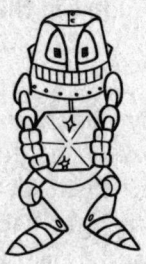

211

Sonic sends the spaceship spiralling into the asteroid field. Chunks of rock whizz past on every side, each one big enough to crush the entire Green Hill Zone. Darting ahead of them, tantalizingly close, is the slim shape of the red ship. Roll on Sonic's Agility, to beat a 5. If he is flying the *Kubrick*, subtract 1 from his score. Add 1 if he is flying the *Toho*. If he misses the roll, the ship scrapes an asteroid and both Sonic and Tails must lose all their rings or, if one of them has no rings, they lose a life (turn back to **191**). If Sonic succeeds, they make it through the asteroids. Turn to **267**.

212

Catching up with the bulldozer is easy, but damaging it is much harder — it's built of solid steel plates. Sonic and Tails leap towards it, spinning like fireworks, but neither of them even dent it. Sonic runs alongside the bulldozer for a second, looking up at its huge bulk. Higher up are two vulnerable spots: the engine, and the driver's cabin which is perched right at the top of the machine. If they could get up there, they might be able to do some damage. Should Sonic and Tails jump onto the bulldozer (turn to **26**), should they follow the road (turn to **107**) or explore the Green Hill Zone to find their friends (turn to **170**)?

213

Sonic swings the pole and knocks the green Chaos Emerald as far as possible from the blue one. It hits the far wall and bounces to the floor. The blue one drops straight into Sonic's waiting paws; he can feel that it's cooling down already. He dashes over to pick up the green Chaos Emerald. Turn to **122**.

214

The fort has battlements on top of it, from which crocodiles are raining rotten fruit down onto the wart-hogs below. There is a solid door in the front of the building, and most of the guards are concentrating their fire there, keeping the invaders away from it. There is a strange greenish glow coming from the windows around the bottom of the building, and it gives Sonic a peculiar prickling feeling all the way down his back. Should Sonic and Tails throw some-thing at the crocodiles to distract their attention (turn to **176**), look for another way in (turn to **75**), or charge the main door with spin-attacks (turn to **24**)?

215

Tails leaps onto the machine and climbs towards the Emerald. It fires two more bolts of light at him, and he must dodge them. Roll on his Agility to beat a 6. If he succeeds, he grabs the Emerald from its cradle of cables, and you must turn to **47**. If he fails, the Chaos-light will mutate him. Roll one die, and count down the abilities on Tails's sheet until you find that one (Speed is 1, Strength is 2 and so on). If that ability is more than 2, it goes down to 2. If it was 2 before, it goes up to 5! The changed Tails rips the Emerald from the wires. Turn to **47**.

216

The monkeys shake their heads. 'Nothing odd hap-pened until it started snowing?' Tails asks.

'There have been some odd things, now you mention

it,' says one. 'A few strange plants have appeared across the Zone, and peaceful animals have been going funny, but we didn't think it was important.'

'It could be,' Tails says. 'It could be chaos from a Chaos Emerald.' Does he ask the monkeys where he is (turn to **158**) or who they are (turn to **274**)?

217

After a few metres the tunnel enters another huge chamber. This one is more like a massive chimney. Far above them the two animals can see a tiny circle of daylight. Filling the chamber is a huge, fat rocket. The bottom half is black, the top half is red and the tip is pinkish. It looks like Robotnik might if he turned into a rocket. Beside it is a huge gantry leading to the top of the rocket; fuel leads join the two together. Another tunnel leads off from here. Four gold rings lie on the floor and our heroes take two each. The voice from the speakers echoes oddly in here: '79. 78. 77.' Should Sonic and Tails climb the gantry (turn to **55**) or head down the tunnel (turn to **137**)?

218

Sonic and Tails dash to the wall, and dig. Tails is the first one to notice something odd. 'Hey, Sonic,' he says, 'there's water seeping into my hole.'

'How much water?' asks his blue friend.

'Lots,' the fox replies glumly.

Sonic looks. 'That's bad,' he says. 'It means there's a lot of water on the other side of the wall. There's no way we can dig under it – the tunnel would turn into mud and collapse.' The two heroes can look at the gate (turn to **108**), go back to the edge of the clearing to watch and wait (turn to **18**) or climb a nearby tree for a better view (turn to **290**).

219

After what seems like eternity, a bright flare explodes in the sky. One of the warriors hurls a grapple over the wall, and Sonic and his forces climb the rope and drop down the other side into the city. Sonic can see most of the cats running towards the gates, where a tremendous battle is going on. The cats are bigger than Sonic remembers and a lot of them are running on all fours. None of them have seen the sneak-attack force come over the wall. Sonic looks around. Nearby he recognizes the prison building that he escaped from. Further away, light streams from all the windows of the highest tower in the city, like a strange, unearthly beacon. Do Sonic and his warriors head to the prison (turn to **93**), the gate (turn to **196**) or the High Tower (turn to **21**)?

220

Sonic opens one eye. Advancing towards him is a huge yellow bulldozer! Its enormous blade is cutting through trees and pushing the ground flat in front of it. A nozzle at the back is spraying something onto the flattened earth, making a road behind it. At the top of the bulldozer is a driver's cab made of mirrored glass. Behind that is the engine, emitting thick dark smoke. Sonic shakes the still-sleeping Tails.

'Creamy buns – ouch!' mutters the fox. 'What did you do that for, Sonic? I was having a lovely dream.' Then he notices the bulldozer. 'Yowks!' he screeches. Should the two friends run out of the bulldozer's way (turn to section **138**) or jump onto the metal machine before it runs them over (turn to section **26**)?

221

The hatch pops open with a whoosh and the rush of wind outside pulls all the loose objects, including Sonic and Tails, out through the gap and into mid-air. The rocket shoots away from them, still heading towards the edge of the atmosphere and into space. The planet is so far below them that it looks like a map, but it's getting closer at an alarming rate.

'Grab my paw!' shouts Tails. 'I'll use my tails as a helicopter to land us safely.'

Sonic falls towards his friend and grabs his outstretched arm. 'Save me from this fall,' he shouts above the roaring of the wind, 'and you'll be a true hero, not a sidekick any more.'

Tails whirls his twin tails, but either Sonic is too heavy or the air this high up is too thin to carry them. They keep falling. Does Tails have a parachute? If he does, turn to **141**. If not, turn to **63**.

222

'Give me a leg up,' asks Sonic. Number Two obliges and Sonic climbs up onto the bird's head. He's still far below the window ledge. He tries to get enough grip on the bricks to pull himself towards it, but the wall is too slippery and he slides down to the floor.

'Perhaps,' says Number Three, 'if I stood on Number Two's head, and you stood on my head, you could get close enough to jump . . .

'No way!' protests Number Two. 'Under no circumstances. You'll just have to think of something else.'

If Sonic has any rope, he can try to lasso the hook in the ceiling (turn to **76**). Otherwise he can use the bricks and planks of the bed to make a see-saw catapult (turn to **182**), or he can try to overpower the guard outside the cell (turn to **133**).

223

Sonic dodges the falling fruit and reaches the inside wall. He swarms up it like a monkey and reaches the top — only to find himself staring into the tooth-filled face of a crocodile guard! Sonic must fight the guard if he's going to get over the wall, using his Strength to do it. The guard's rating is 7. If Sonic loses a life, cross it off his *Vital Statistics* and turn back to **31**. If he wins, turn to **44**.

224

The ship plummets out of the sky; it wasn't built to fly in an atmosphere, and it has the aerodynamics of a dodo. The ocean rushes up fast and the ship hits with a WHUMPH! that knocks the breath and all the rings out of Sonic and Tails. (If either of them has no rings, they lose a life and you must turn back to **191**.) Waves lap around the cockpit as the two animals peer out. They've crashed close to the little red ship, and can see the robot climbing onto its cockpit with the Emeralds beside it. There is no land in sight in any direction. The water around the two ships bubbles and suddenly a giant golden submarine breaks the surface. A hatch on it opens and robots rush out, jumping across to the red ship. It must be one of Robotnik's constructions! What should the two heroes do?

Jump from the cockpit to the red ship?   Turn to **130**

Abandon their ship and swim towards
    the submarine?   Turn to **6**

Use their ship to ram the submarine?   Turn to **35**

225

The battle isn't going well for the figures on the shore. After watching for a while, Tails has worked out that they are monkeys. They keep jabbing spears at the big grey shape, but it stays out of their range. As the grey shape cruises out from under the ice, a brave monkey dashes to the edge and thrusts its spear deep into the water. The shape rears high into the air, and Tails sees that it is a huge shark, made entirely of metal. It grabs the monkey in its metal jaws. Does

Tails dash in to attack the robot shark (turn to **268**) or the other monkeys (turn to **10**)?

226

Tails leaps into the air and grabs the young monkey by the collar of its coat. The collar rips in two and Tails lands beyond the crevasse as the monkey slides away, down into the blue-green-grey depths of the ice. The other monkeys cluster on the other side of the crevasse, watching. A few seconds later, the monkey hits the bottom and stands up. It isn't hurt, but it can't get out either. The other monkeys look at Tails.

'Well?' asks one. 'You're the hero, you get him out.'

Tails can climb down into the crevasse (turn to **28**) or use his two tails like helicopter rotors to fly down (turn to **115**).

227

If Sonic and Tails want to avoid becoming Hedgehog Hors d'Oeuvres with a Foxy Fricassee to follow, they have to fight it! The Warcat has a rating of **10**, and Sonic and Tails must use their combined Agilities to fight it. If either Sonic or Tails loses a life, cross it off their *Vital Statistics* and turn back to **8**. If they beat the Warcat, turn to **33**.

228

The door opens to reveal a large room. Half of it is filled with humming, clicking machinery covered in dials, meters, screens and read-outs, while the other is filled with identical white suits, hanging from hooks on the wall. 'Someone's got a very boring taste in clothes,' observes one of the warriors.

'They're contamination suits,' says Sonic. 'You wear them in dangerous places, to protect you.' He tries to work out what the machinery does, but all he can see is that all the dials and meters are in the red: something is overloading. He can't work out the controls and thinks it would be safer not to touch them. Should Sonic and his friends put on the contamination suits (turn to **265**) or go straight up the stairs (turn to **150**)?

229

-ZZZZZAM! Sonic appears above the largest white bed he's ever seen. Actually it's a cloud, as he soon realizes when he falls through it.

'Wooah!' he screams as he plummets downwards. Far below him is the ground, but it's getting closer very fast. He's falling towards a large city with tall buildings and high walls. Outside the city, everything is a deserted desert; nothing stirs out there. Sonic can shout for Tails (turn to **279**), roll into a ball to soften the impact of landing (turn to **184**) or he can quickly make a parachute out of the leafy clothes the warthogs gave him (turn to **16**).

Two large robots step out of the throng and lay metal hands on the shoulders of Sonic and Tails. 'We'll take them from here,' they say, and lead the animals down the smaller of the two tunnels. The tunnel leads into a large, long room filled with computers and machines with flashing lights. At the far end of the room is Dr Robotnik sitting at the controls of his Egg-o-matic machine; it has a massive twin-barrelled gun fixed to the front, sides, back and underneath of it. There is so much gun that it dwarfs Robotnik.

'What's that thing?' Tails asks.

'It is a Zap Cannon, my small and insignificant friend. Do not move or I shall fry you to your component molecules.'

'That sounds bad,' Tails whispers to Sonic. 'What does it mean?'

'Just don't move,' Sonic whispers back.

'Move all you want, Sonic!' shouts Robotnik, who must have overheard. 'With the Chaos Emeralds back in my grasp, in a few hours I shall eggs-ercise control over Mobius. I tricked you and you never realized! Ha ha ha ha!'

Over the racket of Robotnik's lunatic laughter, the heroes can hear another voice, still counting backwards: '69. 68. 67. 66.' What should they do now?

Not do anything?	Turn to **11**
Demand that Robotnik tell them how he tricked them?	Turn to **152**
Pretend to be very impressed by Robotnik's cleverness?	Turn to **90**
Attack Robotnik?	Turn to **67**

231

The three creatures study him. 'I thought I recognized him,' says the badger. 'He's obviously one of us, sent by our leader to give us support and advice.'

'I'm not so sure, Number One,' says the tall bird. 'I've never seen him before, and nobody told us he was coming. He could be an informer for Galen.'

'Stuff and nonsense, Number Two,' says the badger. 'I don't believe that Galen has planted an informer among us. You're just paranoid.'

'I think he looks like Sonic the Hedgehog,' pipes up the dog.

'Shut up, Number Three,' says the badger.

If Sonic tells them that he is indeed Sonic the Hedgehog, turn to **195**. If not, roll on his Good Looks to beat a 5. If he makes the roll, turn to **14**. If he fails it, turn to **164**.

232

Sonic and Tails dash down the corridor. It twists and turns through the space station, but from time to time they catch a glimpse of a fleeing red robot's heels that let them know they're going the right way. Suddenly a voice breaks in. 'Pardon me for interrupting your jog,' it says, 'but the space station is under attack. You must evacuate immediately. Follow the flashing signs to the escape pods, please.' Do Sonic and Tails keep chasing the robot (turn to **191**) or follow the signs to the escape pods (turn to **3**)?

233

Sonic closes his eyes tightly and tries to ignore the rumbling sound in the distance. It's no good; the noise is definitely getting louder. There's an odd smell on the breeze as well, a horrible burning smell that reminds Sonic of the last time Robotnik tried to take over the planet and Sonic had to journey through the Oil Ocean Zone. He didn't like the smell then, and he doesn't like it now. If you think Sonic should lie where he is, hoping the noise and the smell will go away, turn to section **59**. If you think that's a silly idea and he should at least open his eyes, turn to section **220**.

234

Sonic stumbles and falls, and the bandits leap on him. With fast hands they take everything he is carrying, apart from his shoes and gloves (cross them all off his *Vital Statistics*). The biggest of the bandits puts his sword at Sonic's throat. 'Go now, and find your precious Outcasts,' he jeers. 'They're out in the endless desert – somewhere.' The bandits go back to their fires, laughing amongst themselves. Sonic knows that if he attacks, he would be completely outnumbered, so he slinks out into the desert. Turn to **58**.

235

Sonic leaps for one of the cables connecting the rocket to the gantry, and pulls it away. A cold liquid pours out and onto the floor.

'They're fuel pipes!' shouts Tails. 'Drain all the fuel from the rocket!' He leaps for another one. In seconds, the whole cavern is awash with fuel.

'6. 5. 4.' continues the count-down. '3. 2. 1. Ignition.'

The chamber explodes in a massive fireball, crumpling the rocket as if it was a child's toy, and sending blast-waves through the rest of Robotnik's complex that collapse ceilings and destroy equipment. Within a minute, there is nothing left. In a way, Sonic and Tails have succeeded, because they've stopped Robotnik's insane quest for world domination. But they didn't make it out of the complex. You had better try again. Close, but no prize.

GAME OVER

236

Sonic looks for something sharp enough to cut the vines. A badly aimed spear thuds into the wall just above his head and he grabs it. 'Thanks, pal!' he shouts, using the spear's flint tip to slice through the vines. The drawbridge creaks, sways and begins to fall. But wait — Sonic's still underneath it! Roll on Sonic's Speed, to beat a 7. If he succeeds, turn to **166**. If he fails, turn to **207**.

237

'Okay, let's do it,' orders Sonic. One of the soldiers throws a grapple; it hooks onto the top of the wall and she climbs up it. By the time Sonic has followed her up, the soldier has fixed another rope here, this one leading down to the dark city street below. Sonic slides down it as quietly as he can. There's still no sound of battle from the front gate. He lands in the street, and looks around him as the soldiers slide down behind him. Suddenly a huge shape pounces out of the shadows, landing in front of them. It seems to be wearing clothes ten sizes too small, and it makes strange mewling, growling sounds. Do Sonic and his soldiers attack (turn to **45**), talk to it (turn to **116**), or quickly climb back up the rope and wait outside the city for the signal (turn to **219**)?

238

The leader sets off into the jungle with his scouts. Another wart-hog leads Tails and Sonic to a hut made of woven branches. 'This is our storehouse,' he explains. 'It is where we keep anything that might be useful, or that we don't know how to use. Please take only one item each, because the other warriors in the raiding party will need equipment too.' Sonic and Tails can each choose one item from the list below. There's only one of each item, so if one of them chooses something, the other can't choose it as well:

Twenty rings
Ten rings

A Shield power-up (the next time the holder
    should lose their rings or a life, they can
    ignore it)

An Invincible power-up (will protect the holder
    against everything until the next time they
    go through a teleporter)

One extra life

Write down the items on their *Vital Statistics*. The
wart-hog also gives them clothes made from leaves.
'It's good camouflage in the jungle,' he explains. 'That's
why we wear them.'

'Why do you wear those masks?' Tails asks.

The wart-hog grimaces. 'You'd wear a mask too, if
you had a face like this,' he says.

Dusk falls. The rest of the village's warriors, together
with Sonic and Tails, meet the scouting party at the
edge of a huge clearing. In the middle is a large
stronghold, with high walls made from sharpened tree-
trunks stood on their end. The large gate in the walls
is firmly closed. 'How do you think we should get in?'
the leader asks Sonic. Sonic looks around. There are
three obvious choices: he can tell the warriors to storm
the gates (turn to **249**); he can tell them to climb the
walls (turn to **120**); or he can suggest that they try
swinging over the walls on vines from nearby trees
(turn to **87**). Alternatively, he can try to think of
something better (turn to **272**).

239

Number One lumbers into the attack. Galen hangs back to defend the Emeralds against other threats. Sonic must use his Strength to fight Number One, and he can add 1 point to his roll for every companion that he has in the room. He will need their help, because Number One's rating is a massive 12! If Sonic is hit during the fight, roll the die. On a 1, 2 or 3 he was hit and loses all his rings. If he has no rings, he loses a life; cross it off his *Vital Statistics* and turn back to **21**. On a roll of 4, 5 or 6 it is one of Sonic's friends who has been hit and they are knocked out of the fight (don't add a point for them). If Sonic beats Number One, turn to **117**.

240

'Who said that?' asks Tails to the thin air. 'Who told me to dig further down?' But he does, until his paws hit something cold and solid: a sheet of solid ice under the snow. He can feel it shaking as something very large hits it – and then there is a cracking noise and it splits. The snow-bank shakes and falls into the freezing water that wells up from underneath, and Tails finds himself in bright sunlight, sitting on a chunk of ice drifting out to sea, away from the mainland. Tails stands up and looks around. He can see a group of small creatures at the edge of the land. They're wearing thick coats and brandishing weapons at a large shape that moves slowly under the water towards them. Suddenly it surfaces, throwing a huge splash of water into the air, and Tails can see that it is a shark. The sunlight reflecting off the snow may be playing tricks with his eyes, but it looks as if it's made entirely from metal. Does Tails jump back towards the shore (turn to **22**) or stay on the ice-floe (turn to **103**)?

241

Tails and Sonic find themselves floating in the rotating, spinning, flashing, dazzling, sparkling and deafening lunacy of the Warps of Confusion. It's like being at the centre of a maze of rotating mirrors — impossible to tell what is real or illusion. There is no sign of their ship, or the red robot's ship, or an exit, or anything that might be any help at all.

'Are you okay, Sonic?' Tails shouts. His voice echoes back at him mockingly: '?cinoS, yako uoy erA'

'Is that you shouting about eras and yaks, Tails?' Sonic shouts, from so close that the young fox is almost deafened by the yell. He and Sonic turn around at the same moment, to find themselves facing each other. Sonic grabs Tails's arm. 'Don't let go of me,' he says. 'If you do, I may never find you again.' Tails nods in acknowledgement. Now, should the pair search for

their ship (turn to **284**) or explore the Warp together
(turn to **51**)?

242

Usually Sonic is too cool to sweat, but right now he
can feel the drops of perspiration rolling down his
forehead as he strains his muscles against the iron bars.
Slowly they bend out of shape, although it feels to
Sonic as if his arms are doing the same thing. Finally
he stops and looks at his work. There's just enough
space between the bars for him to squeeze through.

'Good luck!' shouts Number Two, from the cell. 'Follow
the brightest star in the sky – it'll lead you to the
Outcast camp in the desert.'

Sonic waves back at his friend, then looks down into
the city. He's quite a way up, but not too far to jump
down – so he does, and lands in an alleyway. Turn
to **91**.

243

Sonic picks up a clod of earth, takes aim and hurls it
over the bulldozer towards the trees where Tails is
still asleep. His aim is good and there's a sudden yelp
from the trees as a small orange foxy shape leaps
several metres into the air – to land on the bulldozer,
just behind the machine's front blade. 'Sonic!' he wails,
'where are you?' Sonic can't let his furry friend be
carried away by the blundering bulldozer. He breaks
into a supersonic sprint, catches up to the machine in
seconds and leaps aboard it, landing beside his friend.
Turn to section **26**.

244

The monkeys are tied to the base of the fridge-machine with ropes fixed in ice which has set around them like concrete. Tails tries to work out a way of cutting through the ropes or breaking them or melting them. Suddenly there is a whizzing, whistling sound from behind him, and he spins round to see a cloud of tiny icicles hurtling towards him. Behind it, the mammoth has its trunk pointed at him. It puffs hard and more icicles fly from its trunk. Does Tails attack the mammoth (turn to **102**) or dodge the flying icicles (turn to **65**)?

245

'Hi,' says Sonic, standing up in the cake. 'I'm real sorry for bursting in like that. I hope that this gift, from a far-off Zone, will make up for it.' He offers the Chaos Emerald to the most impressively dressed cat in the room, who bows deeply to him and takes the proffered gift.

'Thank you,' he says, a trace of a smile on his lips. 'You should be warned that attempting to bribe an official of Scrap Brain City is punishable by death. Guards! Grab him.' Two heavily muscled cats take Sonic's arms, lift him out of the cake and put him on the floor. The impressive cat looks at him and smiles widely, showing a full set of bright white sharp teeth. He claps his paws twice. 'Let the trial begin,' he shouts. Turn to **69**.

The screen changes to show a map of Mobius. 'CHOOSE NEW DESTINATION,' it reads. Sonic moves the cross-hairs over the map with the joystick, but he doesn't really want to land the Chaos Emeralds anywhere on his home world.

'What happens if you move it out into space?' suggests Tails.

Sonic tries it, and the map changes to a star-chart. 'Wahoo!' he whoops. 'How far away should we send this thing?'

'As far as possible,' says Tails.

'I've got a better idea,' says Sonic. 'Let's send them to Ross on Space Station Eyrie. He can put them back in the Warps of Confusion, and guard them as well.' He moves the cross-hairs over the blip marking the space station on the map and presses the button. 'NEW DESTINATION REGISTERED,' reads the screen, 'MAKE NEXT CHOICE.'

What does Sonic choose now?

Self-destruct?   Turn to **206**

Open hatch?   Turn to **221**

Jettison Chaos Emeralds?   Turn to **57**

247

'Sorry,' says Tails, 'but you're looking for your friends and I'm after a Chaos Emerald and a teleporter device, and I don't think they'll be in the same place. Your friends will probably be stuck in a snowdrift, and the Chaos Emerald will be deep inside some secret stronghold, guarded by fearsome foes who will do anything to stop me getting through.' He shivers a little at the thought and wonders if he should go with the monkeys after all. 'No,' he says, 'you go your way, and I'll go mine. It's been nice meeting you and I hope you find your friends, but I've got to go.' He turns away and walks off along the edge of the ice. Behind him he hears grumbling and a few muffled boos before the monkeys set off towards a tall mountain peak, and the glacier on it. Suddenly something strikes the ice under Tails's feet, and there is an ominous cracking noise. 'Help!' he shouts. The thing hits the ice again, and the nose of the great metal shark breaks through, sending splinters of ice flying. 'Help!' Tails shouts again, as the machine's massive mouth, with its rows of sharp, shining teeth, closes around the unfortunate fox.

GAME OVER

248

Little bits of robot fly off in all directions and Sonic sighs with relief. He switches on the suit's jets which propel him to the outside of the station where Tails is waiting for him. 'The airlock's closed itself,' the fox says. 'I can't reopen it. We'll have to look for another way in.' The two friends set off across the outer wall of the station, the magnets on their boots clunking with every step. After a while they see the pale blue-white bubble of a large force-field ahead of them, sealing off a large opening in the side of the ship. Beside it is an airlock, with the outer door open. Sonic and Tails climb in, press the button to cycle the airlock and wait as the outer door closes and the inner one opens. Turn to **191**.

249

'CHAAARGE!' shouts Sonic. He rushes towards the gate, followed by the rest of the attackers. They hit the wooden gate with a tremendous thud, and it splinters and falls inwards. Unfortunately, on the other side is a moat, and the mighty invading force is moving too fast to stop. With a colossal splash, they fall into the muddy water! Sonic bobs to the surface and looks around. There is another wall on the other side of the moat, with a raised drawbridge set in it. On top of the inner wall are crocodile guards, armed with crossbows, firing rotten fruit at the spluttering wart-hogs. Sonic can swim to the inner wall and climb over it (turn to **223**), he can swim to the drawbridge and lower it (turn to **64**) or he can swim back to the outer wall, climb out and try to find a better way into the stronghold (turn to **31**).

'A good choice,' says the computer and the spacecraft's cockpit opens. Sonic and Tails scramble in and sit down, Sonic in the pilot's seat and Tails beside him. They strap themselves in, the canopy closes and they blast off through the force-field and away from the space station.

Tails is inspecting the controls. They look very simple: just a joystick, a speed control and a single unmarked red button. 'Can I press the button?' he asks. 'It's the only way we'll find out what it does. Oh, go on, Sonic. You're hogging all the fun, let me do this. I'll be your best friend.'

'Hey! You are my best friend!' says Sonic, trying to concentrate on controlling the ship.

'Then let me press the button,' begs Tails. If Sonic says no, turn to **30**. If he says yes, Tails leans forward and presses it. Which ship are they in?

The *Kubrick*?   Turn to **173**
The *Yuzna*?   Turn to **88**
The *Toho*?   Turn to **43**

251

The engine is a thundering collection of whirling wheels, flying pistons, flashing sparks and raw power. It smells of boiling oil and burnt metal, and sounds like a herd of angry rhinoceroses. Sonic and Tails look at it. 'What are you waiting for?' asks Tails.

'I'm working out which part will stop the whole engine if I smash it,' explains Sonic. 'The pistons won't do it. The flywheel's too dangerous, and so is the fan. The fuel tank would blow everything up, including us. Maybe the distributor . . .'

The engine coughs and rattles into silence. The bulldozer stops. Tails stands up, holding something small and white in his paw. 'The spark plugs,' he says, grinning.

'Nice one!' says Sonic. 'Let's get to work.' Should the two animals investigate the bulldozer's cabin (turn to **204**) or the road (turn to **107**)?

252

The two animals dive into the water with hardly a splash, and swim towards a deserted corner of the docks. They climb out and watch as the submarine moors to the dock. A gangplank is placed between sub and dock, and the crew of robots begin to carry things to the shore. First off the sub are two crates marked 'Chaos Emeralds. Do Not Drop'. The robots carrying them disappear into the larger of the two tunnels that lead away from the dock. Next off are four unmarked crates, which are taken down the smaller tunnel. After that, nothing happens for a while.

'Time for us to make our move,' whispers Sonic. 'Which way should we go?'

Down the larger tunnel?   Turn to **217**
Down the smaller tunnel?   Turn to **137**

253

Number Three is polishing his sword with his tail as Sonic approaches. 'Hello!' he barks. 'How can I help you, Sonic — I mean, Number Four?'

Sonic bends close to one of the dog's ears. 'I think you should know,' he whispers, 'that one of your friends is actually an informant for Galen and the cats who run the city.'

Number Three looks at him in surprise. 'An informant? Do you think so? You must have been really clever to work that out, because you've only been here a couple of minutes. Who do you think it is, or don't you know? What'll you do when you find out who it is? I hope it isn't me.' Either Number Three is a brilliant actor, or he really is as stupid as he looks; Sonic can't quite decide. Whichever it is, he knows he's not going to learn much from the dog. What should he do next?

Talk to Number One?   Turn to **38**
Talk to Number Two?   Turn to **126**
Ask the group what their plans are?   Turn to **101**

With his tails spinning faster than they ever have before, Tails carries the stranded monkey up between the icy walls of the crevasse and out, to land on the soft snow. The monkeys on the other side of the crevasse clap loudly. Tails lies back and pants because he's exhausted from the effort. His tails ache and he won't be able to do another trick like that for a week! Turn to **41**.

255

With the chieftain disorientated, Sonic and Tails have a good chance of beating him. 'On three,' shouts Sonic. 'THREE!' The two animals attack. The chief croc is a mean fighter. Sonic and Tails must use their combined Strength to fight him, and his rating is 11. If either of the heroes lose a life, cross it off their *Vital Statistics* and turn back to 31. If they beat the croc, Sonic picks up the Emerald and rushes towards the teleporter on the other side of the room. The strange white light surrounds him, and Tails jumps into its beam a moment later. Once again they hear a loud FAZZZZZZZZ-. Turn to 229.

256

Sonic looks up at you from the deck of the submarine. 'Who are you calling a brute?' he asks. Then he notices that sea water is lapping around his feet. 'Hey, Tails — make with a paw,' he shouts, and the two animals bend to the hatch and heave. Add Sonic's Strength to Tails's Strength, and roll on the total to beat a 9. If they make the roll, turn to 84. If not, the hatchway refuses to budge, and in desperation Tails suggests knocking on it; turn to 155.

257

There is a squeal of brakes from behind them. Sonic and Tails dive out of the way as a huge forklift-truck driven by a tiny red robot races forward, grabs the pile of scaffolding poles they were hiding behind, and races away down the road.

'That was close!' exclaims Tails, wiping his forehead.

'Yes, but now we've got nothing to hide behind,' replies Sonic. Should the fearless pair go into the building (turn to section **193**) or see what's happening in the Green Hill Zone first (turn to section **170**)?

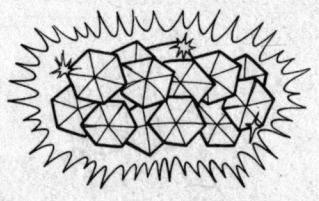

258

Robotnik's eyes gleam. 'I'm eggs-tremely pleased that you're taking such an interest,' he declares. 'The rocket will be guided by internal gyroscopic computers, designed and programmed by myself. They're absolutely infallible. Now, I hear the countdown getting low.' He shuts up for a second and in the background the voice intones, '36. 35. 34.' 'Take-off is imminent,' continues Robotnik, 'and I'm afraid I have to kill you now.' He flicks a switch and the Zap Cannon hums into life, energy pulsing through the coils around its barrels. Should Sonic and Tails attack Robotnik (turn to **67**) or run away (turn to **109**)?

259

The cats applaud as the guards drag Sonic from the courtroom, down a long corridor to a small cell. They hurl him in and slam the door. The cell is bleak. There is a small window with bars on it, a small bed which looks very hard, and the door which is made of steel. Previous prisoners have scratched messages into the stone wall: 'The Outcasts will win', 'Watch out for Galen – he's tricky!', 'I wish I had a "Get Out Of Jail Free" card.' At the top of the wall is a large sign that reads 'Defacing the wall is punishable by death.' Someone has crossed out 'Defacing the wall' and written 'Anything Galen doesn't like' underneath it. What should Sonic examine?

The window?	Turn to **202**
The bed?	Turn to **83**
The door?	Turn to **29**

260

'The radar is activated,' says a computerized voice and coloured symbols flash on the windscreen in front of Sonic's face.

'I can't see. Turn it off!' he shouts, and Tails obeys.

'Sorry, Sonic,' he says, 'I thought it might help. I was wrong.' Turn to **224**.

261

The leader of the wart-hogs launches into a long and boring history of his tribe, full of famines, droughts, floods, arguments with other tribes, attacks by wild creatures, battles, injuries, deaths and the sentence, 'But we are a peaceful people.' After half an hour Sonic notices Tails falling asleep, and nudges him with an elbow. Tails wakes up with a yelp.

'But what about the spears you were carrying today?' asks Sonic quickly, to cover Tails's indiscretion.

'Ah. That,' says the leader. 'We were patrolling in case the crocodiles attacked us again. A week ago they attacked us, shouting about a glowing rock they'd found which had made them strong and how they were going to take over the Zone. We were planning to attack them soon, to try to destroy this rock of theirs and return the jungle to normal. Will you help?' Sonic and Tails can agree to help (turn to **160**), refuse to help (turn to **2**), or ask why the food is so bad (turn to **209**) or if the wart-hogs have seen Dr Robotnik (turn to **147**).

262

'You won't regret this,' Ross says. 'We'll do an excellent job — we were built for it. Computer, display charts.' Behind him, a section of the wall darkens, and a star-chart for the surrounding area of space appears. 'We're here, in orbit around Mobius,' says Ross, pointing. 'Here are the six Warps of Confusion, much closer to the planet. Between us and them is a belt of rocky asteroids, created when Ovi Kintobor blew up a small moon.'

'I thought you said he was a good guy!' Tails exclaims.

'He was,' says Ross. 'He was also absent-minded and clumsy. Good is a variable term.' He, Sonic and Tails study the charts and work out the best course for their journey, then leave the room to prepare. Turn to **288**.

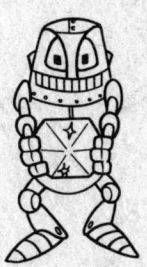

263

The confused crocodiles don't have time to react as a small streak of blue dashes to the inner gate and pulls down the lever that controls the drawbridge. With a crash it falls into place and the wart-hog warriors charge across it and into the stronghold. Turn to **44**.

264

After walking down corridors and passing through several heavy doors, Sonic, Tails and their two guards enter a huge room, filled with flashing, humming, beeping machines. It smells of new paint, hot metal, rotten eggs and the odour of ozone you get when electrical wires aren't connected properly. In the middle of all this, standing on a pedestal and surrounded by controls, screens and keyboards, is the familiar fat figure of Dr Ivo Robotnik. He's just as bald as ever and his bright orange moustache still looks like he has a squirrel up his nose, but now he's wearing a sash that reads 'President of Mobius'.

'Sonic and Tails! Ha ha ha ha!' he laughs, and the tips of his moustache wiggle. 'Welcome to the new Planet Mobius — or Planet Robotnik, as it will soon be known!' The mad scientist's mad laughter continues for minutes. Just as Sonic and Tails are getting bored and looking for escape routes, Robotnik stops and looks at them with a serious expression. 'Of course,' he says, 'you have worked out my dastardly plans, or you'd never have escaped my mind-control devices.' He pauses for a moment and looks at them again. 'You *have* worked out my plans, haven't you?' he asks. Do Sonic and Tails nod (turn to **197**) or shake their heads (turn to **20**)?

265

The contamination suits come in all shapes and sizes. Everyone can find one to fit them and they help each other to zip them up and fasten the hoods. The suits are comfortable, if a little stuffy. There's also a large net on the end of a long pole, like a fishing net, and Sonic picks it up (write this down).

'What now, boss?' says one of the warriors, his voice muffled by the suit.

'We go up — and find the Emeralds,' says Sonic. Turn to 150.

266

Sonic and Tails must roll against their combined Speed, to beat a 13. If they get away, turn to 52. If the total is less than 13, the crocs roar and chase after them — it's a fight! Turn to 181.

267

The last rock zips by outside the cockpit and the ship is past the asteroids. The red ship is still ahead of them but its lead has been cut. Sonic and Tails are so close now that they can see the robot in its cockpit, surrounded by Chaos Emeralds. The small machine looks back over its shoulder, pushes its rocket's engines to full thrust and dives towards the swirling Warps of Confusion that lie ahead!

'Oh no!' shouts Tails. 'It's a robot, so it won't be affected by the Warps. We will. Be careful, Sonic!'

Sonic has three choices. He can fly straight through the Warps (turn to 241), he can zip the ship between them, hoping the Warps won't confuse him too much (turn to 100), or he can avoid them completely by flying around the outside (turn to 77).

268

Tails dashes across the ice, spinning like a gyroscope, and smacks into the side of the shark. With a metallic roar it drops the monkey it was holding and turns to snap its huge jaws at the furry fighting fox. Tails will use his Speed to fight the shark. It has a rating of 12, but Tails can add 1 point for each of the monkeys who are also fighting it; there are four of them, so his attack is his Speed plus the die roll plus 4. If the shark hits him, roll the die again. On a 1, 2 or 3 Tails is hit and loses all his rings or, if he has no rings left, a life (cross it off his *Vital Statistics* and turn back to **123**). On a 4, 5 or 6 one of the monkeys is hit and knocked out of the fight. Don't add a point for a monkey once it's been knocked out. If Tails and the monkeys defeat the shark, it sinks into the water and disappears. Turn to **42**.

269

Sonic ducks down behind the dune and moves around it slowly. He can't see any movement from inside the camp, but he gets the feeling that someone or something is down there, hiding from him. Looking down, he notices a trail of footprints in the sand, leading away from the camp.

'So if they were walking away,' Sonic ponders out loud, 'does that mean the camp's deserted? Not if just one person was leaving, unless it was a lot of people all walking in each other's footprints. But what sort of people would do that?'

'Highly trained warriors,' comes a voice. 'Don't turn round.' Unfortunately, Sonic has already turned round, only to find himself facing a group of cloaked figures, each carrying a curved sword that gleams in the starlight. 'Come quietly, or there will be trouble,' says the one in front. Sonic quickly counts the group and, although confident that he can defeat ten warriors armed with swords, decides to save his strength for later, and is led down into the cluster of tents. Turn to **125**.

270

The two heroes dash forward towards the airlock. Their space suits slow them down a little, giving the red robot just enough time to look up, see them coming, pick up two wires and touch them together. A spark jumps and the outer door of the airlock slams open. The air rushes out of the station like a hurricane, dragging Sonic and Tails with it, out into space! Did the animals finish putting on their space suits in the changing room? If they did, turn to **98**. If not, turn to **49**.

'Keep your hands off our gloves, Egg-face!' yells Sonic as he and Tails dash across the room.

'Shoot them! Perforate them! Eggs-terminate them!' shouts Robotnik as Porker and Sally open fire with their machine-guns. 'Just keep them away from the white cross on the floor!'

'Aha!' Sonic shouts and leaps to the white marker, with Tails an instant behind. They land on it and try to take a step forward – but their shoes are stuck fast to the floor, held down by a sticky liquid.

'It's a trap!' Tails exclaims, stating the obvious.

'That's obvious,' Sonic replies, pulling at his feet with his hands. The sticky liquid gets onto his gloves, and sticks them fast to his shoes. He's completely stuck now, doubled over, and he can see that poor Tails is in an even worse mess. Robotnik laughs madly and pulls a huge switch. A strange device on the ceiling begins to pulse with energy. The two animals can't dodge as the device shoots a beam of pure light straight down at them. Everything disappears, apart from a strange noise that goes FAZZZZZZZZZZZZZZ-. Turn to **8**.

272

Sonic looks out of the page at you, crosses his arms, and sighs. 'Look, sunshine, I've told you before, I'm not the sort of hero who does a lot of standing around and thinking. That's why you're here; you do the brain-work and I risk life and limb trying it all out. Didn't I tell you that before? Oh, I didn't?' He looks confused for a moment. 'Sorry, that's in another game-book.'

'Stop talking to the reader and GET ON WITH IT!' chorus the wart-hogs. Turn to **31**.

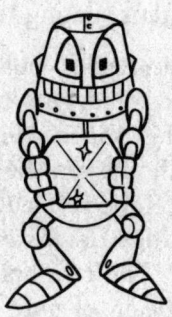

273

'Ah — hello,' says Sonic, a little taken aback. 'We're Sonic and Tails, freelance heroes.'

'I know,' says the robot. 'My name is RO-55, or Ross for short. I'm an android, part of the crew of this space station. We've been watching your adventures, and may I say that you've done very well so far. Is there anything I can do for you, or anything you would like to know?'

Several questions come pouring into the heroes' minds, but they can only ask one at a time. What do you think should come first?

'Do you know how to dispose of
  Chaos Emeralds safely?'   Turn to **9**
'How do we teleport out of here?'   Turn to **74**
'If this is a space station, who built it
  – and you?'   Turn to **159**

274

'We're a search party,' says one of the monkeys. 'We're looking for food, shelter and the other search party. We were also trying to find out what was making all this ice and cold. All in all,' he says, sniffing a bit, 'it hasn't been a good day for us. We've lost our home and we've lost our friends. Will you help us?' Tails can agree to help (turn to **94**), refuse to help (turn to **247**), ask the monkeys where this is (turn to **158**) or whether they have seen a Chaos Emerald recently (turn to **216**).

275

Tails and Mildred walk along the bottom of the crevasse for what seems like hours. It twists and turns and goes past ice-caverns filled with icicles like stalactites and stalagmites. After a while the thin line of sky disappears and it becomes a tunnel. Light still filters down through the ice, making everything a grey-blue colour. Eventually the tunnel widens out into a cavern, with a flat floor of solid ice and icicles hanging from the high, domed ceiling. On the far side stands a large machine that hums faintly. It reminds Tails of a huge fridge. On top of it is a teleport device and, connected by wires and cables, is a Chaos Emerald, glowing with a strange orange light. Tied around the bottom of the fridge-machine are three figures, dressed in heavy coats like Mildred's. Mildred is about to dash over to them when Tails stops her. A dark shape lumbers into the room; it's at least ten times as tall as Tails, with long white tusks and a heavy, matted fur coat. You recognize it as a woolly mammoth, but Tails has never seen anything like it before. The mammoth trundles over to the fridge-machine and stands in front of it, as if on guard. Should Tails and Mildred attack the mammoth (turn to **102**), free the monkeys (turn to **244**) or make a dash for the Chaos Emerald and the teleporter (turn to **17**)?

276

The whirling patterns on the screen fill the minds of our heroes. All they can see are spinning dots, all they hear is humming music, all they feel is happiness. When the screen clears and the face of Dr Robotnik appears on it, they don't mind at all. 'Sonic and Tails! Ha ha ha ha ha!' laughs the mad scientist. 'At last I have you in my power, hypnotized by my television set. Now you'll work for me, and you'll enjoy it! Go out, get eggs-cavating and build something pointless and ugly.' Unthinkingly the two animals turn and march into the sunshine, just two more creatures that Robotnik will use to take over the world. The adventure ends here. Turn back to section **1** and try again.

GAME OVER

277

Leaving Tails in the middle of his trip by teleporter, we return to our hero, Sonic, who right at this moment is being dragged towards a large tent in the centre of the Outcasts' camp. 'You could let me walk,' he protests. 'It's more dignified.'

'Dragging is traditional,' replies the guard, tugging him into the tent and throwing him onto a large mat. Sonic looks up, to find his way out blocked by guards of all species with swords of all types. In front of him, in the middle of the tent, is a tall dog, dressed in the white robes of the desert people, with a belt of gold around his waist. As he bends down to look at Sonic, the hedgehog notices that the dog has pointed ears that remind him of someone else he has met recently.

'I am Ravis, leader of the Outcasts,' he says. 'And you have come from the city to spy on us.'

'No I haven't!' Sonic exclaims. 'I came here to warn you about what's happening in the city. Your spies have been captured —'

'If you know what is happening in the city, you must be from there,' interrupts the dog. 'And since all the city dwellers hate us, you must be an agent for them. Either you will tell us the truth, or we will torture it out of you. You will admit you are a spy — or die.'

What a conundrum! Does Sonic admit to being a spy even though he isn't (turn to 25) or let the Outcasts torture him (turn to 167)?

278

Sonic hammers on the cell door with his fists. After a while he hears footsteps in the corridor outside, and the small panel in the door slides open. An ugly cat guard with a scarred face looks in. 'What?' demands the guard. 'This had better be important. I was torturing a fly to death, and just getting to the exciting bit.' He looks around the cell. 'False alarm eh? Now shut up, or you'll get no food – ever.' The panel clicks shut. Sonic can try to overpower the guard (turn to **133**), he can search the rest of the cell (turn to **27**) or ask the other two to show him what they have in their pockets (turn to **105**).

279

There is no answer. Sonic looks all around him, but there is no sign of Tails at all. The ground hurtles up – too fast! 'Aaaaaaaaaaaaah!' he screams, and just has time to roll himself into a ball. Turn to **184**.

280

Sonic dashes away from his pals, dodging around the equipment at the edge of the room to avoid Galen and Number One and, more importantly, the spinning, whirling shapes of the Emeralds. The two hulking enemies are easy to elude, but the Emeralds seem to sense that Sonic is coming and spiral down towards him, spinning faster and brighter to form an impenetrable barrier of searing heat and flashing lights. There's simply no way past them, and Sonic must turn back. If Sonic picked up the net in the control room, he can use it to capture the spinning Emeralds (turn to 95). Otherwise he can jump up to grab them with his bare paws (turn to 15) or attack Galen and Number One (turn to 239).

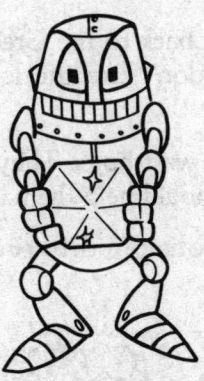

281

Sonic and Tails fight with all their strength, but the native warriors are too practised with their spears. After a hard-fought battle, the two heroes find themselves with their backs against a tree and spears prodding their stomachs. The leader of the natives steps forward and takes off his wooden mask. Underneath he is very much like a scruffy pig to look at. He's got big knobbly warts and lumps all over his long, hairy face, and is very, very ugly indeed. 'You,' he says slowly, 'are valiant warriors, and we need as many of those as we can get. Listen to what I say and you will not be killed. For years we have lived in the jungle, in peace with the other creatures here. Suddenly, some days ago, our village was attacked by crocodiles. They spoke of a glowing rock that fell from the sky and gave them powers and urges to conquer and destroy. Will you help us defeat them, and rid the Zone of this glowing rock?'

Sonic and Tails look at each other. 'It sounds like a Chaos Emerald,' says Sonic.

'Shouldn't we get back to the Green Hill Zone to stop Robotnik first? I don't like the look of these people,' replies Tails.

'Oh, they're only wart-hogs. They seem cool enough,' says Sonic. 'We should help them.'

Do the two agree to help (turn to **160**) or refuse (turn to **2**)? (turn to **160**) or refuse (turn to **2**)

282

In Scrap Brain City, Ravis and his troops are fighting a losing battle against the onslaught of the cat forces. Desperately the Outcast leader looks up at the High Tower. 'Why hasn't Sonic got the Emeralds yet?' he mutters. As if in answer, there is a colossal explosion and the top of the tower disintegrates in a flash of blue-green light, with a crash and boom so loud that the animals far away in the Green Hill Zone stop working for a second to listen. Dust and tiny pieces of brick rain down on the city, rattling against the weapons and armour of the two armies. There is nothing left of the tower, and no sign of the people who were in it when it exploded. 'Ah,' sighs Ravis. 'A shame. Sonic was a brave warrior — a little impulsive, but he had a good heart. Still, there will be time to mourn the departed later, but now I have a battle to fight.'

GAME OVER

283

'Who said that?' asks Tails. 'Who told me to investigate? Sonic, was that you?' There is no answer. He turns himself right way up, digs his way out of the snow and heads off towards the source of the noises. Tails doesn't have far to go until he sees something. He ducks behind another snow-bank so that he isn't spotted and peers out. There is a group of figures, all wearing warm coats and carrying primitive weapons, standing on the edge of the ice-field and looking out over the open water beyond at something large, grey and metallic which is bumping its head against the ice. It could be trying to smash the ice to attack the figures, or it could be trapped there. What should Tails do?

Keep watching the figures?	Turn to **225**
Look for a teleporter device?	Turn to **145**
Shout to the small figures?	Turn to **62**
Attack the small figures?	Turn to **10**
Attack the shape under the ice?	Turn to **168**

284

'Remember,' says Sonic, 'in the Warp, things can look different to how they really are.'

'Like what?' asks his furry companion.

'Just different.' The two animals start hunting for any trace of the spaceship, or anything that might be vaguely spacey or shippy. Finding the ship will take a good look, so roll against Sonic's and Tails's combined Good Looks scores, to beat a 7. If they make the roll, turn to **194**. If they fail, turn to **70**.

285

Sonic punches the OFF button on the television set. The screen goes blank and Chirps blinks. 'Sonic? Tails?' he says. 'Where are we? What's going on?'

'You were driving this bulldozer, building a bypass through the Green Hill Zone,' says Tails.

'Was I?' says Chirps, sounding very confused. 'The last thing I remember is watching *Zone Alone* last night, and then there was a commercial for Robotnik Industries and everything went funny – ooh, I hope I haven't caused too much trouble. Can I go home and have a nice lie-down?'

'Good idea,' says Sonic. 'If you can remember anything else, come and tell us.' Chirps nods, and flaps out of the cab. Sonic and Tails can search the cab (turn to section **143**), they can follow the black road (turn to section **107**) or they can explore the rest of the Zone (turn to section **170**).

286

Tails and Mildred get closer to the strange plant and its trembling and shivering gets more violent. Suddenly it pulls its three branches out of the snow, and Tails just has time to realize that each one is carrying a large snowball before it hurls them at him! Tails and Mildred must each roll on their Quick Thinking to beat a 6 to dodge the snowballs. Mildred has a Quick Thinking of 2. If either of them fail, turn to **161**; otherwise they dodge away out of the plant's range (turn to **111**).

287

Sonic can't see any other way forward, so he jumps down into the moat. The water is cold and deep, and he wonders if he's doing the right thing. He can swim over to the closed drawbridge and try to open it (turn to **64**), he can swim to the inner wall and climb up (turn to **223**) or he can climb back over the outer wall and find some other way to get in (turn to **31**).

'This way,' Ross says and leads them down a passage-way, past rooms where other androids are working, to a large empty chamber. 'This is the changing room,' he says.

'What's he going to change us into?' wonders Tails. Sonic shushes him as Ross speaks into the empty air.

'Computer! One hedgehog-sized spacesuit and one fox-sized spacesuit with extra tail-room,' he says. A concealed door swings open with a concealed hum and two white suits emerge on hangers, steaming slightly. 'Put them on,' says Ross. 'You may need them. Things out here are rarely what they seem, and in space no one can hear you shout for help.' Sonic and Tails start to slip into the suits, which fit perfectly. Suddenly there is a knock, as if someone is rapping on the door. 'Come in,' says Ross, but the door does not move. The knocking comes again. 'I said COME IN!' Ross repeats, raising his voice.

'I'm not coming in, I'm coming out!' shouts a little voice. A section of metal on Ross's stomach dents, then splits in two. Half of it falls to the floor, trailing wires. From inside the android's body a small red robot leaps to the floor, sprints to where Sonic and Tails have left the Chaos Emeralds floating while they are putting on their suits, grabs them and dashes out into the corridor! Should Sonic and Tails give chase immediately (turn to 135) or finish putting on their spacesuits (turn to 80)?

289

The crackle of loudspeakers breaks through the early evening quiet. 'ATTENTION ALL INHABITANTS OF SCRAP BRAIN CITY,' blares Galen's voice. 'A PRISONER HAS ESCAPED. HE IS BLUE AND VERY DANGEROUS. APPREHEND HIM AT ALL COSTS.' Something flashes through the air in front of the sprinting Sonic, and melts a hole in the road ahead. It was a laser beam, and others are flying round his ears. Sonic must roll on his Quick Wits to beat a 5 to dodge the lasers. If he fails the roll, a beam hits him and he loses all his rings. If he has no rings, he loses a life (cross it off his *Vital Statistics*) and must turn back to 91. If he makes the roll then the beams flash harmlessly past him, and he sprints on to the gates. Turn to 154.

290

'Give me a leg up,' Sonic asks Tails. The young fox obliges, and Sonic reaches down to help his friend climb up. Together they scale the tree until they are at the very top, looking out over the stronghold and the forest beyond.

'Look!' says Tails. 'There's another wall inside — and water between the two of them.'

'It's a moat,' says Sonic. 'Very cunning — and very hard to get past. But there's a drawbridge on the inside. Shame it's raised at the moment.'

'We need to get closer,' says Tails. 'There are plenty

of vines around here. Do you think we could swing across on them?'

'There's only one way to find out,' replies Sonic, 'and it'll wait until we're attacking for real, this evening.' The two friends climb down the tree and rejoin the other scouts. Do they stand and watch for a while (turn to **18**), get closer to the gate (turn to **108**), tunnel under the wall (turn to **218**) or wait for the other warthogs to join them for the attack (turn to **52**)?

291

Sonic leaps out of the remains of the cake, sees the most impressively dressed cat-person in the room and hurtles across the floor towards him. Two heavy swords thud into the floor just in front of him and he screeches to a halt. His arms are grabbed and two muscular guards lift him off the floor. The Chaos Emerald drops from his paws. One of the guards picks it up and passes it to the impressive cat, who studies it. 'Interesting,' he says. 'He looks like a kamikaze agent for the Outcasts, but that doesn't explain why he would be carrying a Chaos Emerald. This could be a fake Chaos Emerald, of course. He may have been told to swap it for our Emerald. We must find out. By the authority vested in me, I'm calling a trial!' Turn to **69**.

292

Ravis takes the talisman from Sonic. 'This belongs to my son,' he says, with emotion in his voice. 'He is one of our agents in the city. He clearly has great trust in you. Tell me everything.' Sonic tells the Outcast leader everything about Galen, the two Chaos Emeralds and the way the Outcasts' spies were betrayed by Number One. Ravis nods in understanding. 'That changes things,' he says. 'We were going to attack the city tonight, but I must rethink our strategy. I will still lead our main assault on the front gates of the city, but you shall lead six of my elite warriors to the city's rear wall. Wait until we launch a flare into the sky, then climb the wall and head for the High Tower. We will not win the battle unless you can get the Chaos Emeralds away from there. Will you do it?' Sonic nods, and Ravis slaps him on the back. 'Excellent fellow! Please have these ten gold rings.' Sonic takes them (write them down) and Ravis continues. 'I will give you your weight in diamonds and bless you with many wives once we have won,' he proclaims. Sonic politely refuses that offer, but goes outside to meet the warriors. Mark down '6 warriors' on Sonic's *Vital Statistics*, and turn to **119**.

As they watch, the rabbit Johnny Lightfoot climbs down the tower to pick up a new bag of rivets. 'Hey, Johnny! My old bunny buddy,' Sonic says. 'What's happening? How are you doing? How are they treating you? What are the hours like here? Do you get many carrot breaks?'

Johnny looks at him coldly. 'I recognize you,' he says slowly. 'You're Sonic the Wart-hog.'

'That's Hedgehog!' corrects the hedgehog.

'Whatever. And that's Tails, also known as Two-Tails, also known as Miles Prower.'

'Well, we're big stars —' starts Sonic, but stops as he feels something dig into his back. It's a submachine-gun held by his friend Porker Harris. Sally Acorn stands behind Tails, with another gun. Something's wrong — there shouldn't be any guns in the Green Hill Zone, and Porker and Sally are their friends!

'You are enemies of President Robotnik,' says Johnny. 'Take them away, guards.' Sally and Porker prod their two captives with their guns, and lead them down the road. A strange metal building with a huge satellite dish on its roof comes into view.

'Did he say President Robotnik?' hisses Tails to Sonic.

'Yes, and I think we're going to meet the man himself,' Sonic mutters back. Turn to section 124.

294

The last, biggest bandit goes sprawling face-down in the sand, and the others back away. Sonic puts his foot on the bandit's head and looks at them. 'I've defeated your leader,' he says. 'Does that make me your new leader?'

'No,' says the bandit in the sand. 'It means we'll give you anything you want if you go away. What do you want?'

'Directions to the Outcasts' camp would do nicely,' declares Sonic. 'And if you've got any gold rings, I'll take them too.'

The bandit points to one of his followers. 'You — get this mighty figher as many rings as you can carry,' he demands. The follower disappears into a tent. 'Follow the brightest star in the sky to get to the Outcasts' camp,' continues the bandit. 'It's two hours' walk.'

'Or five minutes if I run,' says Sonic. The bandit's follower reappears from the tent, staggering under the load of the rings he is carrying — 23 of them! Write them down on Sonic's sheet. Sonic thanks his host and takes his foot off his head, then sprints away from the camp towards the brightest star he can see. Turn to **58**.

The two bolts of light streak over Sonic's head and into his friends, still standing by the door. They scream, clutching at their heads, and begin to change before Sonic's eyes. Their bodies swell and grow, new muscles bulge on their arms and legs, and their clothes rip and fall away. Within seconds two different creatures are standing there. They snarl, gnash their new fangs, and dive towards Sonic. He must fight them! Sonic must use his Strength to fight off these mutuated chaos creatures. They have a rating of 7 each, but Sonic can add 1 point to his roll for each of his friends who haven't been mutated yet. If he loses a life, cross it off his *Vital Statistics* and turn back to **21**. If he beats his former friends, he can either keep going towards the Emeralds (turn to **187**) or fight Galen and Number One (turn to **239**).

296

The stairs lead to an underground space glowing with an unearthly light. There are hooks all over the walls with crossbows hung on them, although there is no sign of any ammunition. At the far side of the room are three things which grab the heroes' attention. There's a large machine that looks just like the teleporter that sent them here; there's a large Chaos Emerald; and there's a very large crocodile holding the Chaos Emerald. If crocodiles choose their chief by which of them has the most teeth and the meanest expression, this guy won by a distance.

Tails nudges Sonic. 'I say we go for the teleport,' he says.

'No way!' exclaims Sonic. 'We've got to get the Emerald back. It must be leaking chaos which has made these crocodiles so warlike. Remember what the wart-hog leader told us?'

Tails nods. 'So what do we do now?' he asks. Good question. If you think that the two heroes should attack the crocodile immediately, turn to **153**. If you think they should stay out of his range and insult him, turn to **56**. If you think they should try being friendly to him, turn to **4**.

Tails can see the Chaos Emerald on top of the fridge-machine glowing hotter and brighter as he dashes towards it. Suddenly there is a flash and three bolts of orange light streak out from it! One of them hits the woolly mammoth, which looks very surprised, turns bright orange and falls over. One of them just misses Tails, hitting the far ice wall and leaving a glowing orange mark. The last one hits Mildred. She stumbles for a second then stands up again — but her friendly monkey face has changed into a twisted orange visage of hatred. 'Mildred! Are you okay?' asks Tails.

'Call me not Mil-dred,' declares the mutated monkey. 'I am Drei-Gunug, the Eater of Foxes, for so the Emerald has made me. Now we fight.' She attacks! Tails must use his Speed to fight her, and she has a rating of 8. If he loses a life, turn back to **41**. If he wins, Mildred's face suddenly relaxes back into its old form and Tails puts her carefully on the ice. She'll be okay. Now, does he grab the Emerald (turn to **215**) or jump straight into the teleporter (turn to **132**)?

298

Sonic turns away from the action for a moment, and looks out of the page towards you. 'Do you mind explaining how I'm supposed to act friendly towards these guys?' he asks.

'Who are you talking to?' Tails asks.

'The reader,' answers Sonic. 'It's a hero thing; you wouldn't understand yet.' He turns back to the natives, smiles at them and holds out his open paws to show he's not carrying any weapons. One of the natives pushes the two spear-carriers out of the way and comes towards Sonic, holding out a single paw. Sonic takes it and shakes it. The leader turns back to the others.

'See? I told you it was Sonic,' he says, 'but you wouldn't believe me. Hopeless, you are. Hopeless.' He turns back to Sonic and pulls off the wooden mask he is wearing. Underneath is a face almost as hideous as the mask was, very much like a scruffy pig. He's got big knobbly warts and lumps all over his long, hairy face. He is very, very ugly indeed.

'You're — you're —' says the hedgehog.

'We're wart-hogs,' says the leader. 'And you are the great Sonic the Pussycat and —'

'Hedgehog!'

'Hedgehog the Pussycat and —'

'SONIC the HEDGEHOG! How do you know about me and Tails?'

'Ah,' the leader says, tapping his long, hairy nose. 'We may be primitive dwellers in this tropical rainforest, but we know you to be the greatest megastars on Mobius. Can we invite you to our village for some food?'

Sonic and Tails follow the wart-hogs back to their village. They gather in the largest hut and food is indeed served — grass, tree-bark, and a few shrivelled fruits. Everyone tucks in, although nobody seems to enjoy it much. Sonic feels that they're waiting for him to ask a question. What does he say?

'Has there been any sign of Dr
   Robotnik around here?'   Turn to **147**
'Why is your tribe so warlike?'   Turn to **261**
'Why is the food so terrible?'   Turn to **209**

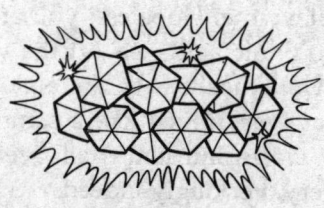

299

Sonic and Tails zip away from the Warp, close behind the red robot's vessel. It tries a zig-zag to throw them off its tail, but Sonic follows its every move. Abruptly a gush of flame erupts from the little rocket's tail, its stubby wings begin to unfold and it plunges down towards the surface of Mobius, far below. Sonic knows he has to follow it if he and Tails are to have any chance of recovering the Emeralds and saving the planet from the clutches of Robotnik, but he's not sure if their spacecraft can take the strain of diving through the planet's atmosphere.

'I think,' interrupts Tails, 'it's time we tried that button.' If Sonic doesn't let him, turn to **224**. If he does, turn to the following section:

If they are in the *Toho*   Turn to **53**
If they are in the *Yuzna*   Turn to **113**
If they are in the *Kubrick*   Turn to **260**

The two heroes pick themselves up and brush the dust and grass off their gloves and knees. Sonic shields his eyes with his hands and looks around. 'It's weird,' he says, 'but there's no sign of all the construction that was going on when we left. No ugly buildings, no stupid roads, no bulldozers, no robots, no televisions, no Robotnik Broadcasting Company.'

'It's them!' comes a shout from the edge of the woods, and Sonic's and Tails's friends rush out to greet them.

'So what happened?' Tails asks.

'The Robotnik Broadcasting Company went off the air about an hour ago, and we all woke up,' replies Porker Harris. 'At first we all thought we were somewhere else, but Chirps remembered what had been going on.'

'So where are the buildings and roads?' Sonic asks.

'Well, all the equipment was lying around and that stuff is even better at taking buildings apart than it is at putting them together,' Porker says a little sheepishly. 'Chainsaws, jackhammers, pneumatic drills. You know.'

'Dynamite too,' adds Johnny Lightfoot. 'That was *fun*.'

'So everything's back to normal?' Tails asks. His pals all nod.

'The bad guys have been defeated, the Chaos Emeralds are safely on their way back to the Warps of Confusion and our home is safe again. You know what that means, Tails?' asks Sonic.

'It means we can watch *Mobzilla Fights Outer-Space Monsters From Planet Z* as many times as we like!' the fox replies ecstatically. 'Anyone want to come with us?'

'Everyone bring food! We'll have a party!' Sally cries. And they do.

'You know,' Sonic says later that evening, after the last of the snacks had been eaten and everyone else had gone home, 'travelling round the world to save hapless civilizations from ruthless tyrants and ultimate evil is all very well, but there's nothing like spending time with your friends. Don't you agree, Tails?'

'Zzzzzzz,' the fox replies. He's fast asleep, slumped in front of the television. Sonic looks at him and yawns himself. Adventuring is tiring work. Sonic lies down next to his friend, safe at home at last, and goes to sleep.

Scoring your adventure

Sonic and Tails get 100 points for every Chaos Emerald that they managed to recover during their adventure. Add another 100 points for every life that they had left, and 1 point for every ring that they were carrying when they reached section **300**. Use the space opposite as a high-score chart, and challenge your friends to see if they can do better. Good luck!

Also in Puffin

SONIC THE HEDGEHOG *Adventure Gamebook 1:*
METAL CITY MAYHEM
James Wallis

Mobius is under threat from the deranged Robotnik. The demented inventor is busy on a master plan building mega-robots. Only you and Sonic can stop him.

Using your skill, speed and agility, you can help Sonic save the day. But think fast and move quickly, Sonic doesn't hang about and there's no time to waste. The future of Mobius depends on you!

SONIC THE HEDGEHOG *Adventure Gamebook 3:*
SONIC V. ZONIK
Nigel Gross & Jon Sutherland

The Green Hill Zone is under attack from a new enemy. Reports come in of a fast-moving blue creature bashing everything in sight. Surely this can't be Sonic? Or has Robotnik cooked up another monstrous plan to crack the blue wonder?

It's up to you to find out. Use your speed, skill and agility in this part-story, part-game adventure. But think fast and move quickly – only the best can keep up with Sonic.

Ideas actuales y tradicionales
Reflexiones
El libro del libro
Una gacela velada: *Viendo cómo ver*
Iluminación especial: *El uso Sufi del humor*

Corpus del Mulá Nasrudín
Las ocurrencias del increíble Mulá Nasrudín
Las sutilezas del inimitable Mulá Nasrudín
Las hazañas del incomparable Mulá Nasrudín
El mundo de Nasrudín

Viajes y exploraciones
Destino: La Meca

Estudios sobre creencias minoritarias
El conocimiento secreto de la magia
Magia oriental

Cuentos selectos y sus trasfondos
Cuentos del mundo

Una novela
Kara Kush

Trabajos sociológicos
La Inglaterra tenebrosa
Los nativos están inquietos
El manual de los ingleses

Traducidos por Idries Shah
Los cien cuentos de la sabiduría (El *Munaqib* de Aflaki)

La sabiduría de los idiotas

los idiotas

Idries Shah

ISF PUBLISHING

Título original: *Wisdom of the Idiots*
Publicado en inglés por ISF Publishing

Traducción de ISF Publishing

Copyright © The Estate of Idries Shah

El derecho de los herederos de Idries Shah a ser identificados
como los dueños de este trabajo ha sido reivindicado según la
ley 1988 de copyright, diseños y patentes (Reino Unido).

Todos los derechos reservados
Copyright mundial

No está permitida la reproducción total ni parcial de este libro,
ni la recopilación en un sistema informático, ni la transmisión
por medios electrónicos, mecánicos, por fotocopias, por
registro o por otros métodos – salvo de breves extractos a
efectos de reseña – sin la autorización previa y por escrito del
editor o del propietario del copyright.

Las solicitudes de permisos para reimprimir,
editar, reproducir, etc., deben ser dirigidas a:
The Permissions Department
ISF Publishing
The Idries Shah Foundation
P.O. Box 71911
London NW2 9QA
United Kingdom
permissions@isf-publishing.org

ISBN 978-1-78479-963-2

Primera edición en inglés: 1969
Edición actual: 2018

En asociación con The Idries Shah Foundation

Nota:

Los Sufis, que por lo general consideran como una locura aquello que los pensadores de mente estrecha imaginan que es sabiduría, a veces se refieren a sí mismos como "Los Idiotas".

También por una feliz casualidad, la palabra árabe para "santo" (*wali*) tiene el mismo equivalente numérico que la palabra para "idiota" (*balid*).

Entonces tenemos un motivo doble para considerar a los grandes Sufis como nuestros propios Idiotas.

Este libro contiene parte de sus conocimientos.

Índice

La fruta del Cielo

HABÍA UNA VEZ una mujer que oyó hablar de la Fruta del Cielo; la codiciaba.

Le preguntó a cierto derviche, a quien llamaremos Sabar:

"¿Cómo puedo encontrar esta fruta, para así lograr el conocimiento instantáneo?"

"Lo mejor sería que estudiases conmigo", dijo el derviche. "Pero si no lo haces, tendrás que viajar con determinación y a veces incasablemente por todo el mundo."

La mujer lo dejó y buscó a otro, Arif el Sabio; y después encontró a Hakim el Docto; luego a Majzub el Loco; más tarde a Alim el Científico y muchos más...

Ella pasó treinta años buscando, al cabo de los cuales llegó a un jardín. Allí se erguía el Árbol del Cielo, de cuyas ramas pendía la resplandeciente Fruta del Cielo.

De pie junto al Árbol estaba Sabar, el primer derviche.

"¿Por qué no me dijiste que *tú* eras el Custodio de la Fruta del Cielo cuando nos encontramos por primera vez?", le preguntó.

"Porque entonces no me habrías creído. Además, el Árbol solamente produce fruta una vez cada treinta años y treinta días."

Arrogantes y generosos

LOS SUFIS, AL contrario que otros místicos o supuestos poseedores de conocimiento especial, tienen fama de ser arrogantes. Esta arrogancia, según ellos mismos, se debe solo a una malinterpretación de su comportamiento por parte de la gente. "Una persona", dicen, "que pudiese encender un fuego sin frotar palos y que lo dijera, le resultaría arrogante a alguien que no pudiera hacerlo".

También tienen fama de ser extremadamente generosos. Su generosidad, dicen ellos, está en las cosas que realmente importan. Su prodigalidad con los bienes materiales es apenas un reflejo de su generosidad con la sabiduría.

La gente que desea estudiar el camino Sufi practica a menudo la generosidad con objetos, como un intento de alcanzar una forma superior de generosidad.

Sea como fuere, se cuenta una entretenida historia acerca de tres hombres generosos de Arabia.

Un día hubo una disputa entre los árabes sobre cuál era el hombre vivo más generoso. Los debates se prolongaron durante varios días y finalmente los candidatos fueron de común acuerdo reducidos a tres.

Como los partidarios de los tres candidatos estaban a punto de llegar a las manos, se nombró un comité para que tomara la decisión final. Decidieron que, como prueba eliminatoria, se enviaría el siguiente mensaje a cada uno de los tres hombres:

"Tu amigo Wais se encuentra en grandes apuros. Te ruega que lo ayudes con bienes materiales."

Tres representantes del comité fueron enviados para localizar a estos hombres, entregar el mensaje e informar de lo sucedido.

El primer mensajero llegó a la casa del Primer Hombre Generoso y le dijo lo que el comité le había encargado.

El Primer Hombre Generoso dijo:

"No me molestes con semejantes nimiedades. Agarra todo lo que quieras de lo mío y dáselo a mi amigo Wais."

Cuando este emisario regresó, la gente reunida pensó que seguramente no podía existir una generosidad mayor que esta... ni tampoco semejante arrogancia.

Pero el segundo mensajero, tras comunicar su mensaje, recibió esta respuesta del criado del Segundo Hombre Generoso:

"Dado que mi amo es realmente muy arrogante, no puedo molestarlo con ningún tipo de mensaje.

Pero te daré todo lo que tiene y también una hipoteca sobre sus bienes inmuebles."

El comité, al recibir este mensaje, imaginó que seguramente este debía de ser el hombre más generoso de Arabia.

Pero todavía no habían considerado el resultado de la misión del tercer mensajero.

Este llegó a la casa del Tercer Hombre Generoso, quien le dijo:

"Empaca todas mis pertenencias, lleva esta nota al prestamista para liquidar todos sus bienes y vuelve aquí para esperar a una persona que llegará de mi parte."

Dicho esto, el Tercer Hombre Generoso se marchó.

Cuando el mensajero hubo terminado esa tarea, se encontró con un agente del mercado en la puerta de la casa; este le dijo:

"Si tú eres el mensajero de Wais, tengo que entregarte el importe de un esclavo que acaba de ser vendido en el mercado de esclavos."

El esclavo era el Tercer Hombre Generoso.

Se cuenta además que el propio Wais, quien había formado parte del comité de jueces, visitó unos meses más tarde una casa en la que el esclavo que le servía resultó ser su amigo, el Tercer Hombre Generoso.

Wais dijo: "¡La broma ha ido demasiado lejos! ¿No es hora ya de que seas liberado?"

El Tercer Hombre Generoso, que era un Sufi, dijo:

"Lo que para unos es una broma puede no serlo para otros. Además, estoy arreglando lo de mi liberación mediante un acuerdo con mi amo y de conformidad con la ley. Será solo una cuestión de dos o tres años antes de que vuelva a ser libre."

El joyero

SE CUENTA LA historia de una mujer que llevaba un cofre con joyas de diversos tamaños a una joyería. Justo tropezó fuera del negocio y la caja cayó al piso: la tapa saltó y las joyas se desparramaron por todas partes.

Los asistentes del joyero salieron corriendo de la tienda para evitar que los transeúntes se llevasen algunas de las gemas y ayudaron a recogerlas.

Un avestruz que vagaba por allí pasó corriendo y, desapercibida en medio de aquel alboroto, se tragó la piedra más grande y valiosa.

Cuando la mujer notó la ausencia de esta joya empezó a lamentarse, y a pesar de buscarla por todas partes no pudo encontrarla.

Alguien dijo: "La única persona que pudo haber agarrado esa joya es aquel derviche que está tranquilamente sentado junto a la tienda."

El derviche había visto al avestruz tragarse la piedra pero no quería que se derramase sangre. Por lo tanto, cuando fue cacheado y empujado e incluso golpeado, dijo apenas: "No he tomado nada en absoluto".

Mientras estaba siendo golpeado, uno de sus compañeros apareció y le recordó a la muchedumbre que tuvieran cuidado con lo que estaban haciendo; pero también lo agarraron y lo acusaron de haber seguramente recibido la piedra del primer derviche, a pesar de que él lo negaba.

Esto es lo que estaba sucediendo cuando apareció un hombre dotado de conocimiento. Advirtiendo la presencia del avestruz, preguntó:

"¿Esa ave estaba aquí en el momento en que cayó el cofre?"

"Sí", respondió la gente.

"En ese caso", dijo, "dirijan su atención al avestruz."

Tras pagarle a su dueño el precio del ave, la mataron. La joya perdida fue encontrada en su estómago.

Ahrar y la pareja adinerada

EMIRUDIN AROSI, QUIEN procedía de una familia conocida por su apego a las creencias de una secta de entusiastas, encontró a un sabio y le dijo:

"Por muchos años, mi esposa y yo hemos intentado resueltamente seguir la vía derviche. Conscientes de que sabíamos menos que muchos otros, nos hemos contentado durante largo tiempo con gastar nuestra riqueza en la causa de la verdad. Hemos seguido a personas que han asumido la responsabilidad de enseñar y de los que ahora dudamos. Sentimos pena, no por lo que hemos perdido en donaciones materiales que fueron despilfarradas en nombre de la Tarea por nuestros últimos mentores en inefectivos emprendimientos comerciales, sino más bien por el desperdicio de tiempo y esfuerzo, y por las personas que aún están en un estado de sometimiento a los ilusos que se autodenominan maestros; gente ocupando irreflexivamente una casa manejada por dos falsos Sufis, en una atmósfera de anormalidad."

El sabio, a quien la tradición llama Khwaja Ahrar, el Señor de los Libres, respondió:

"Ustedes se han arrepentido de su apego a esos 'maestros' imitativos, pero todavía no se han arrepentido de su autoestima que les hace imaginar que tienen una responsabilidad para con los prisioneros de lo falso. Muchos de los prisioneros todavía están atrapados en la telaraña del engaño porque ellos tampoco se han arrepentido del engaño y además quieren conocimiento fácil."

"¿Qué deberíamos hacer?"

"Vengan a mí sin condiciones y con un corazón abierto, incluso si tales condiciones son el servicio a la humanidad o que yo me muestre ante ustedes como un ser razonable", dijo el Maestro, "pues puede que la liberación de sus compañeros sea un asunto para expertos, no para ustedes. Incluso su capacidad para formarse una opinión sobre mí está deteriorada, y yo por lo menos me niego a depender de ella".

Pero, naturalmente, temerosos de acaso estar cometiendo otro error, Arosi y su mujer dejaron pasar la oportunidad… para luego encontrar a otro hombre: uno que los consolaría. Y lo hicieron; resultó ser otro fraude más.

Volvieron a pasar los años y la pareja regresó a la casa de Khwaja Ahrar.

"Hemos venido en total sumisión", le informaron al guardián de la puerta, "a ponernos en manos del Señor de los Libres como si fuéramos cadáveres en las manos del que lava a los muertos".

"Buena gente", respondió el portero, "su resolución parece excelente, propia de personas que el Señor de los Libres no dudaría en aceptar como discípulos. Pero en esta vida no tendrán una segunda oportunidad... porque Khwaja Ahrar está muerto".

Bahaudin y el vagabundo

BAHAUDIN EL-SHAH, GRAN maestro de los derviches
Naqshbandi, se topó un día con un cofrade en la
plaza principal de Bujara.

El recién llegado era un Kalendar errante de
los Malamati, los "Reprobables". Bahaudin
estaba rodeado de discípulos.

"¿De dónde vienes?", le preguntó al viajero con
la habitual frase Sufi.

"No tengo idea", dijo el otro, sonriendo
tontamente.

Algunos de los discípulos de Bahaudin
murmuraron su desaprobación por esta falta de
respeto.

"¿A dónde vas?", persistió Bahaudin.

"No sé", gritó el derviche.

"¿Qué es el Bien?" Para entonces ya se había
reunido una gran multitud.

"No lo sé."

"¿Qué es el Mal?"

"No tengo ni idea."

"¿Qué es lo Correcto?"

"Lo que es bueno para mí."

"¿Qué es lo Equivocado?"

12

"Lo que es malo para mí."

La multitud, irritada más allá de su paciencia por este derviche, lo ahuyentó. Así fue que partió dando decididas zancadas en una dirección que, hasta donde se sabía, no llevaba a ninguna parte.

"¡Tontos!", dijo Bahaudin Naqshband, "este hombre está representando el papel de la humanidad. Mientras ustedes lo despreciaban, él estaba demostrando deliberadamente el descuido que cada uno de ustedes ostenta, de forma inconsciente, todos los días de sus vidas."

Comida y plumas

Érase una vez (y esta es una historia verdadera) un estudiante que solía ir todos los días a sentarse a los pies de un maestro Sufi para anotar en un papel todo lo que este decía.

Debido a que estaba tan inmerso en sus estudios, era incapaz de realizar cualquier tipo de ocupación que le diese dinero. Una noche, al llegar a casa, su mujer le puso delante un cuenco cubierto con una servilleta.

Él tomó la tela, se la puso alrededor de su cuello y entonces vio que el plato estaba lleno de... plumas y papel.

"Dado que esto es lo que haces todo el día", dijo ella, "intenta comértelo".

A la mañana siguiente, como de costumbre, el estudiante fue a aprender de su maestro. Aunque las palabras de su mujer lo habían afligido, continuó con la rutina habitual de estudios sin ponerse a buscar un empleo.

Después de unos minutos de estar escribiendo, notó que su pluma no funcionaba bien. "No importa", dijo el maestro, "ve a ese rincón, trae la caja que encontrarás allí y ponla delante de ti."

Cuando se sentó con la caja y abrió la tapa, descubrió que estaba llena de... comida.

El vislumbre de poder

A UN DERVICHE que había estudiado a los pies de un gran maestro Sufi se le dijo que perfeccionase su conocimiento del ejercicio sensorial y que luego regresase a su maestro para recibir más instrucción. Retirándose a un bosque, se concentró en meditaciones interiores con gran tesón hasta que prácticamente nada podía molestarlo.

Sin embargo, no se había concentrado lo suficiente en la necesidad de mantener equitativamente en su corazón todos sus objetivos, y su celo por tener éxito en este ejercicio resultó ser algo más fuerte que su determinación de regresar a la escuela desde la que había sido enviado a meditar.

Y resulta que un día, mientras estaba concentrándose en su yo interior, un ligero sonido atrapó la atención de su oído. Irritado por esto, el derviche miró hacia arriba entre las ramas de un árbol que parecía haber sido el origen del sonido y vio un pájaro. Por su mente cruzó el pensamiento de que este ave no tenía derecho a interrumpir los ejercicios de un hombre tan dedicado. Apenas hubo concebido esta idea, el pájaro cayó muerto a sus pies.

Ahora bien, resulta que el derviche no había avanzado lo suficiente en la vía Sufí como para darse cuenta de que existen pruebas a lo largo de todo el camino. Lo único que podía ver en aquel momento era que había alcanzado un poder como el que jamás había tenido: podía matar a un ser vivo; o incluso podría ser que el pájaro fue muerto por alguna fuerza distinta a la de aquella que estaba en su interior... ¡y todo porque había interrumpido sus oraciones!

"Realmente debo ser un gran Sufí", pensó el derviche.

Se puso de pie y comenzó a caminar hacia el pueblo más cercano.

Cuando arribó, vio una elegante casa y decidió pedir allí algo para comer. Golpeó la puerta y una mujer le abrió; el derviche dijo:

"Mujer, tráeme comida pues soy un derviche avanzado y hay mérito en alimentar a los que están en el Camino."

"De inmediato, venerable sabio", respondió la dama antes de desaparecer dentro de la casa.

Pero pasó un largo rato y aún la mujer no volvía. A cada momento que transcurría, el derviche se ponía más y más impaciente. Cuando la mujer regresó, le dijo:

"Considérate afortunada de que no descargue sobre ti la furia del derviche, ¿pues acaso no sabe todo el mundo que la desdicha puede llegar mediante la desobediencia a los Elegidos?"

"Es cierto que la desdicha puede llegar, a menos que uno sea capaz de resistirla mediante algunas experiencias propias", dijo la mujer.

"¡Cómo te atreves a contestarme así!" gritó el derviche. "Y en todo caso, ¿a qué te refieres?"

"Solo me refiero", dijo la mujer, "al hecho de que no soy un pájaro en un claro del bosque."

El derviche estaba atónito ante estas palabras. "Mi ira no te está lastimando e incluso puedes leer mis pensamientos", balbuceó.

Y le rogó a la mujer que se convirtiese en su maestra.

"Si has desobedecido a tu propio maestro original, también me fallarás a mí", dijo la mujer.

"Bueno, al menos dime cómo llegaste a un estadio de comprensión muchísimo más elevado que el mío", pidió el derviche.

"Obedeciendo a mi maestro. Me dijo que asistiese a sus conferencias y ejercicios cuando me lo indicase; de lo contrario, debía considerar mis tareas mundanas como si fueran mis ejercicios. De esta manera, aunque hace años no sé nada de él, mi vida interior se ha expandido constantemente, dándome poderes tales como el que has visto y muchos otros."

El derviche regresó a la Tekkia de su maestro buscando más consejos. El maestro se negó a permitirle discutir cualquier asunto, pero meramente dijo cuando apareció:

"Ve y trabaja para cierto barrendero que limpia las calles de tal y tal pueblo."

El derviche, dado que le tenía una gran estima a su maestro, fue a ese pueblo; pero cuando llegó al lugar donde trabajaba el barrendero y lo vio allí de pie cubierto de mugre, reculó del asco sin poder imaginarse a sí mismo como su sirviente.

Mientras permanecía apresado por la indecisión, el basurero le dijo llamándolo por su nombre:

"Lajaward, ¿qué pájaro matarás hoy? Lajaward, ¿qué mujer podrá hoy leer tus pensamientos? Lajaward, ¿qué deber repugnante te impondrá mañana tu maestro?"

Lajaward le preguntó:

"¿Cómo haces para ver dentro de mi mente? ¿Cómo puede un basurero hacer cosas que los ermitaños piadosos no son capaces de hacer? ¿Quién eres?"

El barrendero dijo:

"Algunos ermitaños pueden hacer estas cosas, pero no las hacen para ti porque tienen otras cosas que hacer. Para ti yo me veo como un barrendero porque esa es mi ocupación. Dado que no te gusta el trabajo, no te gusta la persona. Como imaginas que la santidad es lavar y acuclillarse y meditar, nunca la encontrarás. He alcanzado mis capacidades actuales porque nunca pensé en la santidad: pensé en el deber. Cuando la gente te enseña el deber para con un maestro o algo sagrado, te están enseñando el *deber*, ¡tonto! Todo lo que puedes ver es el "deber para con el hombre" o el "deber con el templo". Dado que no puedes concentrarte sobre el deber, date por perdido."

Y Lajaward, cuando fue capaz de olvidar que era el sirviente de un barrendero y se dio cuenta de que ser un sirviente era un deber, se convirtió en el hombre que conocemos como El Iluminado, el Hacedor de Milagros, el Excepcionalmente Perfumado Sheikh Abdurrazaq Lajawardi de Badakhxan.

Para el humano, nada excepto lo que se ha ganado

LA EXPERIENCIA Y el conocimiento superior serán puestos a disposición del hombre o de la mujer, exactamente según su valía, capacidad y esfuerzo puesto en ello. Por ende, si un asno ve un melón se comerá la cáscara; las hormigas comerán todo lo que puedan conseguir; el ser humano consumirá sin saber que ha consumido.

Nuestro objetivo es lograr, mediante la comprensión del Origen, el Conocimiento que procede de la experiencia.

Esto es realizado, como en un viaje, solo con aquellos que ya conocen el Camino.

La justicia de este estado es la mayor que existe: porque este conocimiento no le puede ser negado a quien lo merece ni tampoco se le puede dar a quien no lo merece.

Es la única sustancia con una discernidora facultad de su propia justicia inherente.

(Yusuf Hamadani)

La leche y su suero

MURID LAKI HUMANYUN le hizo esta pregunta a Maulana Bahaudin:

"En el pueblo de Gulafshan hay un círculo de seguidores. Algunos de ellos están en la etapa de los ejercicios, pero la mayoría son aquellos que se reúnen semanalmente para aprender de las transacciones y enseñanzas del *murshid* (guía).

"Muchos de los *murids* (discípulos) comprenden el significado de los cuentos y los eventos, y usan estos para corregir su comportamiento interno y externo.

"Sin embargo, muchos de los seguidores superficiales parecen no beneficiarse de los eventos y de las transacciones, buscando en cambio libros y enseñanzas que les ofrecerán promesas precisas de progreso.

"¿Cómo es que los discípulos sienten dolor cuando los seguidores ordinarios no logran comprender el significado de las historias y de los eventos, especialmente cuando estos últimos son sus amigos cercanos y cada uno de ellos desea que hubiese una unificación entre discípulos y seguidores de tipo superficial?"

Bahaudin contestó:

"El discipulado fue instituido para reunir a aquellos que pueden aprender sin tener objetivos burdos. Los discípulos que se lamentan porque sus compañeros no aprenden de la misma manera y al mismo ritmo, se están lamentando porque han imaginado que el afecto debe producir capacidad. Sin embargo, a la capacidad hay que ganársela: el afecto se da y se recibe.

"Los rejuntes accidentales de personas centradas en una enseñanza siempre sufrirán una división en presencia del agente agitador, como cuando ocurre la separación entre la manteca y la leche, el cual puede estar manifiesto u oculto pero no obstante presente cada vez que comienza a operar una renovación de la enseñanza: esta es la sacudida del recipiente que contiene la leche. Las personas imaginan que cuando hay un movimiento (*jumbish*) se verán afectados todos por igual, tal como sucede con el suero lácteo; pero tanto la manteca como la leche descremada tienen sus funciones, aunque puede que en terrenos diferentes."

Talismán

SE CUENTA QUE un faquir que quería aprender sin esfuerzo fue apartado después de un tiempo del círculo del Sheikh Shah Gwath Shattar. Cuando Shattar lo estaba despidiendo, el faquir dijo:

"Tienes la reputación de poder enseñar toda la sabiduría en un abrir y cerrar de ojos, ¡y no obstante pretendes que yo pase mucho tiempo contigo!"

"Aún no has aprendido a aprender cómo aprender; pero descubrirás lo que quiero decir", dijo el Sufi.

El faquir fingió irse, pero solía ingresar en la Tekkia a hurtadillas para ver qué hacía el Sheikh. Poco después vio a Shah Gwath sacar una joya de cierto cofre de metal grabado. Sostuvo esta gema sobre las cabezas de sus discípulos, diciendo: "Este es el repositorio de mi conocimiento y no es otro que el Talismán de la Iluminación."

"Así que este es el secreto del poder del Sheikh", pensó el faquir.

En las horas postreras de esa misma noche, entró nuevamente en el salón de meditación y robó el talismán; pero en sus manos, por mucho que lo intentara, la joya no ofrecía ni poder ni secretos. Estaba amargamente decepcionado.

Se estableció como maestro, admitió discípulos e intentó, una y otra vez, iluminarlos o iluminarse mediante el talismán... pero todo fue en vano.

Un día estaba sentado en su santuario, luego de que sus discípulos se hubieran acostado, meditando sobre sus problemas cuando Shattar apareció ante él.

"¡Oh Faquir!" dijo Shah Gwath, "siempre puedes robar algo, pero no siempre puedes hacerlo funcionar. Incluso puedes robar conocimiento pero acaso te resulte inútil, como el ladrón que robó la navaja del barbero, hecha mediante el conocimiento del cuchillero, pero sin tener el conocimiento del afeitar. Se estableció como barbero y murió en la miseria cuando no pudo siquiera afeitar una mísera barba pero sí cortar varias gargantas."

"Pero yo tengo el talismán y tú no", dijo el faquir.

"Sí, *tú* tienes el talismán pero *yo* soy Shattar", replicó el Sufi. "Puedo, con mi habilidad, hacer otro talismán; tú, con el talismán, no puedes convertirte en Shattar."

"Entonces, ¿por qué has venido? ¿Solamente para torturarme?" exclamó el faquir.

"Vine para decirte que, si no hubieses tomado todo al pie de la letra imaginando que tener una cosa es lo mismo que poder ser transformado por ella, habrías estado listo para aprender cómo aprender."

Pero el faquir creyó que el Sufi solamente estaba tratando de recuperar su talismán y, debido a que no estaba listo para aprender cómo aprender, decidió persistir en los experimentos con la joya.

Sus discípulos continuaron haciéndolo; y sus seguidores y los seguidores de sus seguidores. De hecho, los rituales que son el resultado de sus incansables experimentos actualmente conforman la esencia de su religión. Nadie podría imaginar, dado lo santificadas que estas prácticas se han vuelto con el tiempo, que su origen yace en las circunstancias que acabamos de relatar.

A los ancianos practicantes de esta fe también se los considera tan venerables e infalibles, que estas creencias jamás morirán.

Discusión con académicos

Está registrado que alguien le preguntó a Bahaudin Naqshband:

"¿Por qué no discutes con los eruditos? Tal y tal sabio lo hace con frecuencia. Esto los confunde totalmente y provoca la constante admiración de sus propios discípulos."

Él contestó: "Ve y pregúntales a aquellos que recuerdan la época en que yo solía lidiar con los académicos; a menudo refutaba sus conjeturas y pruebas imaginadas con relativa facilidad. Aquellos que entonces estuvieron presentes podrán contártelo. Pero un día, un hombre más sabio que yo me dijo:

"'Avergüenzas a los hombres de la lengua tan a menudo y de forma tan previsible, que hay una cierta monotonía en ello. Esto es especialmente así porque no tiene un propósito final, dado que los académicos carecen de comprensión y siguen discutiendo mucho después de que sus posturas han sido demolidas.'

"Agregó: 'Tus discípulos están en un constante estado de asombro ante tus victorias. Han aprendido a admirarte. En cambio deberían haber percibido la inutilidad y falta de importancia de tus adversarios. Por ende, incluso en la victoria, digamos que has fallado en una cuarta parte.'

"'Además, su asombro ocupa una gran porción de su tiempo cuando podrían estar apreciando algo más provechoso. Entonces has fallado quizá en otra cuarta parte. Dos cuartos son igual a una mitad. Te queda media oportunidad.'

"Eso fue hace veinte años. Es por ello que los eruditos ya no me conciernen ni a mí ni a los demás, ya sea para la victoria o la derrota.

"Puede que de vez en cuando uno le aseste un golpe a los eruditos autoproclamados para demostrarles su vacuidad a los discípulos: es como si uno golpeara una olla vacía. Hacer más es un derroche que equivale a darles una importancia a los intelectuales, mediante el otorgamiento de una atención inútil, que ciertamente no podrían alcanzar por sí mismos."

La historia de Hiravi

EN TIEMPOS DEL rey Mahmud el Conquistador de Gazna vivía un joven llamado Haidar Ali Jan. Su padre, Iskandar Khan, decidió obtener para él el patronazgo del emperador y lo envió a estudiar asuntos espirituales bajo la guía de los sabios más importantes de la época.

Haidar Ali, cuando hubo dominado las repeticiones y los ejercicios y conocía las recitaciones y las posturas corporales de las escuelas Sufis, fue llevado por su padre ante la presencia del emperador.

"Poderoso Mahmud", dijo Iskandar, "me he ocupado de que este joven, mi hijo mayor y el más inteligente, fuese entrenado especialmente a la manera de los Sufis para que acaso pueda obtener un puesto digno en la corte de su majestad, sabiendo que eres el patrón de la enseñanza de nuestra época."

Mahmud no levantó la mirada y meramente dijo: "Tráelo en un año."

Ligeramente decepcionado, mas alimentando grandes esperanzas, Iskandar envió a Ali a estudiar las obras de los grandes Sufis del pasado y a visitar los santuarios de los antiguos maestros de Bagdad, para no desperdiciar el tiempo de la espera.

Cuando trajo al joven de regreso a la corte, dijo:

"¡Pavorreal de la Era! Mi hijo ha llevado a cabo largos y dificultosos viajes, y al mismo tiempo le agregó a su conocimiento de los ejercicios una completa familiaridad con los clásicos de la Gente del Sendero. Te ruego que lo examines para que se demuestre que podría ser un adorno de la corte de su majestad."

"Permítele", dijo inmediatamente Mahmud, "que vuelva después de otro año."

Durante los siguientes doce meses Haidar Ali cruzó el Oxus y visitó Bujara y Samarcanda, Qasr-i-Arifin y Tashqand, Dusambé y los *turbat* de los santos Sufis del Turquestán.

Cuando volvió a la corte, Mahmud de Gazna le echó un vistazo y dijo:

"Puede que tenga ganas de regresar después de un año más."

Haidar Ali hizo el peregrinaje a La Meca ese año. Viajó a la India y en Persia consultó libros extraños, y nunca dejó pasar la oportunidad de buscar y presentar sus respetos a los grandes derviches de la época.

Cuando volvió a Gazna, Mahmud le dijo:

"Ahora elige un maestro, si es que te acepta, y regresa en un año."

Cuando ese año hubo transcurrido e Iskandar se

preparaba para llevar a su hijo a la corte, Haidar Alí no mostró ningún interés en ir. Simplemente se sentó a los pies de su maestro en Herat y nada de lo que su padre dijo pudo moverlo de allí.

"He perdido mi tiempo y mi dinero, y este joven ha fallado las pruebas impuestas por Mahmud el Rey", se lamentó, abandonando todo el asunto.

Finalmente llegó, y pasó, el día en que el joven debía presentarse, y entonces Mahmud dijo a sus cortesanos:

"Prepárense para una visita a Herat; allí hay alguien a quien tengo que ver."

Mientras la comitiva del emperador ingresaba a Herat al son de la fanfarria de las trompetas, el maestro de Haidar Alí lo tomó de la mano conduciéndolo hacia la puerta de la Tekkia, y allí esperaron.

Poco después, Mahmud y su cortesano Ayaz se adentraron descalzos en el santuario.

"Aquí, Mahmud", dijo el sheikh Sufí, "está el hombre que no era nada mientras fue un visitante de reyes, pero que ahora es alguien visitado por reyes. Llévatelo como tu consejero Sufí, pues ya está listo."

Esta es la historia de los estudios de Hiravi, Haidar Alí Jan, el Sabio de Herat.

Algo que aprender de Miri

EL RENOMBRADO SABIO Sufi Baba Saifdar tenía un discípulo llamado Miri, que solía quejarse de que Saifdar no lo veía casi nunca luego de haberlo admitido a su discipulado.

"Estaba mejor antes de convertirme en discípulo suyo", decía él, "pues entonces al menos se me trataba como un amigo y podía beneficiarme de su compañía."

Baba Saifdar, sin embargo, conocía la condición interna de su discípulo pero no hacía referencia a ella en sus infrecuentes encuentros; prefería esperar la chance de proporcionarle una demostración efectiva de la relación y su significado.

Un día, Miri estaba testificando en un tribunal al aire libre cuando por allí pasó Baba Saifdar.

El juez justo le había dicho al testigo:

"¿Recuerdas con certeza haber visto al acusado participar del robo?"

Miri, viendo a su maestro y acordándose así del ejercicio de "recordar" que había aprendido de él, exclamó involuntariamente: "¡Recuerdo!"

El supuesto ladrón fue condenado de inmediato por la declaración del "testigo ocular"; era inocente. Y cuando Miri se retractó de aquella identificación, estuvo a punto de ser juzgado por perjurio.

Cuando finalmente fue liberado, el Baba le dijo:

"Eso fue un paralelo, en cuestiones ordinarias, con lo que puede suceder en asuntos más profundos. La alabanza y la queja del maestro propio conducen a la locura; también lo hace el desprecio por sus reglas. Lo que es visible para ellos es invisible para el discípulo."

"Solamente me queda esperar que mi ejemplo sea valioso para otros de modo que, lejos de tener que inevitablemente atravesar esta clase de experiencia, les posibilite dirigirse hacia cosas más elevadas", dijo Miri.

Es por esa razón que esta historia se llama "La lección de Miri".

El ídolo del rey loco

HABÍA UNA VEZ un rey violento, ignorante e idólatra. Un día juró que, si su ídolo personal le concedía cierta ventaja, capturaría a las tres primeras personas que pasasen por su castillo y las forzaría a adorar a dicho ídolo.

Efectivamente, el deseo del rey se cumplió y enseguida envió soldados a la carretera para que le trajeran las primeras tres personas que pudiesen encontrar.

Resulta que estos tres eran un erudito, un Sayed (descendiente del Profeta Muhammad) y una prostituta.

Luego de hacer que los arrojaran a los pies de su ídolo, el desequilibrado rey les contó de su juramento y les ordenó que se postrasen ante la imagen.

El erudito dijo:

"Indudablemente esta situación cae dentro de la doctrina de 'fuerza mayor'. Hay numerosos precedentes que a uno le permiten, de ser obligado, ajustarse a la costumbre sin que hubiere una verdadera culpabilidad moral o legal."

Entonces hizo una profunda reverencia al ídolo.

El Sayed, cuando fue su turno, dijo:

"Como una persona especialmente protegida, teniendo en mis venas la sangre del Sagrado Profeta, mis propias acciones purifican cualquier cosa que haga y por lo tanto no hay nada que me impida actuar tal como lo exige este hombre."

Y se inclinó ante el ídolo.

La prostituta dijo:

"Lamentablemente no tengo ni entrenamiento intelectual ni prerrogativas especiales y me temo que, sin importar lo que me hagas, no puedo adorar a este ídolo… ni siquiera fingiéndolo."

Esta observación hizo que la enfermedad del rey desapareciese inmediatamente. Como por arte de magia vio el engaño de los dos adoradores de la imagen. Al instante mandó a decapitar al erudito y al Sayed, y liberó a la prostituta.

Dos lados

LOS MANTOS BICOLORES de los derviches, empleados con fines didácticos y finalmente imitados para un uso meramente decorativo, fueron introducidos en la España de la Edad Media de esta forma:

Un rey franco tenía cierto gusto por la pompa y también se enorgullecía de su comprensión de la filosofía. Le pidió a un Sufi conocido como "El Agarin" que lo instruyera en la Sabiduría Superior. El Agarin dijo:

"Te ofrecemos observación y reflexión, pero primero debes aprender hasta dónde llegan."

"Ya sabemos cómo aumentar nuestra atención, habiendo estudiado correctamente todos los pasos preliminares hacia la sabiduría desde nuestra propia tradición", dijo el rey.

"Muy bien", dijo el Agarin, "mañana en el desfile le daremos a su majestad una demostración de nuestra enseñanza."

Se hicieron los preparativos necesarios y al otro día los derviches del *ribat* (centro de enseñanza) del Agarin desfilaron por las angostas calles del pueblo andalusí. El rey y sus cortesanos estaban agrupados a ambos lados de la ruta: los nobles a la derecha y los hombres de armas a la izquierda.

Cuando terminó la procesión, el Agarin se volvió hacia el rey y dijo:

"Majestad, por favor, pregúntales a tus caballeros que están al otro lado de qué color eran los mantos de los derviches."

Todos los caballeros juraron sobre las escrituras y por su honor que los atuendos eran azules.

El rey y el resto de la corte quedaron asombrados y confundidos, pues esto no era en absoluto lo que ellos habían visto. "Todos vimos claramente que estaban vestidos con túnicas *marrones*", dijo el rey, "y entre nosotros hay respetadísimos hombres de gran santidad."

Ordenó a todos sus caballeros que se preparasen para ser castigados y degradados.

Aquellos que habían visto que las ropas eran marrones fueron apartados para ser recompensados.

Este proceso llevó un tiempo. Luego el rey le dijo al Agarin:

"¿Qué embrujo has realizado, malvado? ¿Qué diablura es esta que puede hacer que los caballeros más honorables de la cristiandad desafíen a la verdad, abandonen sus esperanzas de redención y den muestras de poca fiabilidad, cosa que los hace inútiles para la batalla?"

El Sufi dijo:

"La parte de las túnicas que se veía desde tu lado era marrón. La otra mitad de cada túnica era azul. Sin preparación, tus expectativas hacen que te engañes a ti mismo acerca de nosotros. ¿Cómo podemos enseñarle algo a alguien bajo tales circunstancias?"

Bienvenidas

DAMOS LA BIENVENIDA a los eruditos que quieran comprender el Camino.

¿Qué hay de los otros? Creen que no les damos la bienvenida, pero en realidad son ellos quienes no nos la dan.

No podrán hacerlo mientras conserven tan extrañas concepciones de la Vía.

Me refiero a dos tipos: aquellos que dicen "Negamos el valor del Sufismo" y los que dicen "Aceptamos el Sufismo, pero esto no lo es."

De los dos, quienes rechazan a los Sufis son mejores que aquellos que imaginan que las personas que no les caen bien no pueden ser, por esta razón, Sufis.

El primer tipo son engañados por otros que les hacen creer que los Sufis son inútiles... y cualquiera puede ser engañado por otros.

Y el segundo tipo son aquellos que se autoengañan al imaginar algo que no es correcto.

Ningún erudito puede decidir quién es o no es un Sufi. Las personas que intentan hacer algo para lo cual están incapacitadas deberían ser siempre una lección para nosotros.

Ajmal Hussein y los eruditos

EL SUFI AJMAL Hussein era constantemente criticado por los eruditos, quienes temían que su reputación eclipsaría la de ellos. No escatimaron esfuerzos en sembrar dudas acerca de su conocimiento, en acusarlo de refugiarse en el misticismo de sus críticas e incluso en insinuar que había sido culpable de prácticas indecorosas.

Finalmente dijo:

"Si les respondo a mis críticos, ellos aprovechan la ocasión para lanzarme nuevas acusaciones que la gente cree porque les divierte creer tales cosas. Si no les respondo, se jactan y pavonean de ello y las personas creen que son eruditos de verdad. Imaginan que nosotros los Sufis nos oponemos a la erudición; no es así. Pero nuestra existencia misma es una amenaza para la fingida erudición de los pequeños eruditos ruidosos. Hace mucho tiempo que desapareció la erudición; lo que ahora tenemos que enfrentar es una erudición falsa."

Los eruditos chillaron más fuerte que nunca. Al fin, Ajmal dijo:

"La argumentación no es tan efectiva como la demostración. Les daré una idea de cómo son estas personas."

Invitó a los eruditos a que enviaran "cuestionarios" para permitirles evaluar su propio conocimiento e ideas; cincuenta profesores y académicos le enviaron sus cuestionarios. Ajmal contestó a todos de diferentes maneras. Cuando los eruditos se reunieron en una conferencia para discutir estos cuestionarios, había tantas versiones diferentes de sus respuestas que todos creían haber desenmascarado a Ajmal y por esto se negaban a abandonar su tesis en favor de cualquier otra. El resultado fue la célebre "trifulca de los eruditos". Se pelearon amargamente durante cinco días.

"Esto", dijo Ajmal, "es una demostración. Lo que más le importa a cada uno es su propia opinión y su propia interpretación; no les importa nada la verdad. Esto es lo que hacen con las enseñanzas de cualquiera. Cuando está vivo, lo atormentan. Cuando muere, se vuelven expertos en sus obras. Sin embargo, el motivo real de la actividad es competir entre sí y contradecir a cualquiera que venga de afuera. ¿Quieres convertirte en uno de ellos? Decide pronto."

Timur y Hafiz

EL POETA SUFI Hafiz de Shiraz escribió el famoso poema:

> Si esa doncella turca Sharazi tomara mi
> corazón en sus manos,
> le daría Bujara por el lunar en su
> mejilla...
> o Samarcanda.

Tamerlán el conquistador hizo que Hafiz fuese llevado ante él y le dijo:

"¿Cómo puedes regalar Bujara y Samarcanda por una mujer? Además se encuentran en mis dominios, ¡y no permitiré a nadie que insinúe que no me pertenecen!"

Hafiz le respondió:

"Acaso tu mezquindad te haya dado poder. Mi generosidad me ha hecho caer en tu poder. Tu mezquindad es, obviamente, más efectiva que mi prodigalidad."

Tamerlán se rió y dejó marchar al Sufi.

Repleto

Un hombre se presentó ante Bahaudin Naqshband y dijo:

"He viajado de un maestro a otro y he estudiado muchos Caminos, los cuales me han brindado grandes beneficios y muchas ventajas de todo tipo.

"Ahora deseo ser aceptado como uno de tus discípulos, para poder beber del pozo del conocimiento y así avanzar cada vez más en la *Tariqa*, la Vía Mística."

Bahaudin, en lugar de responder a la pregunta directamente, mandó a que sirvieran la cena. Cuando trajeron la fuente de arroz y estofado de carne, apuró a su invitado con un plato tras otro. Después le ofreció fruta y pasteles, y luego ordenó que se le trajera más pilau, y más y más platos de comida, verduras, ensaladas y dulces.

Al principio, el hombre se sintió halagado; y dado que Bahaudin daba muestras de placer por cada bocado que tragaba, engulló todo lo que pudo. Cuando comenzó a comer más despacio, el Sheikh Sufi pareció molestarse mucho y para impedir su disgusto el desgraciado se comió prácticamente otra cena.

Cuando fue incapaz de tragar ni siquiera un grano de arroz más, recostándose sobre un almohadón con un gran malestar, Bahaudin se dirigió a él de esta manera:

"Cuando viniste a verme, estabas tan lleno de enseñanzas indigestas como lo estás ahora de carne, arroz y fruta. Te sentías mal y, debido a que estabas desacostumbrado al auténtico malestar espiritual, lo interpretaste como un hambre de más conocimiento. Tu verdadera condición era la indigestión.

"Puedo enseñarte si a partir de ahora sigues mis indicaciones y te quedas aquí conmigo haciendo la digestión mediante actividades que no te parecerán iniciáticas, pero que actuarán como si tomaras algo para digerir la comida y transformarla en nutrientes, no en peso."

El hombre aceptó. Muchas décadas después, siendo el famoso gran maestro Sufi Khalil Ashrafzada, él contó su historia.

Charkhi y su tío

SE CUENTA QUE un joven discípulo de Baba Charkhi estaba sentado en el zaguán de su casa cuando un hombre llegó y dijo: "¿Quién eres?"

El discípulo contestó: "Soy un seguidor de Baba Charkhi."

El hombre dijo: "¿Cómo es posible que Charkhi tenga seguidores? Soy su tío y si fuese así, yo lo sabría. Y en cuanto a que es un 'Baba', querido, te han informado mal."

El tío de Charkhi se quedó en la casa por muchos años después de este intercambio, hasta que murió. Se negaba a participar de las "asambleas de la cultura" organizadas por el Baba y nunca creyó que Charkhi fuese un maestro Sufi. "Lo conozco desde que era un niño", decía, "y no puedo verlo enseñando nada, pues nunca fue capaz de aprender nada."

Incluso cuando Charkhi murió hubo muchas personas, entre ellas algunos asiduos visitantes de su casa – incluyendo mercaderes con quienes había tenido tratos comerciales –, que no creían que era un santo.

Yunus Abu-Aswad Kamali, el teólogo, habló en nombre de algunos cuando dijo: "Conocí a Charkhi durante treinta años y jamás discutió conmigo cuestiones superiores. En mi opinión, semejante comportamiento no es el de un hombre instruido. Nunca intentó describir sus teorías ni hacerme su discípulo; sólo escuché de su supuesta condición de Sufi a través de mi carnicero."

El prisionero de
Samarcanda

Hakim Iskandar Zaramez y Abdulwahab
el Hindi pasaban un día por la esquina de una
gran casa de Samarcanda cuando oyeron un grito
salvaje.

"Están torturando a algún pobre desdichado",
dijo El Hindi, deteniéndose hasta quedar
quietísimo mientras los gritos aumentaban.

"¿Te gustaría aliviar el sufrimiento?" preguntó
Zaramez.

"Por supuesto. Dado que eres un Wali – un
santo – seguramente puedes hacerlo… si es que
Dios lo permite."

"Muy bien", dijo el Hakim, "y además voy a
demostrarte algo."

Zaramez se alejó cinco pasos de la esquina de la
casa; los gritos se detuvieron.

"¡Tú te retiras y el tumulto cesa! Siempre
he escuchado que es el acercarse a una persona
afligida lo que alivia el dolor", dijo El Hindi.

El Hakim sonrió sin decir nada más, haciendo
el signo que entre los Sufis significa: "Una

pregunta puede no tener respuesta en un momento determinado debido al estado del inquiridor."

Muchos años después, cuando El Hindi estaba en Marruecos, una noche escuchó a un derviche contar sus experiencias a un grupo de estudiantes en la amurallada ciudad de Moulay Idriss.

Entre otras cosas, el derviche dijo:

"Durante tal y tal día del mes de Ramadán el-Mubarak, hace muchísimos años, fui detenido por parecer un vagabundo debido a mi aparente pobreza y aspecto raquítico. Me dejaron a la espera del juicio en una celda de piedra ubicada en una de las esquinas del muro exterior de la casa de Kazi. Esto fue en las afueras de Samarcanda, al norte.

"Había estado sentado allí en silenciosa contemplación por un rato, contento con mi suerte, cuando sentí inconfundiblemente una presencia cercana que venía desde afuera... la presencia de un santo. Comencé a aullar y gritar y a revolcarme por el piso, pues había un poder sobre mí y porque no podía escaparme por mucho que quisiese acercarme.

"Entonces sentí que se había alejado como si mi clamor le hubiese molestado. Intenté dejarlo acercarse nuevamente al volverme inactivo y silencioso como la noche."

El sheikh del círculo derviche dijo:

"Tu experiencia podría haberte enseñado que las personas son afectadas más profundamente por la *baraka* (poder espiritual) cuando parece que se encuentra más allá de su alcance. El Wali te estaba enseñando esto a pesar de que estabas en prisión, aunque a los observadores externos les pudo haber parecido que él estaba haciendo algo completamente diferente... o incluso nada en absoluto."

El Hindi relata:

"A partir de este acontecimiento pude realmente comprender que no es maravilloso que la gente tenga 'experiencias espirituales'; acaso lo maravilloso es que tan pocos las tengan. Pero aun más maravilloso es que, en vez de aprender de ellas, adoran la experiencia y la consideran algo que no es."

El libro en turco

Un aspirante a discípulo se presentó ante Bahaudin.

El maestro estaba en un jardín después de la cena, rodeado por treinta de sus discípulos.

El recién llegado dijo:

"Deseo servirte."

Bahaudin contestó:

"Me puedes servir mejor leyendo mi *Risalat* (Cartas)."

"Ya lo he hecho", respondió el recién llegado.

"Si realmente lo hubieras hecho, y no sólo en apariencia, no me habrías abordado de esta forma", dijo Bahaudin; y añadió:

"¿Por qué crees que eres capaz de aprender?"

"Estoy preparado para estudiar contigo."

Bahaudin dijo:

"Que se levante el murid (discípulo) más joven."

Anwari, que tenía dieciséis años, se puso de pie.

"¿Cuánto tiempo llevas con nosotros?", le preguntó El-Shah.

"Tres semanas, oh Murshid."

"¿Te he enseñado algo?"

"No lo sé."

"¿Tú qué crees?"

"Yo creo que no."

Bahaudin le dijo:

"En la bolsa del recién llegado encontrarás un libro de poemas. Tómalo y recita su contenido sin cometer errores y sin siquiera abrirlo."

Anwari encontró el libro. No lo abrió, pero dijo: "Me temo que está en turco."

Bahaudin le ordenó:

"¡Recítalo!"

Anwari así lo hizo; y mientras finalizaba, el forastero se iba sintiendo más y más conmovido por esta maravilla: un libro que estaba siendo leído, sin ser abierto, por alguien que no conocía el idioma turco.

Cayendo a los pies de Bahaudin, rogó ser admitido en su Círculo.

Bahaudin le dijo:

"Este es el tipo de fenómeno que te atrae... y mientras sea así, no podrás realmente beneficiarte de él. Es por esto que, aunque hayas leído mi *Risalat*, realmente no lo has leído."

"Vuelve", continuó, "cuando lo hayas leído como acaba de leerlo este joven imberbe. Fue solamente tal estudio el que le dio el poder de recitar un libro que no había abierto y que al mismo tiempo le impidió postrarse asombrado ante semejante evento."

Mendigos y trabajadores

SE CUENTA DE Ibn el-Arabi que la gente le decía:

"Tu círculo está compuesto principalmente por mendigos, labradores y artesanos. ¿No puedes encontrar intelectuales que te sigan, para que acaso se preste una atención más acreditada a tus enseñanzas?"

Contestó:

"El Día de la Calamidad estará infinitamente más cerca cuando tenga a hombres influyentes y eruditos cantándome alabanzas: ¡porque sin duda lo estarán haciendo por su propio bien y no por el bien de nuestro trabajo!"

Inalterado

EL NAWAB MUHAMMAD Khan, Jan-Fishan, estaba un día caminando por Delhi cuando se topó con varias personas que parecían estar involucradas en un altercado.

Le preguntó a un transeúnte:

"¿Qué está pasando aquí?"

El hombre dijo: "Sublime Alteza, uno de tus discípulos está objetando el comportamiento de la gente de este barrio."

Jan-Fishan se abrió paso entre la muchedumbre y le dijo a su seguidor:

"Explícate."

El discípulo dijo: "Estas personas han sido hostiles conmigo."

La gente exclamó: "Eso no es cierto; al contrario... le estábamos rindiendo honores en tu nombre."

"¿Qué dijeron?" preguntó el Nawab.

"Dijeron: '¡Salve, Gran Erudito!' Yo les estaba explicando que a menudo la ignorancia de los eruditos es la responsable de la confusión y desesperación del hombre."

Jan-Fishan Khan dijo: "La arrogancia de los eruditos es, muy a menudo, la responsable de la miseria del hombre; y es *tu* arrogancia, al afirmar que no eres un erudito, la que ha causado este tumulto. No ser un erudito, lo cual implica desapego de lo insignificante, es un logro. Raramente los eruditos son sabios, pues apenas son personas inalteradas repletas de pensamientos y libros.

"Esta gente estaba intentando honrarte. Si algunos creen que el barro es oro y es su barro... respétalo. No eres su maestro.

"¿No te das cuenta de que, al comportarte de ese modo tan susceptible y obstinado, estás actuando igual que un erudito y por lo tanto te mereces el nombre, aunque sea como insulto?

"Cuidado, hijo mío. Demasiados traspiés en el Camino del Logro Supremo... y puede que te conviertas en un erudito."

Diagnóstico

BAHAUDIN NAQSHBAND VISITÓ una vez el pueblo de Alucha después de que una delegación de ciudadanos, enterándose de que estaba pasando por una ruta cercana, lo esperara y rogase que pasara un tiempo con ellos.

"¿Quieren satisfacer su curiosidad en lo que respecta a mí, entretenerme y honrarme, o invitarme a que les imparta mis enseñanzas?" les preguntó.

El líder del grupo, luego de una consulta con sus compañeros, respondió:

"Hemos escuchado mucho acerca de ti y puede que no hayas escuchado nada sobre nosotros. Dado que aparentemente nos brindas el inusual privilegio de recibir tu enseñanza, aceptaremos con gratitud esta opción de las alternativas que nos has ofrecido."

Bahaudin entró al pueblo.

Toda la población estaba reunida en la plaza pública. Sus propios maestros espirituales escoltaron a Bahaudin hacia el lugar de honor; y cuando se sentó, el jefe de los filósofos de Alucha comenzó a dirigirse a él en estos términos:

"¡Presencia sublime y gran Maestro! Todos hemos oído hablar de ti, pues ¿quién no lo ha hecho? Pero, dado que sin dudas no estás familiarizado con los pensamientos de gente tan insignificante como nosotros, te rogamos que nos permitas delinearte nuestras ideas para que acaso puedas apoyarlas, enmendarlas o refutarlas, y seguramente todos nos beneficiemos de…"

Pero Bahaudin lo interrumpió, diciendo:

"Sin dudas les diré lo que pueden hacer, pero no hace falta que me digan nada acerca de ustedes."

Entonces procedió a describirle a la gente sus métodos de pensamiento y también sus propias dificultades y la forma precisa en que consideran los diversos problemas de la vida y del ser humano.

Después de esto les dijo a los asombrados ciudadanos:

"Ahora, antes de explicarles cómo remediar esta situación, acaso quieran expresar algunos sentimientos reprimidos en sus corazones para que yo pueda explicarme en pos de su edificación; y de esta forma podrán prestar una atención completa a lo que estoy por decir."

El mismo portavoz, después de consultar con la gente, dijo:

"¡Oh anciano y guía! La causa unánime de nuestro asombro y curiosidad es cómo puedes saber tanto de nosotros y nuestros problemas y nuestras especulaciones. ¿Estamos en lo cierto al inferir que semejante conocimiento solamente puede existir donde hay una forma superior de percepción directa, en un individuo inusualmente bendecido?"

Como respuesta, Bahaudin pidió una jarra, un cuenco con agua, un poco de sal y harina; echó la sal, la harina y el agua en la jarra. Luego le dijo al portavoz principal:

"Por favor, ¿serías tan amable de decirme qué hay en esta jarra?"

El hombre dijo:

"Reverencia, hay una mezcla de harina, agua y sal."

"¿Cómo sabes la composición de la mezcla?" preguntó Bahaudin.

"Cuando los ingredientes son conocidos", dijo el portavoz, "no puede haber duda alguna acerca de la naturaleza de la mezcla."

"Esa es la respuesta a tu pregunta, que seguramente no requiere más explicaciones de mi parte", dijo Bahaudin Naqshband.

El kashkul

Se cuenta que, una vez, un derviche detuvo a un rey en la calle. El rey dijo: "¿Cómo te atreves tú, un hombre insignificante, a interrumpir el avance de tu soberano?"

El derviche respondió:

"¿Puedes ser un soberano si ni siquiera eres capaz de llenar mi kashkul, el cuenco de un mendigo?"

Tendió su cuenco y el rey ordenó que se lo llenaran de oro.

Pero en cuanto parecía que el cuenco estaba lleno de monedas, estas desaparecían y de nuevo el cuenco se mostraba vacío.

Trajeron un saco de oro tras otro y el asombroso cuenco seguía devorando monedas.

"¡Alto!", gritó el rey, "¡pues este embaucador está vaciando mi tesoro!"

"Para ti, yo estoy vaciando tu tesoro", dijo el derviche, "pero para otros apenas estoy ilustrando una verdad."

"¿Y la verdad?", preguntó el rey.

"La verdad es que el cuenco representa los deseos del hombre y el oro lo que se le da al hombre. La capacidad de devorar del hombre no tiene fin, a menos que cambie de alguna manera. Mira, el cuenco se ha comido prácticamente toda tu riqueza pero sigue siendo un coco tallado y no comparte en absoluto la naturaleza del oro.

"Si te metes dentro de este cuenco", continuó el derviche, "te devorará a ti también. ¿Cómo puede un rey, entonces, considerarse importante?"

La vaca

Érase una vez una vaca. No había un animal en todo el mundo que diera regularmente tanta leche y de semejante calidad.

La gente venía de todas partes para ver esta maravilla; la vaca era ensalzada por todos. Los padres les hablaban a sus hijos de su dedicación con respecto a la tarea que le habían asignado. Los ministros de la religión exhortaban a sus rebaños a que la emularan como pudieran. Los funcionarios del gobierno se referían a ella como un modelo de comportamiento, planificación y pensamiento correctos que podría ser aplicado en la comunidad humana. En resumen, todos pudieron beneficiarse de la existencia de este animal maravilloso.

Había, sin embargo, una característica que la mayoría de la gente, absorta en las obvias ventajas de la vaca, no fue capaz de observar. Verás, tenía una pequeña costumbre: apenas se llenaba un balde con su leche verdaderamente inigualable… lo volcaba de una patada.

Individualidad y calidad

Yaqub, el hijo del juez, contaba que un día cuestionó de esta manera a Bahaudin:

"Cuando estaba en compañía del Murshid de Tabriz, él solía hacer un gesto para que no se le hablase cuando estaba en una estado de reflexión especial; pero tú estás a nuestra disposición todo el tiempo. ¿Estoy en lo correcto si infiero que esta diferencia se debe a tu indudablemente mayor capacidad de desapego, pues esta capacidad está bajo tu control en vez de ser una fugitiva?"

Bahaudin le contestó:

"No, siempre estás buscando comparaciones entre personas y estados; siempre estás buscando evidencias y diferencias; y cuando no lo estás, buscas similitudes. Realmente no necesitas mucha explicación para cuestiones que escapan a tales mediciones. Ha de considerarse que los diversos modos de comportamiento de parte de los sabios se deben a diferencias en su individualidad, no de su calidad."

El paraíso de la canción

AHANGAR ERA UN grandísimo espadero que vivía en uno de los remotos valles orientales de Afganistán. En tiempos de paz hacía arados de acero, herraba caballos y, sobre todo, cantaba.

Las canciones de Ahangar, quien es conocido por distintos nombres en varias zonas del Asia Central, eran escuchadas entusiastamente por los habitantes de los valles. Venían desde los bosques de nogales gigantes, desde las nevadas cumbres del Hindu Kush, desde Qataghan y Badakhxan, desde Khanabad y Kunar, desde Herat y Pagman, para escuchar sus canciones.

Sobre todo, la gente venía a escuchar la canción de las canciones, que era la Canción del Valle del Paraíso, de Ahangar.

Esta canción tenía cierta característica inquietante y una cadencia extraña; pero por encima de todo poseía una historia que era tan fuera de lo común que la gente sentía que conocía el remoto Valle del Paraíso acerca del cual cantaba el espadero. A menudo le pedían que la cantara cuando no estaba de humor para hacerlo, y se negaba; a veces la gente le preguntaba si el Valle era verdaderamente real, y Ahangar solamente podía decir:

"El Valle de la canción es tan real como la realidad misma."

"Pero, ¿cómo lo sabes?" preguntaba la gente. "¿Has estado allí alguna vez?"

"No de un modo ordinario", decía Ahangar.

Para él, y para casi todas las personas que lo escucharon, el Valle de la canción era, sin embargo, real como la realidad misma.

Aisha, una doncella local amada por Ahangar, dudaba de que pudiera existir un lugar así; también lo hacía Hasan, un fanfarrón y temible espadachín que había jurado casarse con Aisha y quien no perdía oportunidad para reírse del espadero.

Un día, cuando los aldeanos estaban sentados en silencio luego de que Ahangar les hubo contado un cuento, Hasan habló:

"Si crees que este valle es tan real y que está, como dices, más allá de las montañas de Sangan donde surge la neblina azul, ¿por qué no intentas encontrarlo?"

"Sé que no sería correcto", dijo Ahangar.

"¡Sabes lo que es conveniente saber y no sabes lo que no quieres saber!" gritó Hasan. "Ahora, amigo mío, te propongo una prueba. Amas a Aisha, pero ella no confía en ti; no tiene fe en tu Valle absurdo. Nunca podrás casarte con ella, porque donde no hay confianza entre marido y mujer no hay felicidad, y ocurren todo tipo de desgracias."

"¿Pretendes que vaya al valle, entonces?" preguntó Ahangar.

"Sí" dijeron al unísono Hasan y todos los presentes.

"Si voy y regreso sano y salvo, ¿aceptará Aisha casarse conmigo?" preguntó Ahangar.

"Sí", murmuró ella.

Entonces Ahangar, recogiendo algunas moras secas y un trozo de pan, partió hacia las lejanas montañas.

Subió y trepó, hasta que se topó con un muro que rodeaba toda la cordillera. Tras haber escalado su escarpada pared lateral, encontró otro muro que era incluso más escarpado que el primero; y luego había un tercero y un cuarto y, finalmente, un quinto muro.

Descendiendo del otro lado, Ahangar descubrió que estaba en un valle sorprendentemente similar al suyo.

La gente salió a darle la bienvenida y al verlos Ahangar se dio cuenta de que algo muy extraño estaba sucediendo.

Meses después y caminando como un anciano, Ahangar el espadero llegó cojeando a su aldea natal y enfiló hacia su humilde choza. Dado que se corrió la voz de su regreso por todos lados, la gente se reunió frente a su hogar para escuchar cuáles habían sido sus aventuras.

Hasan el espadachín habló en nombre de todos y desde la ventana llamó a Ahangar.

Todos quedaron boquiabiertos cuando vieron cuánto había envejecido.

"Bueno, Maestro Ahangar, ¿lograste llegar al Valle del Paraíso?"

"Lo logré."

"¿Y cómo era?"

Ahangar, buscando palabras a tientas, miró a la gente allí reunida con un cansancio y una desesperanza que jamás había sentido. Dijo:

"Escalé y subí y trepé. Cuando parecía que ya no podía haber vida humana en semejante sitio desolado, y luego de muchas vicisitudes y desilusiones, encontré un valle; era exactamente igual al nuestro. Y luego vi la gente; ellos no solo son como nosotros: son *nosotros mismos*. Por cada Hasan, cada Aisha, cada Ahangar, por cada uno de los que estamos aquí, hay otro exactamente igual en aquel valle.

"Cuando vemos tales cosas nos parecen retratos o reflejos nuestros; pero somos nosotros los retratos y reflejos de ellos... Aquellos que estamos aquí, somos sus dobles."

Todos creyeron que Ahangar se había vuelto loco debido a sus privaciones y Aisha se casó con Hasan el espadachín. Ahangar envejeció rápidamente y murió; y toda la gente, cada uno de los que habían escuchado esta historia de labios de Ahangar, se desanimó, para luego envejecer y dejarse morir pues sentían que iba a suceder algo incontrolable y ante lo cual no tenían esperanzas, perdiendo así el interés por la vida misma.

Es solo una vez cada mil años que el hombre ve este secreto. Cuando lo hace, sufre un cambio. Cuando les cuenta a otros la realidad de los hechos, se marchitan y mueren.

La gente cree que semejante evento es una catástrofe y es por ello que no quieren saber nada acerca de eso, pues no pueden comprender (tal es la naturaleza de sus vidas ordinarias) que tienen más de un yo, más de una esperanza, más de una chance... allí arriba, en el Paraíso de la Canción de Ahangar, el grandísimo espadero.

El tesoro de los custodios

UN PRÍNCIPE DE la ilustre Casa de Abbas, pariente del tío del Profeta, llevaba una existencia humilde en Mosul, Irak. Su familia había sufrido desgracias y regresado al destino común del hombre: el trabajo. Después de tres generaciones, la familia había logrado restablecerse un poco y el príncipe tenía el estatus de un pequeño comerciante.

Este hombre, cuyo nombre era Daud el Abbassi, meramente se llamaba a sí mismo Daud, hijo de Altaf, tal como es costumbre entre los nobles árabes. Pasaba días enteros en el mercado vendiendo frijoles y hierbas, intentando recuperar la fortuna familiar.

Este proceso continuó durante varios años, hasta que Daud se enamoró de la hija de un rico mercader: Zobeida Ibnat Tawil; ella estaba más que dispuesta a casarse con él, pero en su familia había una costumbre según la cual cualquier futuro yerno debía producir una gema excepcional que pudiese ser comparada a aquella elegida especialmente por el padre de la novia, con el fin de evidenciar su ingenio y también su riqueza material.

Luego de las negociaciones preliminares, cuando a Daud se le mostró el brillante rubí que Tawil había elegido para la prueba, el corazón del joven tendero se entristeció. No solo esta gema era de la más excelsa calidad, sino que su tamaño y color eran tales que seguramente las minas de Badakhxan nunca habían podido producir algo semejante más que una vez cada mil años...

Transcurría el tiempo mientras Daud pensaba en todas las formas posibles de conseguir el dinero con el cual podría, al menos, igualar el precio de la joya. Finalmente descubrió, gracias a un joyero, que apenas tenía una oportunidad. Si enviaba a pregoneros para que le hicieran ofertas a cualquiera que pudiese fabricar una copia exacta, ofreciendo no solamente su casa y todas sus posesiones sino también tres cuartos de cada centavo que ganara durante el resto de su vida, quizá tendría una chance de encontrar un rubí similar.

Por consiguiente, Daud hizo pública su intención.

Día tras día corría la voz de que se estaba buscando un rubí de valor, brillo y color asombrosos, y muchas personas llegaron presurosamente de todas partes a la casa del mercader para ver si podían proporcionar algo tan magnífico; pero luego de un lapso de casi tres años Daud descubrió que ni en Arabistán o Ajam o en el Jorasán o el subcontinente indio o ni siquiera en África, Java o Ceilán, había ningún rubí que se aproximara a la excelencia del que su probable futuro suegro había encontrado.

Zobeida y Daud estaban al borde de la desesperación. Parecía como si nunca fueran a casarse, pues el padre de la joven se negaba rotundamente a aceptar cualquier cosa que no fuese, al menos, tan excelsa como su rubí.

Una noche, sentado en su pequeño jardín pensando por milésima vez en algún medio para ganar la mano de Zobeida, Daud se percató de que una figura alta y demacrada estaba de pie junto a él; en su mano tenía un bastón, sobre su cabeza un gorro derviche y colgando de su cintura había un cuenco metálico de mendigo.

"¡La paz sea contigo, oh mi rey!" dijo Daud con el saludo acostumbrado, poniéndose de pie.

"Daud, el Abbassi, ¡vástago de la Casa de Quraysh!" dijo la aparición, "soy uno de los guardianes de los tesoros del Apóstol y he venido a ayudarte en tu extrema necesidad. Buscas un rubí sin parangón; te lo daré, ¡de los tesoros de nuestro patrimonio que han sido dejados a salvo en las manos de los custodios pobres!"

Daud lo miró y dijo: "Todo el tesoro que estaba en poder de nuestra Casa fue gastado, vendido y saqueado hace siglos. No nos queda más que nuestro nombre y ni siquiera lo usamos por miedo a deshonrarlo; ¿cómo es que queda algún tesoro de mi patrimonio?"

"Todavía queda algo de tesoro, precisamente porque no todo fue dejado en manos de la Casa", dijo el derviche; "pues la gente siempre roba primero a aquellos de quienes se sabe que tienen algo para robarles. Sin embargo, cuando eso ya no está, los ladrones no saben dónde buscar. Esta es la primera medida de seguridad de los Custodios."

Daud reflexionó que muchos derviches tienen fama de ser excéntricos y por ende solamente dijo:

"¿Quién dejaría valiosísimos tesoros, como la gema de Tawil, en manos de un mendigo harapiento? ¿Y qué mendigo andrajoso, habiendo recibido semejante joya, se abstendría de desperdiciarla o venderla y despilfarrar el dinero en un frenesí gastador?"

El derviche contestó:

"Hijo mío, esto es exactamente lo que se espera que crea la gente. Debido a que los mendigos son harapientos, las personas imaginan que desean ropa; porque un hombre tiene una joya, la gente imagina que la desperdiciará si no es un mercader próspero. Tus pensamientos son las cosas que ayudan a asegurar nuestro tesoro."

"Entonces llévame al tesoro", dijo Daud, "para que pueda ponerle fin a mis insoportables dudas y miedos."

El derviche le vendó los ojos a Daud y lo hizo andar, vestido como ciego, día y noche montado en un burro arisco. Se apearon y caminaron a través de una hendidura montañosa; y cuando se le quitó la tela de sus ojos, Daud vio que estaba en una bóveda donde incalculables cantidades e increíbles variedades de piedras preciosas brillaban desde los estantes tallados en las paredes rocosas.

"¿Es posible que este sea el tesoro de mis antepasados? Pues jamás he escuchado hablar de algo ni remotamente parecido, incluso en los tiempos de Harún el-Rashid", dijo Daud.

"Puedes estar seguro de que lo es", dijo el derviche, "y mucho más que eso. Esta es apenas una caverna, la que contiene las joyas que puedes elegir… hay mucho más."

"¿Y es mío?"

"Es tuyo."

"Entonces me llevaré todo", dijo Daud, que estaba prácticamente vencido por la codicia que sus ojos le presentaban.

"Te llevarás solamente lo que has venido a buscar", dijo el derviche, "pues estás tan poco preparado para administrar esta riqueza correctamente como lo estaban tus antepasados. Si esto no fuese así, los Custodios habrían devuelto todo el tesoro hace siglos."

Daud eligió el único rubí que podía ser comparado con el de Tawil y el derviche lo llevó de regreso a su casa del mismo modo en que lo había traído. Daud y Zobeida se casaron.

Y de esta manera se cuenta que los tesoros de la Casa son entregados a los pertinentes herederos cuando tienen una verdadera necesidad de ellos. Hoy los Custodios no siempre se presentan como derviches con mantos emparchados; a veces se ven como los hombres más comunes. Pero no cederán los tesoros a menos que haya una necesidad real.

El apego llamado gracia

Un dedicado y estudioso buscador de la verdad llegó a la Tekkia de Bahaudin Naqshband.

Según la costumbre, asistió a las conferencias y no hizo preguntas.

Cuando finalmente Bahaudin le dijo: "Pídeme algo", este hombre dijo:

"Shah, antes de venir a verte estudié tal y tal filosofía con fulano de tal. Viajé hasta tu Tekkia atraído por tu reputación.

"Al escuchar tus conferencias he quedado muy impresionado con lo que dices y me gustaría continuar mis estudios contigo.

"Pero, dado que tengo semejante gratitud y apego a mis estudios previos y maestros, me gustaría que explicases su conexión con tu trabajo o al menos que me hagas olvidarlos, para que pueda continuar sin una mente dividida."

Bahaudin dijo:

"No puedo hacer ninguna de esas cosas. Lo que *puedo* hacer, sin embargo, es informarte de que el estar apegado a una persona y a un credo e imaginar que semejante apego proviene de una fuente superior, es una de las señas más obvias de la vanidad humana. Si una persona se obsesiona con los dulces, los llamaría divinos si alguien se lo permitiese.

"Con esta información puedes aprender sabiduría. Sin ella, solamente puedes aprender apego y llamarlo gracia."

> "El hombre que necesita *malumat*
> (información), siempre supone que
> necesita *maarifat* (sabiduría)
> Si realmente es un hombre de
> información, verá que lo siguiente
> que necesita es sabiduría.
> Si es un hombre de sabiduría,
> solamente entonces estará libre de la
> necesidad de información."

Corrección

Abdullah ben Yahya le estaba mostrando a un visitante un manuscrito que había producido.

Este hombre dijo: "Pero esta palabra ha sido escrita incorrectamente."

De inmediato borró la palabra y la escribió según el parecer del invitado.

Cuando este se hubo ido le preguntaron a Abdullah: "¿Por qué hiciste eso, sobre todo cuando de hecho la 'corrección' era errónea, y escribiste la palabra equivocada en lugar de la original que era correcta?"

Contestó: "Fue una ocasión social. El hombre creyó que me estaba ayudando y que la expresión de su ignorancia era un indicio de conocimiento. Apliqué el comportamiento de la cultura y la amabilidad, no el de la verdad, pues cuando la gente quiere amabilidad e intercambio social no pueden tolerar la verdad. Si hubiese tenido con este hombre una relación de maestro-discípulo, las cosas habrían sido diferentes. Solo los estúpidos y los pedantes imaginan que su deber es enseñarles a todo el mundo, cuando generalmente la motivación de la gente no es buscar instrucción, sino atraer atención."

El santo y el pecador

HABÍA UNA VEZ un devoto derviche que creía que su tarea era reprochar a aquellos que hacían maldades e imponerles pensamientos espirituales para que pudiesen encontrar el sendero correcto. Lo que este derviche no sabía, sin embargo, era que un maestro no es solamente alguien que les dice a otros que actúen según principios fijos. A menos que el maestro sepa exactamente cuál es la situación interna de cada estudiante, puede que produzca lo contrario de lo que busca.

Sin embargo, un día este devoto encontró a un hombre que apostaba excesivamente y no sabía cómo curar el hábito. El derviche se ubicó justo afuera de la casa del apostador. Cada vez que salía rumbo a la casa de apuestas, el derviche colocaba una piedra por cada pecado sobre una pila que estaba armando como un recordatorio visible de la maldad.

Cada vez que salía, el apostador se sentía culpable; cada vez que regresaba, veía otra piedra sobre la pila; cada vez que ponía una piedra en la pila, el devoto sentía bronca para con el apostador y cierto placer personal (que llamaba "piedad") por haber registrado su pecado.

Este proceso continuó durante veinte años. Cada vez que el apostador veía al devoto, pensaba:

"¡Ojalá pudiese entender la bondad! ¡Cómo trabaja por mi redención ese santo! Ojalá pudiera arrepentirme, y sobre todo ser como él, pues seguramente tendrá un lugar entre los elegidos cuando llegue el día de la recompensa!"

Resulta que, debido a una catástrofe natural, ambos murieron al mismo tiempo. Un ángel vino a buscar el alma del apostador y gentilmente le dijo:

"Tú has de venir conmigo al paraíso."

"Pero", dijo el apostador, "¿cómo puede ser? Soy un pecador y debo ir al infierno. Seguramente estás buscando al devoto que se sentaba frente a mi casa y que estuvo intentando reformarme durante veinte años."

"¿El devoto?" dijo el ángel. "No, está siendo llevado a las regiones inferiores pues tiene que ser asado al espiedo."

"¿Qué clase de justicia es esta?" gritó el apostador, olvidándose de su situación, "¡debes de haber recibido las instrucciones al revés!"

"No es así", dijo el ángel, "y te explicaré por qué no: el devoto ha estado regodeándose durante veinte años con sentimientos de superioridad y mérito. Ahora le toca reequilibrar la balanza.

Realmente él puso esas piedras en la pila para él mismo, no para ti."

"¿Y qué hay acerca de mi recompensa? ¿Qué *me he* ganado?", preguntó el apostador.

"Has de ser recompensado porque cada vez que pasabas al lado del derviche primero pensabas en la bondad y después en el derviche. Es la bondad, no el hombre, la que te está recompensando por tu fidelidad."

Los sheikhs de los casquetes

BAHAUDIN NAQSHBAND FUE contactado por los sheikhs de cuatro grupos Sufis de la India, Egipto, Turquía y Persia. Le pidieron, en cartas elocuentemente escritas, que les enviara enseñanzas que pudiesen impartir a sus seguidores.

Primero, Bahaudin dijo: "Lo que tengo no es nuevo; ustedes lo tienen y no lo usan correctamente. Por lo tanto, cuando reciban mis mensajes simplemente dirán: 'Estas no son nuevas'."

Los sheikhs contestaron: "Con respeto, creemos que nuestros discípulos no pensarán así."

Bahaudin no respondió a estas cartas; pero las leyó en sus asambleas, diciendo: "Desde lejos podremos ver lo que ocurra. Sin embargo, aquellos que están en el medio del acontecimiento no harán el esfuerzo para ver qué les está sucediendo."

Entonces los sheikhs le escribieron a Bahaudin pidiéndole que diese alguna muestra de interés. Bahaudin les envió casquetes, el *araqia*, para que los repartiesen entre sus discípulos diciendo que los mandaba él pero sin revelar el por qué.

Dijo a su asamblea: "He hecho tal y tal cosa. Nosotros los que estamos lejos veremos lo que aquellos que están cerca de los eventos no verán."

Después de un tiempo les escribió a cada uno de los sheikhs, preguntándoles si habían respetado sus deseos y cuál había sido el resultado.

Los sheikhs escribieron: "Hemos respetado tus deseos." Pero en lo referido a los resultados, el sheikh de Egipto escribió: "Mi comunidad aceptó de buena gana tu regalo como un símbolo de santidad y bendición especiales, y apenas se repartieron los casquetes cada discípulo lo consideró como algo del más grande significado interior y como portador de tu autoridad."

Por otro lado, el sheikh de los turcos escribió: "La comunidad observa tus casquetes con cierto recelo; imaginan que presagian tu deseo de asumir su liderazgo. Algunos temen que incluso puedas influenciarlos desde lejos mediante este objeto."

Hubo otra reacción del sheikh de la India, quien escribió: "Nuestros discípulos están sumidos en una gran confusión y diariamente me piden que les interprete el significado de la distribución de *araqias*. No sabrán cómo actuar hasta que les diga algo acerca de ello."

La carta del sheikh de Persia decía: "El resultado de tu distribución de los casquetes es que los buscadores, contentos con lo que les has enviado, esperan tu siguiente regalo para que puedan realizar los esfuerzos que deberían ser puestos a disposición de su enseñanza y de ellos mismos"

Bahaudin le explicó a un grupo de Bujara:

"La característica superficial dominante de las personas en los círculos de la India, Egipto, Turquía y Persia fue manifestada en cada caso por las reacciones de sus miembros. Su comportamiento, cuando fueron enfrentados a un objeto trivial como es un casquete, habría sido exactamente igual si se hubieran enfrentado a mí en persona o con mis enseñanzas. Ni los discípulos ni los sheikhs han aprendido que deben buscar entre ellos mismos sus peculiaridades sofocantes. No deberían usar estas peculiaridades triviales como métodos para evaluar a los demás.

"Entre los discípulos del sheikh persa hay una posibilidad de comprensión, pues no tienen la arrogancia de imaginar que 'comprenden' que mis casquetes *los* bendecirán, *los* amenazarán, *los* confundirán. Según los tres casos, las características son: esperanza egipcia, miedo turco e incertidumbre india."

Algunas de las epístolas de Bahaudin Naqshbandi habían sido copiadas en el interín como acto piadoso y distribuidas por derviches bienintencionados – pero no iluminados – en El Cairo, el subcontinente indio y en diversas zonas persas y turcas; pero finalmente cayeron en manos de los círculos que rodeaban a estos mismos "Sheikhs de los Casquetes".

Es por ello que Bahaudin le pidió a un Kalendar errante que visitase a cada una de estas comunidades y que le informara cómo se sentían acerca de sus epístolas. A su regreso, este hombre dijo:

"Todos dijeron: 'Esto no es nada nuevo. Ya estamos haciendo todas estas cosas. No solo eso, sino que estamos basando en ello nuestras vidas cotidianas y así, mediante nuestra tradición existente, nos mantenemos ocupados día y noche con el recuerdo de estas cuestiones.'"

Acto seguido, El-Shah Bahaudin Naqshband convocó a sus discípulos; les dijo:

"Ustedes que están alejados de ciertos eventos conectados con estos cuatro grupos dirigidos por sheikhs, podrán ver qué poco se ha logrado mediante la operación del Conocimiento entre ellos. Aquellos que están allí presentes han aprendido tan poco que ya no pueden beneficiarse de sus propias experiencias. ¿Dónde, entonces, está la ventaja del 'recuerdo y la lucha diarios'?

"Tómense el trabajo de recopilar toda la información disponible acerca de este evento, infórmense de la historia completa, incluyendo el intercambio de cartas y lo que he dicho y el reporte del Kalendar que está aquí. Sean testigos de que hemos ofrecido los medios con los cuales otros pueden aprender. Hagan que este material sea puesto por escrito y estudiado, y permitan que aquellos que han estado presentes sean testigos para que, Dios mediante, acaso su lectura pueda prevenir que semejantes cosas sucedan frecuentemente en el futuro e incluso ello permita que les llegue a los ojos y oídos de quienes fueron afectados tan poderosamente por la 'acción' de casquetes inactivados."

El secreto de la habitación cerrada

AYAZ ERA AMIGO íntimo y esclavo del gran conquistador Mahmud el Destructor de Ídolos, monarca de Gazna; primero había llegado a la corte como un esclavo muy pobre y luego Mahmud lo convirtió en su consejero y amigo.

Los otros cortesanos estaban celosos de Ayaz y observaban todos sus movimientos, con la intención de denunciarlo por alguna falla suya y así provocar su caída.

Un día, estos celosos fueron a ver a Mahmud y dijeron:

"¡Sombra de Alá sobre la tierra! Has de saber que, infatigablemente entregados a tu servicio, hemos estado vigilando de cerca a tu esclavo Ayaz. Ahora debemos reportar que todos los días, apenas se va de la corte, Ayaz se encierra en una habitación pequeña donde no se le permite la entrada a nadie; pasa un rato allí y luego va a sus propios aposentos. Tememos que este hábito suyo pueda estar relacionado con un secreto inconfesable; acaso allí se junte con conspiradores que tienen planes de quitarle la vida a su majestad."

Durante mucho tiempo Mahmud se negó a escuchar nada en contra de Ayaz; mas el misterio de la habitación cerrada asedió su mente hasta que sintió que tenía que interrogar a Ayaz.

Un día, cuando Ayaz salía de su cuarto privado, un Mahmud rodeado de cortesanos apareció y exigió que se le mostrase la habitación.

"No", dijo Ayaz.

"Si no me permites entrar a la habitación, toda la confianza que tengo puesta en ti como hombre fidedigno y leal se habrá evaporado, y en adelante jamás podremos mantener nuestra relación en los mismos términos. Elige", dijo el feroz conquistador.

Ayaz lloró; luego abrió la puerta de la habitación y permitió que entrasen Mahmud y su personal.

El cuarto no tenía ni un mueble; todo lo que había era un gancho en la pared, del cual colgaba una andrajosa túnica emparchada, un bastón y un cuenco de mendigo.

El rey y sus cortesanos eran incapaces de comprender el significado de este descubrimiento.

Cuando Mahmud exigió una explicación, Ayaz dijo:

"Mahmud, durante años he sido tu esclavo, tu amigo y consejero. He intentando nunca olvidar

mis orígenes y es por esta razón que he venido
aquí día tras día para recordarme lo que yo fui.
Te pertenezco, y todo lo que me pertenece a mí
son mis harapos, mi palo, mi cuenco y mi errancia
sobre la faz de la tierra."

El milagro del derviche real

Se cuenta que, un día, el maestro Sufí Ibrahim ben Adam estaba sentado en el claro de un bosque cuando dos derviches errantes se le acercaron; les dio la bienvenida y hablaron de asuntos espirituales hasta el atardecer.

Apenas anocheció, Ibrahim invitó a los viajeros a que cenaran con él. Ellos aceptaron inmediatamente y ante sus ojos apareció una mesa servida con los manjares más exquisitos.

"¿Hace cuánto que eres un derviche?", preguntó uno de ellos a Ibrahim. "Hace dos años", contestó él.

"Yo he estado siguiendo el Camino Sufí durante casi tres décadas y jamás se me ha manifestado una capacidad como la que nos has mostrado", comentó el hombre.

Ibrahim no dijo nada.

Cuando la comida casi se había terminado, un forastero de túnica verde penetró en el calvero; se sentó y comió algo de las sobras.

Todos se dieron cuenta, a través de una sensación interna, de que este era Khidr, el Guía inmortal de todos los Sufis; y esperaron que les impartiera algo de sabiduría.

Cuando se levantó para irse, Khidr simplemente dijo:

"Ustedes dos, derviches, se preguntan acerca de Ibrahim. Pero ¿a qué han renunciado para poder seguir el Sendero derviche?

"Abandonaron toda expectativa de seguridad y de una vida ordinaria. Ibrahim ben Adam era un poderoso rey y descartó la soberanía del sultanato de Balkh para convertirse en un Sufi. Es por ello que está muy por delante de ustedes. Durante sus treinta años, ustedes también han obtenido satisfacciones a través de la misma renuncia: esta ha sido su recompensa. Él siempre se ha abstenido de reclamar pago alguno por su sacrificio."

Y un momento después Khidr desapareció.

La prueba de Ishan Wali

Ishan Wali, cuando apareció repentinamente en Siria procedente del Turquestán, mostró que tenía un notable repertorio de técnicas (que los externalistas denominaban sus "sabidurías") con las cuales era capaz de lograr un avance en el entonces lento estudio del Sufismo.

Descubrió, por ejemplo, que las escuelas Sufis se habían convertido en organizaciones unidas por el tradicionalismo y su consideración para con un maestro a expensas de las enseñanzas de los Sufis como un todo. Trabajaban con ejercicios e ideas que pertenecían justamente a otras personas, a otros tiempos e incluso a otros lugares.

La forma en que Wali abordó este problema impresionó enormemente a aquellos que, ignorando sus métodos, creían que debían ayudarlo. Entre ellos se encontraban Mustafá Ali Darazi, Ali-Muhammad Husseini y Tawil Tirmidhi; sus reportes aún sobreviven.

Les dijo:

"Al ojo externo que ve este rejunte de gente, quienes en realidad quizá se han convertido en molinos de harina en vez de escuelas, le resulta imposible diferenciar entre aquellos que han de ser abordados y los que no tienen capacidad de aprender. Como bien saben, les he mostrado que actualmente todos son inadecuados para el Trabajo. ¿Pero cuál de ellos es capaz de renacer?"

Señaló una fila de palmeras que estaban sufriendo el calor. "Si el agua es limitada, ¿qué árbol regamos? Les he mostrado que están marchitos, algo que no habían percibido antes. Ahora les voy a mostrar una manera de comprobar si un árbol puede revivir o no."

A manera de demostración, Ishan Wali se encontró con todos los sheikhs de las escuelas repetitivas, quienes en su mayoría le dieron amablemente la bienvenida y le hicieron saber que estarían encantados de recibir su ayuda para restablecer las enseñanzas.

No les aseguró nada. Separándose de ellos, les escribió a cada uno de la siguiente manera:

"Tengo algo de suma importancia que decirles *a* ustedes y nada en absoluto que decir *a través* de ustedes. Esto significa que se me debe permitir que me dirija directamente a sus seguidores. Si lo permiten, revelaré mis métodos. Si, por otro lado, no lo permiten, podré con el tiempo dirigirme a estas personas de forma indirecta. Pero de esa manera se habrán distanciado de mí mediante el rechazo y no seré capaz de dirigirme *a* ustedes.

Dado que soy responsable o bien de todos ustedes o de ninguno, al comienzo no puedo utilizarlos a ustedes como canal cuando puedo abordarlos directamente. Ya que han desarrollado semejante afinidad íntima con su comunidad, debo considerarlos a ustedes como una parte esencial de la comunidad y por ende no puedo tratarlos por separado."

Les explicó a sus ayudantes que aquellos sheikhs que estaban dispuestos a considerarse a sí mismos como alumnos del mismo modo que consideraban a sus propios estudiantes como discípulos, serían quienes dirigirían las Escuelas que podían ser revivificadas.

Algunos sheikhs respondieron con comprensión y otros reaccionaron con intensa desconfianza, abierta o encubiertamente, al enterarse del enfoque de Ishan Wali.

Aunque apreció la comprensión de aquellos que se consideraban a sí mismos como sus discípulos y que al mismo tiempo no creían ser superiores a sus propios discípulos más inexpertos a este respecto, se entristeció por las plantas marchitas.

Ali-Muhammad Husseini dijo: "¿Entonces debemos entristecernos por aquello que, según se ha demostrado, está muerto?"

Ishan Wali contestó: "No todos están muertos; es solamente su sospecha la que los hace comportarse como si estuviesen muertos."

Apenas hubo dicho esto, algunos sheikhs de las escuelas divididas cambiaron su actitud – como si hubieran escuchado una perceptiva voz interna – y pusieron sus turbantes a los pies de Ishan Wali.

Majzub, uno de los sheikhs previamente desconcertados, dijo a continuación:

"Sentí como si se me hubiese quitado un peso opresivo de encima; y entonces supe que era *mi* miedo y sospecha."

Pero Ishan Wali dijo: "Fueron las oraciones de los sheikhs 'marchitantes', más fuertes que sus miedos y sospechas, lo que hizo que viniesen a nosotros para recibir lo que teníamos para darles. De hecho, el mérito es todo suyo. ¿Qué mérito hay en hacer algo que sabemos? En el pasado se nos ha ensalzado por ejercitar virtudes; pero fueron *ellos* quienes en este caso, al empujar contra sus naturalezas llenas de óxido, han pulido el espejo de la comprensión."

Y así fue que los recelosos sheikhs conservaron su importancia en sus propias escuelas y se ganaron aún más respeto de sus propios discípulos. Los pocos que permanecieron distanciados descubrieron que sus estudiantes se inclinaban cada vez más hacia la confusión mental o la adhesión al Wali, quien les escribió diciendo:

"No acepto a sus estudiantes, pero no por cortesía para con ustedes sino porque la extremidad, sin la comprensión de todo el cuerpo, no puede funcionar. Si temen la pérdida de discípulos por mi presencia, entonces no teman: pues no puedo ayudarlos y siempre lo diré. Pero sí tengo miedo por vuestra situación futura."

Las plantas marchitas, a excepción de unas pocas, no respondieron a esta amable lluvia. Hoy, por supuesto, no hay rastro sobre la tierra de los seguidores de aquellos sheikhs que no adoptaron los métodos de Ishan Wali durante su estadía en Siria.

Milagros ocultos

ALGUIEN LE PREGUNTÓ a Fuwad Ashiq, viejo discípulo de Bahaudin Naqshband:

"¿Puedes decirme por qué es que el Maulana disimula sus milagros? A menudo lo he visto en algún lugar y al mismo tiempo otros han testificado que en ese momento estaban con él en otro lado. Similarmente, cuando cura a alguien mediante la oración, puede que diga: 'Habría sucedido de todas maneras.' La gente que le pide favores, o que son favorecidas por su interés, obtienen grandes ventajas en el mundo aunque él niegue su influencia o atribuya dichos sucesos al azar o incluso al trabajo de otros."

Fuwad dijo:

"Yo mismo he observado esto muchas veces; de hecho, desde que estoy tan a menudo con él esto es parte de mi experiencia cotidiana. La razón es que los milagros son el 'servicio extraordinario' en acción. No se hacen para hacer feliz o entristecer a la gente. Si impresionan, esto hará que la persona infantil se vuelva crédula y excitada, en lugar de hacerla aprender algo."

La entrada a un círculo Sufi

Si lees, si practicas, puede que estés cualificado para un círculo Sufi. Si solamente lees, no lo estarás. Si piensas que has tenido experiencias sobre las que puedes construir, puede que no estés cualificado.

Las palabras solas no comunican: debe haber algo ya preparado, de lo cual las palabras son un indicio.

La práctica por sí sola no perfecciona a la humanidad. El ser humano necesita el contacto con la verdad, inicialmente en una forma que lo ayudará.

Lo que es conveniente e impecable para un tiempo y lugar, es generalmente limitado, inadecuado o un obstáculo para otro tiempo y lugar. Esto es cierto en la búsqueda y también en muchos ámbitos de la vida ordinaria.

Ten esperanza y trabaja para que puedas ser aceptable para un círculo Sufi. No intentes juzgarlo, o a sus miembros, a menos que estés libre de codicia. La codicia te hace creer cosas que normalmente no creerías; te hace descreer de cosas que por lo general creerías.

Si no puedes superar la codicia, ejercítala únicamente donde puedas verla actuar; no la traigas al círculo de los iniciados.

Nazir el-Kazwini, "Las observaciones solitarias"

La historia de Ibn Halim

HUBO DOS HOMBRES de gran renombre como maestros del Camino Correcto. Ibn Halim cuenta que primero fue a ver a uno de ellos, cuyo nombre era Pir Ardeshir de Qazwin.

Le dijo a Pir Ardeshir: "¿Me aconsejarías qué hacer y qué no hacer?"

El Pir contestó:

"Sí, pero te daré tales instrucciones que te serán muy difíciles de realizar, dado que van en contra de tus preferencias... incluso aunque a veces tengas preferencia por la dificultad."

Ibn Halim pasó unos meses con Pir Ardeshir y descubrió que efectivamente la enseñanza le resultaba muy difícil. A pesar de que ahora los anteriores discípulos de Pir Ardeshir eran famosos en todo el mundo como maestros iluminados, él no podía tolerar los cambios, las incertidumbres y las asignaturas que se le imponían.

Finalmente le solicitó al Pir permiso para irse; viajó a la Tekkia del segundo maestro, Murshid Amali.

Le preguntó al Murshid: "¿Me impondrás cargas que acaso me resulten casi intolerables?"

Amali contestó:

"No te impondré tales cargas."

Ibn Halim preguntó:

"¿Me aceptarás como discípulo?"

El Murshid dijo:

"No hasta que me hayas preguntado por qué mi entrenamiento no sería tan arduo como el del Pir Ardeshir."

Ibn Halim preguntó: "¿Por qué no sería tan arduo?"

El Murshid le contó: "Porque entonces ni tú ni tu bienestar real me importarían como le importaban a Ardeshir. Por lo tanto no debes pedirme que te acepte como discípulo."

La mujer Sufi y la reina

Cierta mujer que pertenecía a la deshonrada familia de los Omeyya, habiéndose convertido en Sufi, fue a visitar a la reina del hogar de el-Mahdi, que había reemplazado a los Omeyya.

La misma reina era conocida como una mujer delicada y compasiva. Cuando vio la figura demacrada y harapienta de la pobre princesa Omeyya ante su puerta, le pidió que entrase y se preparó para brindarle palabras de consuelo y regalos que seguramente aliviarían su evidente penuria.

Pero apenas la princesa dijo:

"Soy una hija de la familia de los Omeyya..." la reina se olvidó de toda su caridad y gritó:

"¡Una mujer de los malditos Omeyya! Sin dudas has venido a pedir limosna, olvidando las cosas que tu gente hizo a mi familia, cómo los oprimieron y trataron sin piedad, dejándolos a la buena de Dios..."

"No", dijo la princesa Omeyya, "no vine buscando simpatía, perdón o dinero. Vine para ver si la familia de el-Mahdi había aprendido cómo comportarse a partir del ejemplo de sus predecesores, quienes no sabían cómo hacerlo: los despiadados hijos de los Omeyya; o si la conducta que deploras fue una enfermedad contagiosa que seguramente provocará la ruina de aquellos que la han contraído."

La princesa Omeyya se fue; no se la vio nunca más.

Pero tenemos esta historia solamente por las palabras de la reina de el-Mahdi, y acaso haya sido la causa de alguna mejora en el comportamiento humano, en algún lugar.

El asistente del cocinero

CIERTO FAMOSO, QUERIDO e influyente mercader visitó a Bahaudin Naqshband; le dijo en asamblea abierta:

"He venido a ofrecerte mi sumisión a ti y a tu enseñanza, y te ruego que me aceptes como discípulo."

Bahaudin le preguntó:

"¿Por qué sientes que eres capaz de sacar provecho de la enseñanza?"

El mercader contestó:

"En ti encuentro todo lo que he conocido y amado en la poesía y en la enseñanza de los antiguos, tal como está registrado en sus libros. En ti realmente encuentro perfecta y completamente todo lo que otros maestros Sufis predican, ensalzan y cuentan de los sabios, pero no en ellos. Te considero como uno de los grandes, pues puedo percibir el aroma de la Verdad en ti y en todo lo que está vinculado contigo."

Bahaudin le pidió al hombre que se retirase, diciendo que le comunicaría su decisión sobre su aceptabilidad a su debido tiempo.

Después de seis meses, Bahaudin convocó al mercader y le dijo:

"¿Estás preparado para tener un diálogo público conmigo?"

Contestó:

"Por mis ojos y mi cabeza que sí."

Cuando la reunión matinal iba progresando, Bahaudin llamó al comerciante e hizo que se sentara a su lado; les dijo a los oyentes:

"Este es fulano, el distinguido rey de los mercaderes de esta ciudad. Hace seis meses vino aquí creyendo que podía percibir el aroma de la verdad en todo lo vinculado conmigo."

El mercader dijo:

"Este período de prueba y separación, estos seis meses sin un atisbo del Maestro, este exilio, han hecho que me sumerja en los clásicos incluso aún más profundamente, para que al menos pudiese mantener algún tipo de relación con aquel a quien deseo servir, Bahaudin el-Shah, el cual es visiblemente idéntico a los Grandes Sabios."

Bahaudin dijo:

"Seis lunas han pasado desde que estuviste aquí por última vez. No has estado ocioso: has estado trabajando en tu tienda y estudiando las vidas de los grandes Sufis. Sin embargo, podrías haberme estudiado a mí, a quien consideras identificable con los Sabedores del pasado, ya que he estado dos veces por semana en tu tienda. Durante estos seis meses, en los cuales 'no hemos estado en contacto', estuve cuarenta y ocho veces en tu tienda; y en la mayoría de dichas ocasiones hice algún tipo de transacción contigo, comprando o vendiendo mercadería. Debido a los bienes o a un simple cambio de vestuario y apariencia, no me reconociste. ¿Es esto 'percibir el aroma de la verdad'?"

El mercader permaneció en silencio.

Bahaudin continuó:

"Cuando te acercas al hombre a quien otros llaman 'Bahaudin', puedes sentir que él es la verdad. Cuando te encuentras con el hombre que se autodenomina mercader Khaja Alavi (uno de los pseudónimos de Bahaudin) no puedes percibir el aroma de la verdad en aquello que está vinculado con Alavi. Obviamente solo descubres en Naqshband lo que otros predican y no son. En Alavi no descubres lo que son los sabios porque no parecen serlo. La poesía y enseñanza a las cuales te has referido son una manifestación exterior; tú alimentas una manifestación exterior. Por favor, no llames a eso espiritualidad."

Este mercader era Mahsud Nadimzada, posteriormente un famoso santo, que se convirtió en discípulo de Bahaudin luego de haberse sometido al estudio bajo la guía del cocinero del Khanqa, quien ignoraba casi todo acerca de la poesía, de las charlas espirituales y de los ejercicios.

Una vez dijo:

"Si no hubiese estudiado lo que imaginaba que era un camino espiritual, no habría tenido que olvidar los numerosos errores y superficialidades que el Khalifa-Ashpaz (el cocinero) evaporó fuera de mí al ignorar mis pretensiones."

¿Por qué lo mojado
no está seco?

ANTES DE SER ampliamente conocido por la gente, Khidr viajó durante miles de años por la tierra buscando a quienes pudiera enseñar.

Cuando encontraba estudiantes apropiados, les brindaba verdades y artes útiles. Pero en cuanto introducía una nueva enseñanza, se la apropiaban para hacer un mal uso de ella.

La gente solo se preocupaba de la aplicación de la capacidad y de las leyes, y no acerca de comprender en profundidad, por lo que el conocimiento no pudo desarrollarse como un todo.

Entonces un día Khidr decidió aplicar un método diferente de aprendizaje: transformó a muchas cosas en sus opuestos. Por ejemplo, hizo que lo que solía estar mojado estuviese seco y lo seco, mojado.

Pronto la gente se acostumbró a esto, y simplemente se amoldaban a considerar lo mojado como seco y lo seco como mojado.

Habiendo invertido un gran número de cosas, Khidr regresará un día para mostrar nuevamente cuál es cuál.

Hasta que lo haga, solo unos pocos serán capaces de beneficiarse del trabajo de Khidr. Los que no podrán son aquellos a quienes les gusta decir: "Yo ya sabía eso", cuando de hecho no lo sabían.

Libros

Si DISTRIBUYO UN libro vacío, lo cual significa: "Aún no puedes beneficiarte con mi libro", acaso pensarás: "Me está insultando."

Pero si ofrezco un libro completo e inteligible, todos los lectores se estimularán con sus superficialidades, exclamando "cuán magnífico, cuán profundo". La gente seguirá estas cuestiones externas una vez que me haya ido, haciéndolas una fuente de estímulo y debate; a partir de ellas inferirán cuestiones didácticas o poesía o ejercicios o historias.

Si no doy libros, o doy uno pequeño, los eruditos se burlarán y arruinarán las mentes de los potenciales y vulnerables estudiantes con literatura alternativa, aún más de lo que ya lo hacen actualmente.

Los estudiantes desconcertados se vuelven destructivos, imaginando soluciones y luego tratando de imponérselas a los demás.

Si doy un libro voluminoso, algunos imaginarán que es pretencioso. Notarás que todas estas suposiciones están allí porque a la gente le conviene tenerlas, no porque exista la mínima posibilidad de que sean verdad.

Si ofrezco un libro críptico, las personas imaginarán que contiene secretos extraños; o puede que se vuelvan innecesariamente ingeniosas por tratar de entenderlo.

Y cuanto más dices estas cosas, más la gente dice petulante o desdeñosamente: "No nos entiendes. No nos comportamos así. La falta de comprensión es tuya."

Pero si yo digo todas estas cosas y tomas nota de todo aunque sea por un rato, prestándole la misma atención a cada afirmación, estaré contento.

(Bahaudin)

Cuando una persona se encuentra a sí misma

UNA DE LAS dificultades más grandes del hombre es también su mayor desventaja. Podría ser corregida si alguien se tomase el trabajo de señalarla con frecuencia y convincentemente.

La dificultad es que el humano se está describiendo a sí mismo cuando cree que está describiendo a otros.

¿Cuán a menudo escuchas a la gente decir sobre mí:

"Considero a este hombre como el Qutub (Polo magnético) de la Era"?

Naturalmente, quiere decir: "*Yo* considero a este hombre..."

Está describiendo sus propios sentimientos o convicciones, cuando en realidad lo que querríamos saber es algo acerca de la persona o cosa que está siendo descripta.

Cuando dice: "Esta enseñanza es sublime", quiere decir: "Esto parece que me conviene." Pero acaso habríamos querido saber algo acerca de la enseñanza, no de cómo cree que lo influencia.

Algunos dicen: "Pero una cosa puede ser verdaderamente conocida mediante su efecto. ¿Por qué no observar el efecto sobre una persona?"

La mayoría de la gente no entiende que, por ejemplo, el efecto de la luz del sol en los árboles es algo constante. Para conocer la naturaleza de la enseñanza deberíamos tener que conocer la naturaleza de aquel sobre la cual ha actuado; la persona ordinaria no puede saber esto; todo lo que puede saber es lo que esa persona supone que es un efecto sobre sí misma... y no tiene una imagen coherente de lo que "ella misma" es. Dado que el observador externo sabe incluso menos que la persona que se describe a sí misma, nos quedamos con una evidencia bastante inútil. No tenemos testigos confiables.

Recuerda que, mientras esta situación persista, generalmente habrá un igual número de personas diciendo: "Esto es maravilloso", que las que dicen: "Esto es ridículo." "Esto es ridículo" verdaderamente significa: "Esto me parece ridículo", y "esto es maravilloso" significa: "Esto me parece maravilloso."

¿En serio disfrutas de ser así?

Mucha gente lo hace, mientras que enérgicamente simulan lo contrario.

¿Te gustaría ser capaz de evaluar qué es realmente ridículo o maravilloso o algo entre dichos extremos?

Puedes hacerlo, pero no cuando supones que lo puedes hacer sin práctica alguna, sin entrenamiento, en medio de cierta confusión en lo referido a qué es lo que eres y por qué te gusta o disgusta algo.

Cuando te hayas encontrado a ti mismo podrás tener conocimiento; hasta entonces solamente podrás tener opiniones. Las opiniones se basan en el hábito y en lo que imaginas que es conveniente para ti.

El estudio de la Vía requiere el autoencuentro a lo largo del camino; aún no te has encontrado. La única ventaja de encontrar a otros en el interín es que acaso uno de ellos te presente a ti mismo.

Antes de que eso ocurra, posiblemente imaginarás que te has encontrado contigo varias veces; pero la verdad es que cuando te encuentras contigo mismo, ingresas a una dotación y legado de conocimiento permanentes que no tiene parangón sobre la tierra.

(Tariqavi)

El Sufi y el cuento de Halaku

Un maestro Sufi fue visitado por varias personas de diversos credos que le dijeron:

"Acéptanos como discípulos, pues vemos que no queda ninguna verdad en nuestras religiones y estamos seguros de que lo que tú enseñas es el único camino verdadero."

El Sufi dijo:

"¿No han oído hablar del mongol Halaku Khan y su invasión de Siria? Permítanme que les cuente. El visir Ahmad del califa Mustasim de Bagdad invitó al mongol a invadir los dominios de su señor. Cuando Halaku hubo ganado la batalla por Bagdad, Ahmad salió a su encuentro para ser recompensado. Halaku le preguntó: '¿Buscas tu recompensa?', y el visir respondió: 'Sí.'

"Halaku le dijo: 'Has traicionado a tu propio señor conmigo y sin embargo esperas que yo crea que me serás fiel.' Tras decir esto, ordenó que Ahmad fuese colgado.

"Antes de pedir a alguien que los acepte, pregúntense si es porque simplemente no han seguido el camino de su propio maestro. Si están satisfechos con la respuesta, entonces vengan y pidan ser aceptados como discípulos."

Peces en la luna

Una vez le preguntaron al Sheikh Bahaudin Naqshband:

"¿Por qué siempre dices que nadie puede aprender Sufismo solo y que cualquiera que crea estar más avanzado que otro en el Camino es insignificante?"

Contestó:

"Porque mi experiencia diaria me muestra que aquellos que creen poder aprender Sufismo solos, de hecho no pueden; son muy egocéntricos. Aquellos que creen no poder aprenderlo solos, de hecho pueden hacerlo. Pero, debido a la vanidad, es solamente un maestro verdadero quien puede autorizarlos a continuar solos, dado que es capaz de diagnosticar su verdadera condición.

"Quienquiera que crea tener más conocimiento que otro es casi completamente ignorante y no es capaz de aprender más. Da vueltas y vueltas en los 'intestinos del diablo' de su propia ignorancia. Esto es porque la experiencia del conocimiento verdadero no es en absoluto similar a creer que uno está más avanzado que otro.

"Notarás que nunca acepto como discípulo a alguien a quien he criticado por ser terco. Esto se debe a que ciertamente sentiría, más allá de lo que imagine, que mi crítica hacia él estaba motivada por un deseo de enseñarle; por lo tanto, siempre despido a quienes critico. Pero hay esperanza de que acaso encuentren en algún lugar a un maestro que no los halague... aunque es tan probable como que haya peces en la luna."

Kilidi y las piezas de oro

EL MAESTRO SUFI Kilidi descubrió que varios de sus discípulos pasaban mucho tiempo difundiendo historias de sus increíbles virtudes y su extraordinario poder de anticiparse a los pensamientos y a las necesidades de instrucción de sus discípulos.

Los reprochaba una y otra vez, pero la tendencia humana a jactarse de alguien a quien se sirve o admira era demasiado fuerte para ellos. Un día les advirtió: "A menos que dejen esta práctica, la cual no solo me mantiene rodeado de turistas sino que me impide impartirles más conocimiento significativo, tendré que aplicar un castigo ejemplar y ello hará que me tengan aversión. Los transformaría en el hazmerreír por haberme seguido."

Dado que esta advertencia no tuvo el efecto deseado, poco después Kilidi le dio a un mendigo que pasaba por allí cien piezas de oro en presencia de varios discípulos y miembros del público.

Al rato el mendigo regresó con el oro, diciendo: "Este oro no me ha servido para nada. Ahora mi esposa dice que ella debería tener la mitad o que al menos debería recibir de ti la misma cantidad, ya que es tan pobre como yo."

Kilidi agarró el oro y se lo pasó a un hombre rico que estaba allí, diciendo:

"Los ricos no se quejan de su dinero."

Dijo al mendigo:

"Ahora que has vuelto a tu estado anterior, retoma la relación naturalmente armoniosa con tu esposa."

Volviéndose a sus discípulos, dijo:

"¿Ven? Kilidi comete errores y el mundo también lo ha visto."

Trigo y cebada

UN DISTINGUIDO ERUDITO que estaba visitando a Bahaudin Naqshband preguntó:

"Mediante tu carácter, ejercicios y capacidad manifiesta para el bien, eres reconocido públicamente – al igual que en el corazón de tus discípulos – como el actual Maestro de la Era. ¿Fue siempre así para ti?"

Bahaudin dijo:

"No, no siempre fue así."

El visitante replicó:

"Los Sufis más antiguos eran considerados frecuentemente como imitadores, ridiculizados por los eruditos, temidos por los intérpretes. Algunos de aquellos a quienes los Adeptos consideraban como sus ejemplares más nobles están registrados en los libros de los formalmente instruidos como indeseables o como influencias que no han de ser bien recibidas por las autoridades; mas si han contribuido al conocimiento y a la práctica de la Vía, ¿seguramente eran notorios Adeptos?"

Bahaudin dijo:

"Algunos son claramente adeptos, otros son claramente nada."

"Entonces, ¿dónde yace la cualidad esencial del derviche?"

"Yace en su realidad, no en su apariencia."

"¿Acaso tales personas no tienen cualidades mediante las cuales cualquiera puede evaluarlas?"

Bahaudin contestó:

"Recuerda el cuento del trigo y la cebada. Hace mucho tiempo alguien plantó trigo en un campo. Todo el mundo se acostumbró a ver crecer el trigo y a vivir del pan hecho con su harina. Pero pasó el tiempo y fue necesario plantar cebada. Cuando esta surgió, mucha gente – literalistas, tal como suelen ser los eruditos ordinarios – exclamó: "¡Esto no es trigo!"

"'Es cierto', dijeron los cultivadores de cebada, 'pero es un cereal, y lo que todos necesitamos son cereales.'

"'Charlatán', exclamaron los literalistas. Muchas veces, cuando se cosechaba la cebada, el clamor para expulsar a los cultivadores era tan fuerte y eficaz que estos eran incapaces de proveerle harina a la gente. La gente se moría de hambre pero creían, persuadidos por sus consejeros de mentalidad literal, que hacían bien en rechazar la cosecha de los cultivadores de cebada."

El visitante preguntó:

"Entonces lo que denominamos 'Sufismo', ¿es realmente el cereal de tu historia? En ese caso, ¿hemos estado llamando 'cereales' al 'trigo' o a la 'cebada', y tenemos que darnos cuenta de que hay algo más profundo de lo cual ambos cultivos son una manifestación?"

"Sí", dijo el Maulana.

"Seguramente sería más deseable si se nos pudiese dar conocimiento de 'cereales' en vez de 'harina' o 'cebada' bajo el nombre de 'cereales', dijo el inquiridor.

"Seguramente sería mejor si pudiese ser hecho", dijo Bahaudin, "pero el caso es que la mayoría de la gente, por su propio bien y el de los demás, aún tiene que trabajar por la cosecha para poder comer. Hay muy pocos que saben qué son los cereales: son aquellos a quienes llamas Guías. Cuando un hombre sabe que acaso la gente muera de hambre, tiene que suministrar el alimento que puede. Solo aquellos que no están trabajando en los campos tienen tiempo para preguntarse acerca del grano; son ellos, también, quienes no tienen derecho a hacerlo, pues no lo han probado ni están trabajando en pos de la producción de harina para la gente."

"Es malo decirles a las personas que hagan cosas cuando no pueden comprender por qué deberían hacerlas", dijo el visitante.

"Peor es explicar que cierto árbol va a caer, con tal detalle, que antes de que hayas terminado de relatarlo tu público habrá muerto aplastado por él", contestó Bahaudin.

El frasco de vino

EN LAS ASAMBLEAS de los sabios se cuenta que había una vez un hombre que deseaba atender a un amigo con la mayor hospitalidad de la que era capaz.

Luego de la cena y de una larga sobremesa con su amigo, el anfitrión dijo:

"Quizá deberíamos beber un poco de vino para sacudir la insulsez de nuestro pensamiento y para estimular la nitidez de nuestros sentimientos."

Su invitado estuvo de acuerdo. Resulta que el anfitrión tenía solamente un frasco de vino en su casa, y se lo dijo a su invitado; pero cuando mandó a su hijo – quien sufría la enfermedad de visión doble – a buscar el vino, regresó y dijo:

"Padre, hay dos botellas; ¿cuál de ellas quieres que traiga?"

Avergonzado de que el invitado pudiese pensar que no le estaba dando todo lo que podía, el padre contestó:

"Rompe una botella y tráenos la otra."

El joven, por supuesto, lanzó una piedra sobre la única botella y como resultado imaginó que había roto ambas sin querer… por lo tanto aquella noche no hubo vino ni para el anfitrión ni para el invitado.

El invitado creyó que el joven era un tonto, cuando de hecho solamente sufría de una discapacidad. El orgullo del anfitrión de su propia hospitalidad fue la causa de la destrucción de la botella. El muchacho estaba apenado porque había hecho algo mal.

Todo esto fue porque el anfitrión temía que, de haberle dicho desde el principio a su invitado que su hijo sufría de visión doble, aquel habría imaginado que era solo un pretexto para no agotar todo el vino.

Bahaudin Naqshband dijo

Estábamos parados sobre una pequeña meseta en las altas montañas de Kohistán.

Mi maestro dijo:

"Mira cómo algunas de esas coníferas son pequeñas y otras son grandes; algunas están bien arraigadas y otras se han torcido; otras, sin razón evidente, tienen varias ramas dañadas."

Pregunté:

"¿Qué podemos inferir de esto?"

Respondió:

"Las altas están llenas de aspiración."

"¿Tienen todas éxito?"

"De ninguna manera."

"¿Y las dañadas?"

"Son aquellas que intentaron justificarse a sí mismas."

"¿Son las pequeñas mejores que las altas?"

"Puede que algo sea pequeño por herencia, debido a falta de oportunidad o a la ausencia de nutrición o al deseo."

"¿Y las profundamente arraigadas?"

"Todo depende de su naturaleza y de la selectividad de sus raíces para obtener verdadera nutrición. Algunas de las bien enraizadas lo están debido a una innecesaria codicia de consumir. A veces son estas las que hachan los leñadores y las utilizan para madera..."

La esponja de problemas

SE CUENTA QUE durante muchos siglos la tumba de Boland-Ashyan curaba enfermedades, concedía deseos, beneficiaba a todos los que la visitaban; era conocida como "La esponja de problemas".

El santuario estaba situado cerca del pequeño pueblo de Murghzar, en Irán, y aquí Faisal Nadim trabajó como cocinero en el Ashkhana (restaurante) por veintitantos años.

Faisal nunca iba al santuario; pero los viajeros que entraban a su cocina y pasaban tiempo con él mientras trabajaba produjeron la línea de iluminados Sufis denominados los Nadimis, mientras que los visitantes de la tumba nunca fueron reconocidos como sabios excepto entre los ignorantes.

Alguien le preguntó al sabio Khorram Ali por qué los piadosos peregrinos no eran transformados por su visita a un lugar de tales milagros... y por qué los frecuentadores de una cocina se convertían en santos Sufis.

Khorram contestó:

"Una esponja absorbe agua que no es necesaria pero que acaso impida, según las circunstancias, un trabajo útil. Es muy insensible, más allá de los méritos que le atribuyas. Un cocinero conoce la medida de los ingredientes y cómo hacerlos digeribles. Puede que un cocinero necesite una esponja para eliminar lo que se interponga en su camino, como por ejemplo agua sucia. Solamente el estúpido, mirando únicamente la esponja, imaginaría que está trabajando por iniciativa propia.

El pez de cristal

UN JOVEN, HABIÉNDOLE hecho un favor a cierto barquero, recibió como agradecimiento un pececito de cristal.

Lo perdió; y en su desesperación por haber perdido semejante objeto raro y hermoso se indignó cuando vio a otro hombre de cuyo cuello pendía un cordón del cual colgaba un pez de cristal.

El joven lo llevó a los tribunales y logró que lo condenaran por robo. A último momento, cuando le preguntaron si tenía algo para decir antes de ser conducido a la prisión, el hombre dijo:

"Pregúntenle a cualquier barquero de este país: todos tenemos el mismo emblema, y este es el mío. No le pertenece a aquel joven. También tengo dos ojos y una boca, ¡pero tampoco son suyos!"

"¿Por qué no hablaste antes?" preguntó el magistrado al barquero.

"Porque hay más mérito para la humanidad si se llega a la verdad cuando desde el principio todos los involucrados ejercitan la consciencia, que si uno tiene que probar algo que, después de todo, quizá sea imposible de probar."

"Sin embargo, todos debemos aprender", remarcó el juez.

"¡Ay!" dijo el barquero, "si se considera que el aprender depende de la producción de pruebas, solo tenemos la mitad del conocimiento y seguramente estamos perdidos."

Los Kishtiwanis, a cuya escuela pertenecía este barquero, se destacaban por su hábito de enfatizar que la gente pasa la mayor parte de su tiempo sacando conclusiones apresuradas o no prestándole ninguna atención a los hechos.

El portador del sello

Muy poco después de la muerte de Maulana Bahaudin Naqshband, un harapiento se acercó a su tumba y exigió:

"Condúzcanme hasta el califa (diputado)." El califa no estaba allí.

Agregó: "Permitan que Bibi Jan, la viuda del Maulana, me identifique."

Todos estaban perplejos ante el forastero y los seguidores que quedaban del Maulana no sabían qué decir o hacer.

El errante dijo:

"¡No hay califa, no hay comprensión! Entonces les voy a mostrar algo que incluso un hombre-asno debería saber."

Produjo el sello de Bahaudin Naqshband.

Ahora este hombre fue tratado con honores, pero pidió que lo condujesen al muro que estaba frente a la colina de Tillaju; derrumbó parte de aquel muro y les dijo a los presentes que excavasen sus cimientos.

Entonces quitó ciertos objetos que estaban enterrados allí y dijo:

"Estos son para mí. Habrían sido para los discípulos si hubiesen sido Adeptos."

Alguien preguntó:

"¿Por qué los discípulos no los recibieron?"

Dijo:

"El-Shah les dijo que excavasen los cimientos del muro, pero en cambio construyeron el muro allí arriba. Así que en algún momento el muro habría caído y los invaluables objetos se hubiesen perdido. La holgazanería de los murids (discípulos) para los trabajos manuales, y su superioridad en la imaginación, ha provocado su anulación en el reino espiritual."

Un murid preguntó:

"¿Podremos saber de aquellos que no son como nosotros, pues ansiamos conocimiento?"

El misterioso derviche dijo:

"Aquellos que podrían saber, ya saben; para aquellos que quedan, es demasiado tarde para saber. Por ende se sienten satisfechos por haber estado cerca de el-Shah. Pero sería mejor si se dispersaran. De lo contrario, simplemente repetirán los nombres y las fórmulas de el-Shah y la gente se extraviará al imaginar que esto es Sufismo."

Alguien comentó:

"¿Cuál de los Iluminados eres, qué Wali, qué Abdal? ¿No te quedarás con nosotros?"

Contestó:

"Soy el sirviente de menor rango de los Maestros, los Khwajagan. Un sirviente solamente puede quedarse donde es capaz de cumplir las órdenes de su maestro. No puedo llevar a cabo el servicio de la humildad en compañía de la arrogancia."

Alguien preguntó:

"¿Cómo podemos reducir nuestra arrogancia?"

Dijo:

"Pueden reducirla dándose cuenta de que no son dignos de ser representantes de las enseñanzas de el-Shah; los indignos están doblemente incapacitados. Se autoengañan al imaginar que están estudiando el Camino. Descaminan a otros cuando pretenden enseñarles, incluso mediante insinuación.

"Esto no es estudio. Esto no es enseñanza. Donde no hay un representante, la imitación de su posición equivale a una usurpación; la usurpación destruye el alma."

Lleno

UN ASTRÓNOMO QUE era vano y estaba lleno de
conocimientos partió de viaje y visitó a Kushyar
el Sabio, maestro de Avicena.

Pero Kushyar no tenía nada que hacer con él y
se negó a enseñarle de todos los modos posibles.

El astrónomo se estaba despidiendo con tristeza,
cuando Kushyar dijo:

"El creerte que sabes tanto produce el efecto de
hacerte igual a un recipiente completamente lleno
de agua. Por ello, como la vasija, eres incapaz de
admitir nada más.

"Pero la completitud es la repleción de la
vanidad, y el hecho es que estás realmente vacío,
más allá de cómo te sientas."

Voz en la noche

ANOCHE UNA VOZ me susurró:
 "¡No existe tal cosa como una voz susurrando en la noche!"

(Haidar Ansari)

Percepción

Está registrado que alguien le dijo a Saadi, el gran filósofo:

"Deseo la percepción, para así volverme sabio."

Saadi dijo:

"La percepción sin sabiduría es peor que nada en absoluto."

Se le preguntó: "¿Cómo puede ser eso?"

Saadi contestó: "Como en el caso del buitre y el milano. El buitre le dijo al milano: 'Tengo una vista mucho mejor que la tuya, ya que puedo ver un grano de trigo allí abajo en el suelo mientras que tú no ves absolutamente nada.'

"Las dos aves se lanzaron en picada para encontrar ese trigo que el buitre podía ver, pero que el milano no. Cuando estuvieron muy cerca del suelo, el milano vio el grano; el buitre continuó con su descenso y se lo tragó. Y luego colapsó... pues el trigo estaba envenenado."

Sobras

Las sobras de la comida del emir son mayores
que los presentes de *halwa* (dulces) del mercader.
(Timur Fazil)

La mosca dorada

Había una vez un hombre llamado Salar, que distinguía entre lo correcto e incorrecto y que sabía lo que debía hacerse y lo que no, y que sabía mucho acerca del aprendizaje mediante libros. Sabía tanto, de hecho, que había sido nombrado como el asistente personal de Mufti Zafrani, un eminente jurisconsulto y juez.

Pero Salar no sabía todo; e incluso en lo referido a las cosas que sí sabía no siempre actuaba según su conocimiento.

Un día, cuando había dejado su vaso de jugo dulce, una pequeña y resplandeciente mosca dorada se posó en el borde y bebió un trago; al otro día sucedió lo mismo; y también al otro, hasta que la mosca creció en tamaño y Salar podía verla fácilmente. Pero la mosca había crecido tan despacio que Salar apenas la notaba.

Finalmente, después de varias semanas en las cuales Salar había estado inmerso en el estudio de un complejo problema legal, levantó la vista y se dio cuenta de que la mosca se veía mucho más grande de lo que debería; la espantó. De inmediato la mosca se elevó en el aire, trazó unos círculos sobre el vaso y se fue.

Pero volvió. Cuando Salar relajaba su ojo vigilante, la mosca volaba hacia el vaso para sentarse en su borde y beber tanto como podía. Con el correr de los días, la mosca se volvía cada vez más y más grande... y mientras más tomaba más diferente se veía.

Primero, Salar la espantó con la mano. Luego se dio cuenta de que tenía que agarrar un palo para pegarle. A veces le parecía que la mosca comenzaba a tener una especie de forma semihumana. Era, por supuesto, un Jinn y no una mosca en absoluto.

Finalmente, Salar le gritó a la mosca; y ella respondió diciendo: "No bebo mucho de tu vaso, y además soy hermosa, ¿no?"

Al principio Salar estaba asombrado, luego asustado y por último completamente confundido.

Comenzó a obtener cierto placer de las visitas de la mosca, a pesar de que bebía de su sorbete. La miraba danzar, pensaba mucho en ella, hacía cada vez menos trabajo; y mientras la mosca se volvía más grande descubrió que se sentía cada vez más y más débil.

Salar solía tener dificultades con el muftí; entonces recobró la compostura y decidió ultimar a la mosca. Invocando toda su resolución, le dio un violento golpe y ella se escapó volando mientras decía: "Me has hecho daño, pues yo solo quería ser tu amiga; pero me iré, si eso es lo que quieres."

Al principio Salar sintió que se había deshecho de la mosca de una vez por todas. Se dijo a sí mismo: "La he derrotado y ello prueba que soy más poderoso que ella, sea o no un humano, un Jinn o una mosca."

Entonces, cuando ya Salar se había convencido a sí mismo de que todo el asunto estaba cerrado, la mosca apareció otra vez; había crecido hasta ser enorme y descendió del techo como un lago resplandeciente con forma de hombre.

Dos enormes manos extendidas agarraron a Salar por el cuello.

Cuando el muftí vino a buscar a su asistente, yacía estrangulado en el suelo. Una de las paredes de la casa había colapsado al paso del Jinn; y todo lo que había allí como testimonio de su enormidad era la huella de su mano en la cal, tan grande como el contorno de un elefante.

Promesa de taberna

Puede que se *diga*: "Vinieron en vano."
No *dejen* que hayan venido en vano.
Dejamos esto, el legado, a ustedes:
Terminamos lo que pudimos, les dejamos el resto a ustedes.
Recuerden: este es el trabajo encomendado;
Recuerden, bienamados, que nos volveremos a encontrar.

Canción derviche

El cuchillo

UN DERVICHE ERRANTE corrió hacia donde un Sufi estaba sentado en profunda contemplación y dijo:

"¡Rápido! Debemos hacer algo. Un mono acaba de agarrar un cuchillo."

"No te preocupes", respondió el Sufi, "siempre y cuando no haya sido un *hombre*."

Cuando el derviche volvió a ver al mono descubrió que, tal como era de esperar, ya había tirado el cuchillo.

(Kardan)

Caravasar

Había una vez un hombre llamado Muin, que en su juventud fue estafado y traicionado por otro hombre, de nombre Halim, el cual era un individuo inusualmente codicioso.

Muin se dijo a sí mismo: "Un día estaré en condiciones de hacérselas pagar. Me volveré rico y su envidia lo arruinará, ¡especialmente si le niego dinero!"

Pero los años pasaron y Muin no se hizo rico. Todo lo que había ahorrado durante su vida habría mantenido a un hombre acaudalado apenas durante un mes. Cuando tenía cuarenta años de edad cayó enfermo y los médicos dijeron que le quedaban solamente unas pocas semanas de vida.

Resulta que Muin tenía un preceptor Sufi – Daud, hijo de Zakaria – y le preguntó qué podía hacer.

"El despertar envidia no forma parte del trabajo de un Sufi", dijo Daud, "pues la envidia es una podredumbre fatal que mata al hombre que la alimenta y solamente puede ser extirpada con enorme dificultad. El único método, de hecho, es que el afectado practique generosidad extrema y verdadera; algo que raramente está dispuesto a hacer. Puedo decirte esto, y el resto depende de ti: los envidiosos se corroen a sí mismos por lo que creen que es verdad, no por la verdad real."

Muin reflexionó profundamente sobre estas palabras. Luego mandó a llamar a su hijo, Aram, y le dijo: "Tengo muy poco que dejarte, pero creo que puedo cancelar una deuda y hacer provisiones para tu futuro por medio de una inversión acertada, si la hago ahora; entonces obedéceme en cada detalle. Me queda poca vida."

Aram, siguiendo sus instrucciones al pie de la letra, tomó todos los ahorros del padre y compró espléndidas túnicas, algunas joyas, dos hermosas casas y mucho más. Luego padre e hijo fueron al caravasar más caro, cerca del hogar del villano, y lo mandaron a llamar. Muin, debilitado por el esfuerzo, estaba acostado en la cama. Cuando vio a Halim, dijo:

"Probablemente estoy en mi lecho de muerte, y tú eres la única persona que conozco en esta localidad. Tengo un hijo, como ves, y a él le impartiré el secreto de un Sufi que produjo todas las cosas que ves aquí, las cuales son mis posesiones. Cuida de este niño, Aram, y en el momento correctamente propicio él te dirá el secreto que le he confiado."

Muin murió poco después. Entonces Halim, que era muy rico, le prodigó regalos al joven e hizo todo lo posible para convencerlo de su amabilidad, codicioso del secreto del Sufi. Permanecía siempre atento en caso de que sucediese el momento oportuno para la transmisión del secreto.

Pero Muin le había dicho a Aram: "Revélale a Halim las palabras del Sufi si ha sido lo suficientemente generoso contigo, y si alguna vez descubres que ya no es codicioso."

Entonces Aram observó a Halim durante muchos años. Halim ofrecía dinero, pero de alguna manera nunca daba tanto como prometía.

Aram tomaba lo que se le daba e incluso pedía más, tanto directamente como por medio de intermediarios, para descubrir si había cierta renuencia de parte de Halim... y encontró mucha.

Este proceso continuó por muchos años. Halim sufría ataques de euforia y depresión, y comenzó a interesarse en toda clase de diversiones, como los chismes, para aliviar las tensiones de su vida.

Entonces, un día, estaba leyendo un libro Sufi que decía: "El prometer y no cumplir impide la transmisión de secretos Sufis." De repente recordó que no había cumplido todas las promesas a Aram. Ese mismo día le ofreció al joven el total de la enorme suma que originalmente había dicho que le daría.

Aram dijo: "No soy quién para juzgar por qué hiciste esto; pero dado que acaso sea por la razón correcta, ahora te diré el secreto del Sufi." Le contó a Halim lo que había ocurrido entre el Sufi y Muin.

Entonces Halim, superada la codicia mediante su admiración por la sabiduría del Sufi, dijo: "Aram, no tengo lugar en mi corazón para estar arrepentido por el dinero que ha sido gastado. Haz solamente una cosa para mí: dime cómo encontrar a este Sufi, para que pueda besarle los pies."

Esta es la historia contada por Halim, el gran sabio Sufi, que con el tiempo sucedió al Sheikh Daud, hijo de Zakaria.

Fantasías

¡AY HOMBRE! SI tan solo supieras cuántas de las
falsas fantasías de la imaginación estaban más
cerca de la Verdad que las cuidadosas conclusiones
de los prudentes. Y cómo estas verdades no
tienen ninguna utilidad hasta que el imaginador,
habiendo hecho su trabajo con la imaginación, se
ha vuelto menos imaginativo.

(Shab-Parak)

Irrelevancia

UNO DE LOS sabios Sufis designó a un representante para transmitir sus instrucciones a los discípulos. Sin embargo, en poco tiempo los discípulos se encargaron de considerar al representante no como un canal sino como un hombre de santidad y autoridad. Él, en cambio, empezó a imaginar que todo lo que decía era significativo. Enseguida, dudando de algunos resultados de las acciones del representante, varios de los discípulos se preguntaban unos a otros: "¿Está este hombre actuando según su mandato?" Algunos consideraban a tales pensamientos como traición, y se cegaron ante todos los abusos.

El sabio escuchó los cuestionamientos y contestó: "La vanidad se ha apoderado de este representante, pero ha sido alimentada por vuestro propio deseo de venerar a alguien."

Los discípulos estaban abatidos y preguntaron: "Si esto puede sucederle a un delegado, ¿qué es lo que no podría sucedernos a nosotros?"

El sabio les dijo: "No podría haber sucedido si ambas partes no fuesen culpables. Si hubiesen estado obedeciendo mis órdenes, en vez de crear su propio maestro imitativo – no satisfechos con las instrucciones y por ende buscando ídolos –, esto no habría sucedido. Pero, por otro lado, donde aquellas tendencias están presentes, no solamente sucede sino que debe suceder. En vez de preguntarse qué es lo que ha acaecido, deberían observar cuán incapaces son para distinguir lo falso de lo verdadero; aunque no sean lo suficientemente humildes para no suponer que lo falso es lo verdadero.

"Esa es vuestra lección."

Dijeron: "¿Qué será de él?"

Contestó: "Eso no les concierne. Es el preocuparse por lo irrelevante lo que ha obstaculizado vuestro desarrollo: y aún lo siguen haciendo. Lejos de estar más avanzados que la gente ordinaria, ahora están bien atrás de ellos. ¿Quieren alcanzarlos?"

Fidelidad

NAJMAINI ("EL HOMBRE de las dos estrellas") echó a un discípulo con las palabras: "Tu fidelidad ha sido puesta a prueba. Me parece tan inconmovible que debes irte."

El discípulo dijo: "Me iré, pero no puedo comprender cómo la fidelidad puede ser causa de despido."

Najmaini dijo: "Durante tres años hemos puesto a prueba tu fidelidad. Tu fidelidad para con el conocimiento inútil y los juicios superficiales es total. Es por ello que debes irte."

El santuario de Juan el Bautista

SAADI, EL AUTOR Sufi del clásico persa *El jardín de rosas*, escribe acerca de una visita a la tumba de Juan el Bautista en Siria.

Un día llegó allí, exhausto y con los pies doloridos. Pero entonces, mientras se compadecía de sí mismo, vio a un hombre que no solamente estaba cansado sino que no tenía pies. Saadi le agradeció a Dios pues, al menos, tenía pies.

Esta historia, en el nivel obvio, significa "sé agradecido por las pequeñas cosas". A esta enseñanza se la puede encontrar en todas las culturas. Es útil ayudar a alguien a encontrar una perspectiva más amplia de su situación si está sufriendo de una autocompasión incapacitante.

El empleo de tales cuentos con propósitos emocionales – el cambiar la actitud mental, incluso el hacer que una persona esté contenta y acaso momentáneamente agradecida con su suerte – es característico de este tipo de instrucción convencional.

Los sofisticados modernos dicen: "Todo lo que hizo Saadi fue inculcar las llamadas virtudes morales… su trabajo pasó de moda." Acaso los burdos y tradicionales sentimentalistas digan: "Qué bello es detenerse en la miseria de los demás y en la propia buena suerte."

Pero Saadi, siendo un Sufi, incluyó en sus escritos materiales que tenían más de una función posible. Este cuento es uno de ellos.

En las escuelas Sufis a la pieza se la toma por lo que es: un ejercicio. Puede que el discípulo se beneficie de cualquier moraleja "edificante" ofrecida por la interpretación convencional; mas, sin introspección pero con autobservación, debería ser capaz de decir: "Me doy cuenta de que mis cambios de humor dependen de estímulos emocionales. ¿*Tengo* que depender siempre de 'ver a un hombre sin pies', o leer acerca de ello, antes de percatarme de que 'tengo pies'? ¿Cuánto se desperdicia de mi vida mientras espero que alguien me diga qué hacer o que algo suceda para que cambie mi condición y actitud?"

Según los Sufis, el ser humano tiene mejores – más confiables – sentidos internos y capacidades para educarlos que los constantes estímulos emocionales.

El objetivo de la interpretación Sufi de esta lección sería anulado si ocasionara que las personas empezasen una orgía de autocuestionamiento de un tipo emocional.

El propósito de señalar este uso Sufi de la narrativa es que sea registrado en la mente de modo que, en el futuro, el estudiante pueda notar una forma superior de evaluar su situación, cuando aquella comienza a operar en él.

El significado

UN HOMBRE QUE había pasado muchos años intentando descifrar significados fue a ver a un Sufi y le contó acerca de su búsqueda.

El Sufi dijo:

"Vete y reflexiona sobre esto: IHMN."

El hombre se fue. Cuando regresó, el Sufi estaba muerto. "¡Ahora nunca sabré la verdad!" gimió el descifrador.

En ese momento apareció el discípulo principal del Sufi; dijo:

"Si estás preocupado por el significado secreto de IHMN, te lo diré. Son las iniciales de la frase persa '*In huruf maani nadarand*'... 'Estas letras no tienen significado.'"

"Pero, ¿por qué se me ha dado semejante tarea?" exclamó el descifrador.

"Porque cuando se te acerca un asno, le das repollos; ese es su alimento, no importa cómo lo llame. Los asnos seguramente piensen que están haciendo algo mucho más significativo que comer repollos."

El método

Cierto maestro Sufi estaba explicando cómo había sido desenmascarado un falso Sufi. "Un Sufi verdadero envió a uno de sus discípulos para que actuase como su sirviente. El discípulo se desvivía por el impostor, día y noche. De a poco todos comenzaron a ver cómo el fraude adoraba estas atenciones, y la gente lo abandonó hasta que se quedó completamente solo."

Uno de los escuchadores de esta historia pensó para sí: "¡Qué idea maravillosa! Me marcharé y haré exactamente lo mismo."

Fue a donde se encontraba un falso hombre santo y deseó apasionadamente convertirse en su discípulo. Después de tres años, era tal su devoción que se habían congregado cientos de devotos. "Realmente este sabio debe de ser un gran hombre", se decían unos a otros, "para inspirar semejante lealtad y autosacrificio en su discípulo."

Entonces el hombre regresó al Sufi del cual había escuchado la historia y le explicó lo sucedido. "Tus cuentos no son confiables", dijo, "porque cuando intenté poner uno en práctica, sucedió lo contrario."

"Por desgracia", dijo el Sufi, "hay apenas un aspecto erróneo en tu intento de aplicar métodos Sufis: y es que no eres un Sufi."

Abu Tahir

MIR ABU TAHIR atrajo a muchos estudiantes mediante sus discursos iluminadores y haciendo circular epístolas que eran comentadas favorablemente por todos los mayores pensadores de aquel entonces.

Sin embargo, cuando la gente se reunía a escucharlo hablar en persona apenas lograban que repitiese una sola frase:

"El deseo por el mérito, no por el hombre."

Esta recomendación fue dada varias veces al día durante cinco años. Alguien visitó al sabio Ibriqi y le rogó que ayudase con algún tipo de explicación sobre la extraña conducta de Abu Tahir.

Ibriqi dijo:

"Te quejas porque el Mir dice algo de forma repetitiva pero no te quejas de que el sol sale y se pone cada día; sin embargo ambas cosas son lo mismo. Como el sol, el Mir está haciendo algo valioso. Si no haces uso de ello, él aún debe continuar 'brillando' en beneficio de aquellos que *pueden* sacar provecho; o para ti, en un momento en que *puedas* beneficiarte."

Contención

Un viajero derviche relata:

Visité a cierto sheikh que era como un imán para gente de todo tipo.

Dije:

"¿Cómo puedes soportar la compañía de personas tan horribles? Ni han mejorado por estar cerca de ti, ni jamás se sintieron atraídas hacia ti por tus virtudes; pues, según confiesan, solo buscan poderes que nadie más posee."

Nunca olvidaré lo que el sheikh respondió:

"Amigo, si todas las serpientes del mundo se dedicaran únicamente a matar, y ninguna fuese distraída por vanas esperanzas que impiden el ejercicio de su maldad, no quedaría un solo ser humano vivo."

Tamizando

¡OH PEDANTE! TAMIZA, toda tu vida, los escritos y dichos de los Sabios. Mas en primer lugar aprende una cosa: estás usando un tamiz que deja pasar la cascarilla y descarta el nutriente... el trigo.

(Shab-Parak)

El Maestro perfecto

Cierto hombre decidió que buscaría al Maestro Perfecto.

Leyó muchos libros, visitó a un sabio tras otro, escuchó, debatió y practicó, pero siempre se hallaba dudando o inseguro.

Luego de veinte años encontró a un hombre cuyas palabras y gestos condecían con su idea del hombre totalmente realizado.

El viajero no perdió el tiempo: "Tú", dijo, "me pareces el Maestro Perfecto. Si lo eres, mi búsqueda ha llegado a su fin."

"Efectivamente, se me describe con ese nombre", dijo el Maestro.

"Entonces, te ruego, acéptame como discípulo."

"Eso", dijo el Maestro, "no lo puedo hacer: pues mientras puede que desees el Maestro Perfecto, él, a su vez, solamente requiere el Discípulo Perfecto".

Dar y tomar

EL JEFE TOMA menos de lo que se le da
Y da más de lo que ha tomado.

(Kitab-i-Amu Daria)

La prueba del zorro

ÉRASE UNA VEZ un zorro que se topó con un joven conejo en el bosque. El conejo dijo: "¿Qué eres?" El zorro dijo: "Soy un zorro y podría devorarte si así lo quisiera."

"¿Cómo puedes demostrar que eres un zorro?" preguntó el conejo. El zorro no sabía qué decir, pues en el pasado los conejos siempre habían huido de él sin hacer semejantes preguntas.

Luego el conejo dijo: "Si puedes mostrarme una prueba escrita de que eres un zorro, te creeré."

Entonces el zorro fue trotando a ver al león, quien le dio un certificado de que él realmente era un zorro.

Cuando regresó al lugar donde el conejo estaba esperando, el zorro comenzó a leer el documento; le agradó tanto que saboreaba cada párrafo con un deleite continuo. Mientras tanto, habiendo captado la esencia del mensaje desde las primeras líneas, el conejo se escabulló dentro de una madriguera y nunca más se lo volvió a ver.

El zorro regresó al cubil del león, donde vio a un ciervo conversando con el león. El ciervo decía:

"Quiero ver una prueba escrita de que eres un león..."

El león dijo:

"Cuando no tengo hambre, nada me importa. Cuando *tengo* hambre, no necesitas nada por escrito."

El zorro le dijo al león: "¿Por qué no me dijiste que hiciera eso cuando te pedí el certificado para el conejo?"

"Mi querido amigo", contestó el león, "deberías haberme dicho que había sido pedido por un conejo. Creí que era para un humano estúpido, de quienes algunos de estos animales idiotas han aprendido este pasatiempo."

Oportunidad

LAS PALABRAS "TIENES una chance", de los labios
de la Autoridad, valen cien veces más que "Eres el
hombre más grande del mundo", del tonto.

(Nuri Falaki)

El préstamo

Un hombre les estaba diciendo a sus amigos en una casa de té:

"He prestado a alguien una moneda de plata y no tengo testigos. Ahora temo que esa persona negará haber recibido alguna vez algo de mí."

Los amigos se compadecieron, pero un Sufi que estaba sentado en una esquina levantó la cabeza de entre sus rodillas y dijo:

"Invítalo aquí y menciónale en una conversación, delante de estas personas, que le prestaste veinte monedas de oro."

"¡Pero yo sólo le presté una moneda de plata!"

"Eso" dijo el Sufi, "es exactamente lo que gritará... y todo el mundo lo oirá. Tú querías testigos, ¿verdad?"

Tejiendo luz

Le preguntaron a Firmani:

"¿Cómo sabías que fulano de tal era tan cruel? Te negaste a conversar en profundidad con él cuando estuvo aquí, a pesar de que todos decían que era un santo."

Firmani dijo:

"Si un forastero se acerca a hombres comunes y dice 'A la luz se la hace tejiendo. Yo tejí toda la luz que hay y que hubo', ¿de qué se dan cuenta?"

Contestaron:

"Se dan cuenta de que lo que dice es falso."

Firmani agregó:

"Del mismo modo, cuando un individuo cruel se presenta ante un hombre de conocimiento, no es difícil juzgar su condición, independientemente de lo que la gente imagine o diga."

Explicación

LA SUPOSICIÓN DE que cualquier persona de
valía puede explicarse con plenitud y lucidez en
el tiempo que le conceden aquellos que quieren
aprender lo que ella sabe, o bien es una broma o
una estupidez.

(Shab-Parak)

Día y noche

Un erudito dijo a un Sufi:

"Ustedes los Sufis suelen decir que nuestras preguntas lógicas son incomprensibles para ustedes. ¿Puedes darme un ejemplo de por qué les parecen así?

El Sufi dijo:

"He aquí tal ejemplo. Una vez yo estaba viajando en tren y atravesamos varios túneles. Frente a mí estaba sentado un campesino que obviamente nunca antes había viajado en tren.

"Después del séptimo túnel, el campesino me tocó y dijo:

"'Este tren es muy complicado. En mi burro puedo llegar a mi pueblo en apenas un día. Pero en tren, que parece estar viajando más rápido que un burro, todavía no hemos llegado a mi casa a pesar de que el sol ha salido y se ha puesto completamente siete veces'."

166

La fuente del ser

Permite que la Fuente del Ser mantenga el contacto contigo: ignora las impresiones y opiniones de tu yo habitual. Si este yo fuese de valor en tu búsqueda, habría encontrado la realización para ti. Pero todo lo que puede hacer es depender de otros.

(Amin Suhrawardi)

Manchada

SE CUENTA QUE un hombre fue a la asamblea del maestro Baqi-Billah de Delhi y dijo:

"He estado leyendo el famoso verso del Maestro Hafiz: 'Si tu maestro te ordena manchar tu alfombra de oración con vino, obedécele'; pero yo tengo una dificultad."

Baqi-Billah dijo:

"Mora lejos de mí por un tiempo y te ilustraré esta cuestión."

Tras un considerable período de tiempo, el discípulo recibió una carta del sabio. Decía: "Toma todo tu dinero y dáselo al portero de algún burdel."

El discípulo quedó sorprendido y, por un tiempo, pensó que el maestro debía de ser un impostor. Sin embargo, tras luchar consigo mismo durante varios días fue a la primera casa de mala fama y le ofreció al hombre que estaba en la puerta todo el dinero que tenía.

"Por esta cantidad de dinero", dijo el portero, "te concederé la más selecta gema de nuestra colección: una mujer intacta."

Apenas entró a la habitación, la mujer que estaba allí dijo:

"Se me ha engañado para estar en esta casa y me mantienen aquí por la fuerza y mediante amenazas. Si tu sentido de la justicia es más fuerte que tu razón para venir aquí, ayúdame a escapar."

Entonces el discípulo comprendió el significado del poema de Hafiz: "Si tu maestro te ordena manchar tu alfombra de oración con vino, obedécele."

Wahab Imri

Un hombre visitó a Wahab Imri y le dijo:

"Enséñame humildad."

Wahab contestó:

"No puedo hacerlo, porque la humildad es una maestra de sí misma. Se la aprende mediante su práctica. Si no la puedes practicar, no la puedes aprender. Si no la puedes aprender, realmente no quieres aprenderla internamente en absoluto."

El pillo y el derviche

Cierto derviche planteó una lección objetiva. Le pagó a un actor para que fuese a un pueblo y se estableciese como un maestro religioso. "Junta todos los discípulos que puedas", dijo, "simulando ser un hombre de gran santidad. Cuando llegue, te desenmascararé. La gente se dará cuenta de que han sido engañados y, una vez que les haya mostrado cuán superficiales son sus creencias, escucharán mis enseñanzas."

Unos meses después, el derviche entró al pueblo y enfiló hacia la casa del místico. Allí estaba el actor, rodeado de discípulos adoradores que lo colmaban de regalos y elogiaban cada una de sus palabras.

El derviche comenzó a hablar:

"¡Oh gente! Sepan que he venido a explicarles todo. Yo envié a este hombre para demostrar cómo las personas creerán cualquier cosa, si así lo quieren. Ahora, en cambio, les daré la verdadera enseñanza."

El actor no dijo nada en absoluto. La gente agarró al derviche y lo llevaron a un manicomio. Una noche, el actor se acercó a la ventana

abarrotada y le dijo: "Aunque tenía la apariencia
de un vagabundo, fui lo suficientemente avispado
para aceptar tu consejo. Aunque según tu opinión
eras sabio, fuiste lo suficientemente insensato para
creer en tus propios planes. Un plan corrupto
beneficiará solo al corrupto y uno sabio, solamente
al sabio."

Esperanza

HABÍA UNA VEZ un rey, descendiente de una antigua y poderosa estirpe, a quien la adversidad lo había expulsado de su posición y forzado a huir de sus enemigos.

El rey estaba empapado por la lluvia, en medio de un desolado páramo, cuando se topó con una pequeña choza utilizada por los pastores. Pensó en descansar un rato allí, y al entrar descubrió que ya había dos pastores envueltos con mantas para protegerse del frío.

Lo recibieron amablemente y compartieron con él su único alimento: un poco de queso y unas cebollas.

El rey dijo:

"Un día, cuando recupere el trono, ¡los recompensaré como es digno de un rey!"

Ahora bien, aunque ambos pastores le habían ofrecido comida al rey – demostrando que los dos eran igualmente generosos – no poseían las mismas cualidades en todos los sentidos.

El primer pastor, por lo tanto, le contaba a todo el mundo pavoneándose de que él era mejor que un noble, pues le había dado comida a un rey cuando nadie más podía hacerlo.

Pero el segundo pastor, reflexionando, se dijo a sí mismo:

"El hecho de que yo haya estado en la choza, y el haber tenido algo de comida conmigo, fueron meros accidentes. Mi ofrenda de alimento al rey fue una acción normal. Pero el rey, con una generosidad verdaderamente real, eligió interpretar estos hechos como resultado del mérito. Ahora me toca ser inspirado por este ejemplo y hacerme verdaderamente digno de semejante nobleza de espíritu."

Dos o tres años después, el rey recuperó su legítimo poder y mandó a buscar a los pastores. Ambos recibieron espléndidos regalos y también obtuvieron posiciones de poder en la corte.

Pero el primer pastor, no habiendo hecho ningún esfuerzo en mejorarse y prepararse a sí mismo, pronto cayó víctima de una intriga y fue ajusticiado por conspirar. Por otro lado, el segundo pastor trabajó tan bien que, cuando el rey alcanzó la vejez, fue nominado y aceptado como su sucesor.

Querer

SI QUIERES ESTAR con el Maestro cuando él quiere
que estés lejos de él, debes obedecerle o evitarlo.
Si discutes sobre ello, eres peor que desobediente.

(Halqavi)

El arquero

EL ARQUERO CAMPEÓN del pueblo de Salimia se quejaba de que no tenía contrincante de categoría.

"Estos, los habitantes de Salimia, no son arqueros... ¡y por ende no pueden juzgar mi excelencia!" repetía una y otra vez a todo aquel que estuviese dispuesto a escucharlo.

Convenció a todos de su infelicidad.

Un día, cierto maestro Sufi pasaba por el pueblo y se detuvo a beber un poco de té.

En el salón de té, la gente le contó del arquero desdichado.

"Acaso crea que está sufriendo", dijo el sabio, "pero, de hecho, el Altísimo ha sido más que amable con este hombre. Si hubiese sido puesto entre arqueros, habría sentido un miedo constante de ser superado.

"Si realmente hubiese necesitado adversarios de su nivel, nada le habría impedido encontrarlos.

"Hasta que el humano – y su público – pueda escuchar el mensaje tácito, y olvidar el pronunciado, permanecerá encadenado."

Mahmud y el derviche

Se relata que Mahmud de Ghazna estaba un día paseando en su jardín cuando tropezó con un derviche ciego que dormía junto a un arbusto.

Apenas se despertó, el derviche exclamó:

"Eh tú, ¡torpe patán! ¿Acaso no tienes ojos, que debes pisotear a los hijos de los hombres?"

El compañero de Mahmud, que era uno de sus cortesanos, gritó:

"¡Tu ceguera solamente tiene parangón con tu estupidez! Puesto que no puedes ver, tendrías que ser doblemente cuidadoso sobre la persona a la que estás acusando de descuido."

"Si por esto estás queriendo decir", dijo el derviche, "que no debería criticar a un sultán, eres tú quien debería darse cuenta de tu superficialidad."

Mahmud quedó impresionado de que un hombre ciego supiera que estaba en presencia del rey, y dijo apaciblemente:

"¿Por qué, oh derviche, debería un rey tener que escuchar tus improperios?"

"Precisamente", dijo el derviche, "porque es la coraza que la gente de cualquier categoría pone ante las críticas apropiadas para ellos lo que causa su perdición. Es el metal bruñido el que reluce con mayor brillo; el cuchillo golpeado con la piedra de afilar el que corta mejor; y el brazo ejercitado el que puede levantar peso."

Etapas

AL PRINCIPIO CREÍA que un Maestro debe tener razón en todo.

Después, imaginé que mi maestro se equivocaba en muchas cosas.

A continuación, me di cuenta de lo que era correcto y de lo que era equivocado.

Lo equivocado era permanecer en cualquiera de las dos primeras etapas.

Lo correcto era transmitir esto a todo el mundo.

(Ardabili)

Lo que hay en él

Cierto derviche Bektashi era respetado por su piedad y aparente virtud. Cada vez que alguien le preguntaba cómo había llegado a ser tan santo, siempre respondía: "Sé lo que hay en el Corán."

Un día acababa de dar esta respuesta a un interrogador en un café, cuando un imbécil preguntó: "Bueno, ¿y qué es lo que *hay* en el Corán?"

"En el Corán", dijo el Bektashi, "hay dos flores prensadas y una carta de mi amigo Abdullah."

Sano y enfermo

Un buscador errante vio a un derviche en una posada y le dijo:

"He estado en cientos de regiones y escuchado las enseñanzas de muchísimos mentores. He aprendido cómo decidir cuándo un maestro no es un hombre espiritual. No puedo darme cuenta si es un guía genuino o cómo encontrar uno, pero completar la mitad del trabajo es mejor que nada."

El derviche rasgó sus vestiduras y dijo:

"¡Desdichado! Convertirse en experto de lo inútil es como ser capaz de detectar manzanas podridas sin aprender las características de las sanas.

"Pero ante ti hay una posibilidad aun peor; ojo con convertirte en alguien igual al doctor de esta historia. Con el fin de poner a prueba el conocimiento de un médico, cierto rey envió a muchas personas sanas para que fueran examinadas por él; el doctor le dio una medicina a cada uno. Cuando el rey lo convocó y acusó de fraude, la sanguijuela contestó: '¡Gran rey! Hacía tanto que solamente atendía a dolientes, ¡que comencé a imaginar que todo el mundo estaba enfermo y confundí los ojos brillantes de la buena salud con los signos de la fiebre!'"

Estofado de cordero

BAHAUDIN SHAH DIO una vez un discurso sobre los principios y las prácticas de los Sufis. Cierto hombre que se creía inteligente y que podría beneficiarse al criticarlo, dijo:

"¡Si solamente este hombre dijese algo nuevo! Esa es mi única crítica."

Bahaudin escuchó esto e invitó al crítico a cenar.

"Espero que apruebes mi estofado de cordero", dijo.

Después de probar el primer bocado, el invitado saltó gritando: "Estás intentando envenenarme... ¡esto no es estofado de cordero!"

"Pero lo *es*", dijo Bahaudin, "aunque, dado que no te gustan las recetas viejas, intenté algo nuevo. Es cierto que contiene cordero, pero también le agregué una buena cantidad de mostaza, miel y emético."

Encontrando los defectos

Isa Ibn Abdulwahab al-Hindi mantuvo, durante varios años, largas y frecuentes conversaciones en las cuales discursaba sobre todos los temas imaginables.

Un día, cierto respetado sheikh pasó a verlo y le dijo:

"Mi corazón está apesadumbrado, pues se cuenta que en numerosas ocasiones has hablado críticamente de mí."

Isa dijo:

"He dicho veinte veces que hay disparidades entre tus palabras y acciones. ¿Puedes dudar de que esto sea cierto?"

El sheikh preguntó:

"Me encantaría escuchar los motivos por los cuales encuentras defectos en mí."

Isa contestó:

"Los sabrás apenas escuches las doscientas ocasiones en las que te he elogiado ante aquellas mismas personas que, en el nombre de la exactitud, ahora internamente buscan separarnos.

El reportar algo a medias es peor que no reportar nada. El reportar un décimo de algo equivale a una falsificación."

Oír

Un visitante, que había venido de un lejano país, le dijo a Bahaudin Shah:

"Permíteme sentarme en tu durbar (corte) y oír tus palabras, pues con razón se ha dicho que la lectura no es un sustituto del oír."

Bahaudin dijo:

"¡Ay! Si no eres sordo, es triste que haya tenido que esperar tanto tiempo para darte la bienvenida. Verás... actualmente nunca doy charlas."

El visitante preguntó por qué.

Bahaudin dijo:

"Nunca he dado ninguna charla desde que un día vino un grupo de personas parcialmente sordas. Yo dije: 'No sean como un perro o un cerdo...', y cuando me dejaron se pelearon al discutir si yo había dicho 'Sean un perro...', o incluso 'Coman carne de cerdo...'. Con la palabra escrita esto no es posible. Si eres ciego, siempre podrá leerte alguien."

El elefante bebé

Érase una vez un elefante bebé que escuchó decir a alguien: "Mira, hay un ratón." La persona que lo dijo estaba mirando a un ratón, pero el elefantito creyó que se estaba refiriendo a él.

Pero resulta que había muy pocos ratones en ese país; y en cualquier caso solían quedarse en sus agujeros y sus voces no eran muy sonoras. Pero el elefante bebé vociferaba yendo de un lado a otro, eufórico por su descubrimiento: "¡Soy un ratón!"

Lo dijo tan fuerte y tantas veces, y a tanta gente, que – aunque no lo creas – ahora hay un país entero donde casi todos creen que los elefantes, y en particular los elefantes bebé, son ratones.

Es cierto que de vez en cuando los ratones han intentado discutir con aquellos que sostienen la creencia mayoritaria: pero siempre han tenido que huir.

Y si a cualquiera se le ocurre reabrir esta cuestión de ratones y elefantes por aquellos lares, más le vale tener una buena razón, nervios de acero y medios efectivos para presentar su caso.

Un pedido

Si disfrutaste este libro, por favor deja una reseña en Goodreads y Amazon (o donde quiera que hayas comprado el libro).

Las reseñas son el mejor amigo de un escritor.

Para estar al tanto de las novedades acerca de nuestros próximos lanzamientos o noticias de la Idries Shah Foundation, apúntate a nuestra lista de correo:

 http://bit.ly/ISFlist

Y para seguirnos en las redes sociales, usa cualquiera de los siguientes enlaces:

 https://twitter.com/IdriesShahES

 https://www.facebook.com/IdriesShah

 http://www.youtube.com/idriesshah999

 http://www.pinterest.com/idriesshah/

 http://bit.ly/ISgoodreads

 http://fundacionidriesshah.tumblr.com

 https://www.instagram.com/idriesshah/

http://idriesshahfoundation.org/es

Printed in April 2021
by Rotomail Italia S.p.A., Vignate (MI) - Italy